ADDITIONAL PRAISE FOR
UNRULY

"Sean has written a must-read guide for a complex, chaotic world, connecting the dots between geopolitics, AI, and law to create a compelling and integrated understanding of the risk landscape. His core message is one that will help CEOs, leaders, and anyone interested in a better future to thrive in our turbulent times."

—**Mustafa Suleyman**, CEO of Microsoft AI

"Sean West provides sharp, practical guidance for CEOs trying to navigate an era where conventional wisdom no longer applies. Whether it is an increasingly inconsistent and fraught regulatory environment, the culture wars around corporate responsibility, or the exponential rise in global volatility, there are few norms and rules to anchor strategic decisions. This book provides tactics and ideas to build resilience in an era where it has never been so difficult to run a business. It's the perfect complement to my own book, *Higher Ground*."

—**Alison Taylor**, Clinical Associate Professor at NYU Stern, and author of *Higher Ground*

"*Unruly* is truly a must-read! Globalism is gone, standards have eroded, expectations are different, and change is everywhere! Sean West presents the 'now and future' of a world writhing under the intertwined impacts of geopolitics, law, and artificial intelligence. With broad scope and deep insights, Mr. West proves his points with incisive interpretations of example after example. Readable, fun, worrisome, profound: this is a book for professionals, business leaders, and the general public. Sean West proves 'we aren't going back.'"

—**Gen. Wesley Clark**, former NATO Supreme Allied Commander Europe

"There are many books about politics, law, or technology. But *Unruly* is one of the very few books designed to help the modern CEO and general counsel take effective action in the midst of volatility that involves all these factors. It's a must-read for any senior executive who is seeking to navigate today's tumult."

—**C. Allen Parker**, former CEO and General Counsel of Wells Fargo

"A truly thought-provoking, compelling book – and a must-read for leaders at every level and in every sector. Sean West's novel and persuasive assertion that politics, AI, and law are converging to generate ever more challenging global risks makes *Unruly* critical reading for those at the helm of companies, government institutions, and nonprofit organizations alike. And his prescriptions for dealing with the increasing unruliness around the world are of enormous value to those trying to navigate the new global order (and the growing disorder in it)."

—**General David Petraeus (US Army, Ret.),**
former Commander of the Surge in Iraq,
US Central Command, and NATO/US Forces in Afghanistan;
former Director of the CIA; and co-author of the
New York Times bestselling book, *Conflict:
The Evolution of Warfare from 1945 to Gaza*

"In a world where technology, geopolitics, and law collide to rewrite the rules of business, *Unruly* offers a bold and indispensable roadmap. Sean's insights empower leaders to navigate volatility, confront novel risks, and shape the future rather than be shaped by it."

—**Enrico Letta,** former Prime Minister of Italy

"West's 'Unruly Triangle' is a powerful new framework for understanding our chaotic present. By showing how technology, law, and politics interact to create novel risks and opportunities, he gives business leaders a practical toolkit for navigating – and thriving in – an increasingly turbulent world."

—**Azeem Azhar,** founder of Exponential View

"A brilliant and thought-provoking analysis, providing CEOs and general counsel alike with an essential framework for anticipating and navigating risk in an increasingly unruly world."

—**Bjarne Tellmann,** former General Counsel of Haleon

"*Unruly* is a masterful synthesis capturing the interplay of current affairs and the law. A fascinating read for every lawyer."

—**Cherie Blair,** CBE, KC

"*Unruly* is a must-read for business leaders and those helping them navigate global risks. West has masterfully captured a fundamental shift underway at the intersections of geopolitics, law, and technology that we risk overlooking, and guides us through a changed world and the new set of rules for operating in it."

—**Lewis Sage-Passant, PhD,**
Global Head of Intelligence at Novo Nordisk,
Adjunct Professor at Sciences Po Paris,
and founder of *Encyclopedia Geopolitica*

"This book should be required reading for every CEO, investor, or regular American who wants to understand – and get ahead of – the coming global, political, legal, and technological risks that are inevitable in our new and unruly world."

—**Brody Mullins,**
Pulitzer-prize winner and co-author
of *The Wolves of K Street*

"Sean West brilliantly captures the compounding threats –breakdowns in politics, legal systems and the employment base of society itself –because of the impact of AI. For the business reader, this is an uncomfortable, but indispensable, guide to navigating the engulfing triple threat."

—**Lord Mark Malloch-Brown,**
former Deputy Secretary General of the United Nations

"*Unruly* brilliantly dissects how the intersections of politics, law, and technology are reshaping global business. Sean West's expertise and insights makes this indispensable guide for leaders facing high-stakes decisions in an increasingly volatile environment."

—**Bridget McCormack,**
President and CEO of American Arbitration
Association, and former Chief Justice of the
Michigan Supreme Court

"Business, politics, technology, law, culture, and inequality are much more interconnected than we realize. For years, Sean West has briefed CEOs and their management teams on unseen systemic risk roiling worldwide. Although facts, data, and technical knowledge are essential to this task, the rarest ability is to make the risk simple, intelligible, and plain. I suggest buying *Unruly* and putting it by your bedside, reading a chapter a night. In a world of empty-calorie pundits, *Unruly* is pure protein."

—Bill Henderson,
Editor of *Legal Evolution,* and Professor of
Law at Indiana Maurer School of Law

"The development of AI, including its potential and risks, is undoubtedly one of the defining topics of our time. Any reflection aimed at organizing our thoughts on the matter is an investment in the future. For that future to be truly human, we must continue considering the implications of AI. Few resources are more valuable for doing so effectively than Sean West's book."

—José María Aznar,
former Prime Minister of the Spanish government

"As the complex and irresistible forces at the intersection of geopolitics, law, and technology wreak havoc on the established perspectives of risk, *Unruly* provides invaluable and practical insights into both the emerging challenges and the techniques needed to successfully navigate what lies ahead. An essential read for every CEO and general counsel leading through complexity *and* every law firm leader seeking to remain their trusted adviser of choice."

—Matthew Layton,
former Global Managing Partner at Clifford Chance

"The future belongs to companies and leaders who can successfully navigate geopolitics and economic statecraft. The rise of AI – which quite literally has the ability to reshape everything we do – further highlights this critical skillset. West's *Unruly* provides a framework for leaders as they attempt to see around corners and find opportunity in an increasingly dynamic, fast-moving, and multi-stakeholder world."

—Rob Beard,
Chief Legal and Global Affairs Officer at Coherent Corp.

"*Unruly* is an original piece of thinking that will do for law what Graham Allison did for bureaucracy or Robert Jervis for psychology. Weaponize *Unruly* for the purposes of geopolitical analysis."

—**Marko Papic,** Macro-Geopolitical Chief Strategist at BCA Research, and author of *Geopolitical Alpha*

"Unruly makes sense of the extraordinary changes in law, geopolitics, and technology that today frame the environment of business. Clearly, understanding these forces and how they interact is vital for planning and implementing a successful corporate strategy."

—**Richard Vietor,** Emeritus Professor at Harvard Business School

UNRULY

FIGHTING BACK WHEN POLITICS, AI, AND LAW UPEND THE RULES OF BUSINESS

SEAN WEST

WILEY

Published by John Wiley & Sons, Inc., Hoboken, New Jersey.
Published simultaneously in Canada.

For general information on our other products and services or for technical support, please contact
our Customer Care Department within the United States at (800) 762-2974, outside the United States
at (317) 572-3993 or fax (317) 572-4002.

Wiley also publishes its books in a variety of electronic formats. Some content that appears in print
may not be available in electronic formats. For more information about Wiley products, visit our
web site at www.wiley.com.

Library of Congress Cataloging-in-Publication Data is Available:

ISBN 9781394318452 (Cloth)
ISBN 9781394318469 (ePub)
ISBN 9781394318476 (ePDF)

Cover Design: Jon Boylan
Cover Image: © malshak_off/Adobe Stock
Author Photo: Courtesy of author

SKY10097793_020425

To my Dad who showed me the world
To my Mom who showed me to care for everyone in it
To my Wife who works to make it better
To my Kids who give me hope for it

CONTENTS

CONTENTS

FOREWORD BY ANDY BIRD

The world is changing in dramatic ways. Politics is nastier and more volatile than it has been in decades. Technological advancement is opening up great promise and potential perils. The law is less clear, less stable, and less predictably enforced than at any point in my decades leading global companies. The world, as Sean puts it, is becoming unruly.

As a result of these changes, the rules of business are also changing. And, as is always the case, it is the modern CEO's responsibility not just to anticipate these changes but to navigate and, indeed, fight back against them when they threaten the businesses we lead.

It's a lonely life being a CEO. There you are at the top of the pedestal with everyone looking at you, watching your every move, and passing judgment on how you look, speak, and act. Your investors, your chairperson, the board, your direct reports and employees, and your customers all hang on every word. The list is endless, and the job can be relentless.

Ultimately, you're paid to ensure the company, employees, and stakeholders thrive. You're paid to make brilliant decisions at breakneck speed. That's much harder in an unruly world.

The stock market, investors, and financial analysts operate in the "black and white" of P&Ls, balance sheets, and operating margins. A successful CEO must be totally on top of these elements. But a CEO must also manage the gray. The "gray" comes with how you create a narrative, how you inject creativity, how you look after the human capital as much as the financial capital in your company, and, most importantly, how you mitigate risk.

Mitigating risk isn't a job solely for your chief risk officer, your chief legal officer, or your chief technology officer. It's ultimately your responsibility and many times risk, legal, and IT are under resourced and not front and center of the "business." I compare this sometimes to the fire extinguisher philosophy. If you work in an environment where there's a potential for fire, it's pretty handy to have a fire extinguisher close by. But most people don't know how to properly utilize it when a fire occurs. It sits in a corner out of sight and out of mind until there is a fire and panic. That's not great for preparedness.

At the heart of all of this is managing risk. Risk should be front and center of everything you do, but the trouble is that risk doesn't work nine to five—events happen at the most inconvenient times and in the most unlikely places. So, when that happens many CEOs are on the backfoot and scrambling for information and advice to make decisions.

But with the advent of technology it's easy to stay current because risk is constantly evolving, constantly changing, literally on a day-to-day basis. You simply have to choose to prioritize this.

I experienced this firsthand, as CEO of Pearson PLC, the world's leading learning company and a member of the FTSE 100 in the United Kingdom. Pearson operates in more than 100 countries around the world with a diverse set of businesses all focused on improving individuals' opportunities to learn and advance themselves in society. To support this mission, we employ tens of thousands of people. Sadly, risk events happened all too frequently and many times without warning.

I can recall when Russia attacked Kyiv and started the invasion of Ukraine in 2022. I was faced with multiple decisions around how to mitigate the risk to our business, our employees, and our stakeholders. I started to triage the multitude of tasks from a legal, product, and people perspective. What is the impact on my business? How do I safely evacuate my employees stuck in Ukraine? How can we maintain business continuity when our talented software engineers are being displaced? Then there were the ensuing Russian sanctions. I had to prepare briefings for my chairman, my board, our investors, and, most importantly, my employees. Having invested in proactive scenario planning and putting desktop exercises to work helped immensely. It was also important to have trusted up-to-date information on the geopolitical ramifications and have that information in real time, as the situation rapidly escalated.

Unfortunately, these occurrences, however big or small, occur with greater frequency. We live in a constantly shifting and unstable geopolitical landscape.

In my prior role as chairman of Walt Disney International, I was responsible for overseeing the company's many business activities outside the United States. How do we make Disney locally relevant to consumers and expand our presence in emerging markets? First and foremost, the question I always asked myself was: How do I mitigate risk for the company? So, understanding the political landscape, the regulatory landscape, infrastructure, and the like was vital.

What's the first step in formulating a market-entry strategy? Too many companies take a global view based around *domestic* and *international*. You cannot go on vacation to *international*. You visit an individual country, culture, people, political, and legislative framework. So, I set about asking a simple question: How do we go from being the *Walt Disney Company, India* to being *the Indian Walt Disney Company*? How do we go from being the *Walt Disney Company, China* to being the *Chinese Walt Disney Company*? We asked that question for every single country we operated in, so that, ultimately, we could be more relevant and not take a *one-size-fits-all* approach. To be relevant to consumers in each of these markets, we had to tailor our strategies accordingly.

It's not just geopolitical risk; there's also risk associated with technology. I remember vividly on November 30, 2022, when Open AI released ChatGPT to the public. Suddenly the world became aware of generative artificial intelligence (AI) and there was a scramble to determine which companies would benefit from generative AI and which would be at risk. Ironically, it was *people* who made those decisions: I found myself spending increasing time assessing the impact for Pearson to quickly relay a narrative to the analysts, investors, our board, and employees. As we've seen, AI provides many compelling opportunities but also many risks, and having the tools at hand to fully comprehend what this means for your business on a country-by-country basis in real time is vitally important.

That's why I love the premise of Sean's book. He is using his decades-long experience advising companies and investors on geopolitical risk and marrying that with deep research and insight about new technology and the law in order to track a new combined phenomenon he calls "unruliness." By connecting the dots across each of these areas, Sean reveals that the world we are entering is riskier than we appreciate, which is to say that the world will be characterized both by volatility and by an erosion of rules of the game we CEOs take for granted. He then takes that new world of risk and tries to show us how we can fight back against it—not just to manage risk but to use it to our competitive advantage.

The world is no longer so simple that CEOs can have a direct report responsible for politics, another for law, and another for technology—all operating within their own silos to control risk. Instead, the risks companies face will be multifaceted, and the CEO will need an integrated team to be successful. Great CEOs fully engage all parts of the business. They proactively integrate sales and growth functions along with risk, legal, and governance functions. When you do this, you get a more disparate set of perspectives and inputs to help your decision-making and if there is ever an event, then risk, legal, and governance functions are totally up to speed with the business leaders and the needs of the business.

Every successful CEO must now look up from their daily fire drills to realize that the world is on fire. I guess the very fact that you're reading this demonstrates you know the importance of a proactive approach to managing risk in an increasingly unruly world. Enjoy!

—Andy Bird
Former CEO, Pearson
Former president and chairman, Disney International

INTRODUCTION

en years ago, I was a high-flying forecaster of U.S. politics. Literally, I was flying hundreds of thousands of miles a year around the world to brief CEOs and investors on the risks they faced from politics. I would see a bank CEO in Johannesburg, and then I'd shower on the plane en route to brief a Gulf sovereign wealth fund. I'd marvel at the quality of the carpet in the C-suites in Tokyo. Then I'd head to New York to be grilled by hedge fund principals who I often spoke to more times a day than to my wife.

The politics in Washington were like nothing the business community had seen in recent memory. President Obama was deep into his second term and couldn't get much done. The government had recently been shut down by an increasingly fractious Republican Party that made good on a once-in-a-generation threat. The U.S. credit rating had been downgraded, and there was a risk of a technical debt default at every turn.

I was churning out tons of research on the rise of populism in American politics and how it was potentially going to bring America to the brink of a catastrophe. In June 2014, I spoke to the *New York Times* about the electoral defeat of a member of Congress who I said was "the hub for big corporations that could trust him to get things done ... the one standing between the conservative pitchforks and the business community."[1]

I read the paper the next day and nearly spat out my coffee: the *Times* had highlighted that statement in its front section, as the "Quotation of the Day." How could something so banal be the day-defining statement? Well, as risky as the world seemed in 2014, it was pretty tame compared to what we see today.

As I pen this introduction, recent Quotations of the Day include a Sudanese refugee lamenting "This is not freedom" as anti-immigrant riots raged in his adopted English town.[2] There is a Russian journalist speaking amid air-raid sirens from a Ukrainian incursion, asserting that "Silence is salvation. We live according to Orwell."[3] There is a Lebanese taxi driver stating that "It was cool to wake up and find that I was alive" as Israel's conflict with Hezbollah escalated.[4] The defeat of Eric Cantor for Congress in 2014, which I had been quoted about, is meaningless against that backdrop.

Back then, politics in developed countries generally existed inside the normal probability curve. Pendulums swung back and forth. Politicians had traditional incentives. Political parties cared about support from business. Candidates could beat up on globalization, free trade, and open markets in public but still vote for them when no one was looking. Politicians rarely used violent rhetoric and were castigated for much less. The hottest issues were about tax breaks and healthcare coverage.

To say that much has changed is a severe understatement.

In today's world, presidential candidates are convicted of felonies and then go on to win the popular and Electoral College vote, with foreign actors and the world's richest person all battling to influence the results. Consumer devices like pagers are weaponized and detonated against adversaries—with no regard for legal consequences. New artificial intelligence (AI) tools scale to 100 million users in weeks—well before lawmakers can figure out how they work let alone how to regulate them. International economic relationships—like that between Western countries and Russia—can be canceled instantly, leading businesses to scramble to salvage value. And, of course, they can be turned back on too.

It's not enough to say this world is characterized by volatility and uncertainty. Politics often rewards outlandish promises, deceit, conflict, and punching down before the pendulum swings back to optimism.

No, to get leverage over the world today, we need to look deeper. When many of the world's political systems shift at the same time—and shift in the ways they interact with each other—something more serious is afoot.

All this turmoil has led some to declare that we live in a world of "polycrisis" where everything that can go wrong will.[5] While certainly we live in a world of overlapping risk, that type of casting rolls together near-term and very far-off risks into the same analysis, while ultimately giving the impression there is little we can do to defend ourselves.

To get leverage over what's ahead, we need to bound our perspective and force ourselves to be concrete in our diagnoses. This book will argue the culprit for today's unruliness is the intersection of three main forces all changing at once.

The first force, geopolitics, is consistently cited as a top worry for CEOs. And it is suddenly more complex than ever before. The United States and China are trying to splinter the world into spheres, while many countries simply want to produce in China and ally with the U.S. military. Wars are raging in Europe, the Middle East, and parts of Africa as a result of geopolitical games being played by Russia and Iran. National politics in many countries is more polarized than ever.

The second force, law, is both eroding and becoming weaponized. Rule of law is receding across the world while the day-to-day rules and laws governing business are becoming tools of conflict.

The third force, technological innovation more generally and AI more specifically, threatens to upend and circumvent politics, law, and the overall organization of the economy. And it is doing so faster than any of us can truly appreciate.

As a result, the traditional rules of business are about to come crashing down in ways we can already see before our eyes. Business leaders need a new toolkit to manage the fallout.

This is not simply a world of political and legal risk or a world undergoing technological change. This is, in fact, a world where politics, technology, and law intersect to create new synthetic risks not previously contemplated. It is an unruly world.

THE UNRULY WORLD

The term "unruly" generally means disorderly or unable to be controlled. No doubt, the ongoing political volatility in the world gives that impression, as do the effects of relentless technological innovation. But I chose the title of *Unruly* for this book because it's not just volatility alone. It's the destruction of rules and laws—the literal "unruling" of the world—that amplifies the challenge to business in the years ahead.

Society is built on mutual acceptance of rules and laws, not just having laws on the books. These laws form the backbone of how citizens and businesses navigate their everyday lives. Companies make business decisions based on protections they expect from the law, or calculated risks based on their best understanding of it. Firms will avoid entering markets that do not have a strong tradition of rules and laws. Today, it is hard to find a market where the law has not become politicized.

As the world globalized over the last few decades, Western conceptions of rule of law were exported to emerging markets. Increased global trade brought billions out of poverty and reinforced a need for a rules-based order that could make everyone rich. Institutions like the United Nations pushed for international development goals that were supposed to reflect an evolving set of universal values and businesses clambered for international standards and arbiters, like the World Trade Organization, to simplify and police international commerce. Great powers, like the United States, Europe, Russia, and China, largely avoided conflict as they focused on consolidating wealth accumulation for the citizens and the state.

The era of globalization was a time characterized by tremendous economic growth as geopolitics and technology combined to bring the world closer together in a way that necessitated constructing legal rules and institutions. This convergence on rules and norms buttressed further growth and expansion, as businesses unleashed massive investment on the basis of increasing legal and regulatory certainty. Even as the world dealt with the COVID-19 pandemic in 2020, countries were able to implement substantial first-wave lockdowns and close down international commerce as if flipping a switch—reinforcing some sense of control and order even at a moment of sheer chaos.

The world is now facing the specter that a number of geopolitical and technological factors risk setting in motion a dramatic unwinding of the rules of business. And because the legal framework that created globalization is receding faster than globalization itself, there is much more exposure to this than commonly appreciated.

On the political side, we are in uncharted territory.

Anti-elitism, xenophobia, and populism converged to deliver or sustain semi-authoritarian leadership in once democratic countries like Hungary. In other cases, such factors made countries look increasingly inward, as the United Kingdom's exit from the European Union demonstrated—undermining decades of legal institution building.

President Donald Trump's return to power as part of a global anti-incumbent trend in 2024 was due in part to a backlash to the world rules created. In the waning days of the pandemic, populations became fatigued with government policies and simply started ignoring them—raising questions about whether they would ever follow such rules again and elevating politicians who didn't play by the rules either. A push toward increasing environmental, social, and governance (ESG) and diversity standards has actually triggered a movement against them, catapulting culture wars back to the national stage and causing divergent perspectives between the United States and Europe. Modern technology companies believe regulators are too slow to regulate properly, so better to break the rules and ask for forgiveness than to be constrained—a mindset that carries over when such figures decide to play politics, as in the case of tech titan Elon Musk.

The last few years have become just as treacherous on an international level. Russia invading Ukraine flies in the face of simply believing that modern European borders are settled law. Conflict in the Middle East raises daily questions about the laws of war—from targeted cross-border assassinations to a staggering human cost of conflict. Tensions between the West and China risk turning companies from independent actors into proxy extensions of the state against their desire not to be that.

Technology is perhaps the most important factor to understand where we are headed, as it can serve either as an accelerant or as a disruptor to the political direction of travel. The rise of AI threatens to upend the entire employment infrastructure of modern economies, which will call into question the social safety net structure of the modern state. It will also present opportunities for leaders to deploy surveillance systems and predictive governance approaches we can barely contemplate to consolidate authoritarian rule. Everything from the space economy to digital assets will hinge on this interplay between technology and law.

Moreover, technology will directly impact rules and laws themselves. Innovation brings the marginal cost of digital products to zero, and it will do the same with law. When it costs nothing to file lawsuits, the law will be weaponized like cyberattacks. Robot lobbyists will serve entrenched interests to reinforce their advantages. Companies will let their AIs negotiate with the AIs of other companies in lieu of going to court or arbitration—turning legal disputes into optimization problems. Citizens will increasingly be able to practice machine-aided law themselves, with profound implications.

This new era requires much more than a sense that politics and technology breed uncertainty, which has been the core thesis of many analysts. Rather, if we appreciate that we face unique variations of political, legal, and technological risk while also facing new risks from the intersections of these factors, then we can start to get leverage over the future.

FIGHTING BACK AGAINST UNRULINESS

You picked this book up because you feel something is fundamentally shifting in the world today. It's not just volatility—there is an increasing sense that the systems we live in are on the ballot at every election. Companies are not just takers in this new world: They can look at how geopolitics, technology, and the law are upending the rules of business and fight back. But to do so, new strategies are needed.

Businesses must realize that they are organized for an old world of siloed risk. Today, political risk is dealt with by monitoring and lobbying while legal risk is mitigated in court with the best legal support money can buy. Technological governance exists almost as an independent entity focused on cybersecurity and data privacy while innovation serves to outcompete in the market rather than in court or in Congress. The new world requires embracing complexity and organizing for risks that change shape and permeate corporate boundaries.

The U.S. banking industry, for example, has been under pressure from all of these forces. Politicians love to beat up on big finance in the name of protecting consumers. Laws and regulations are passed by many jurisdictions—often with an eye toward past crises—creating a cat-and-mouse game of compliance or hoping to skate by undetected. Traditional players reconstitute themselves to go around the letter of the law. Financial technology moves faster than regulators can keep up with while innovative challengers do their best to disrupt traditional banking. And the intersection of these factors—politicized regulatory actions and pushes for digitally open banking—create additional layers of challenge.

Jamie Dimon, CEO of America's largest bank, JP Morgan Chase, had enough of the unruliness. He recently told the American Bankers Association "It is time to fight back … if you're in a knife fight, you better bring a knife, and that's where we are."[6] Dimon noted that many banks are afraid to fight with their regulators because they fear retaliation but at some point that becomes a risk worth taking. "Things are becoming unfair and unjust, and they are hurting companies," he asserted.

What may seem like a uniquely pugnacious position taken by one of the world's top bankers is the mindset all businesses must adopt going forward. Businesses must shift to a war footing, anticipating threats that are attacking from every angle and proactively defeating them.

Those threats might be new policies from a change in government made more likely due to voter manipulation via deepfakes. It might be thousands of legal cases filed against your company via robot lawyers steered by disgruntled employees. It might be unbridled technological advancement by competitors who simply ignore the law to steal market share—or steal your intellectual property because they have a finger on the scales of justice. It might be some confluence of politics, law, and technology that manifests in completely novel ways.

Today's political and innovation cycles move too fast to ignore for very long. Businesses that favor a reactive posture will find themselves overwhelmed by change and unable to catch up. Those that fight back have a real chance of success.

Core to success will be learning to embrace the chaos around you and to use it to your advantage. If you can correctly diagnose which force you are fighting—politics, technology, law, or some combination—you can implement strategies that will give you significant advantages over competitors who will be whipsawed around by change.

Fighting back against the forces upending business—and using these same forces to your advantage—will enable you to thrive in an unruly world.

PART I

UNRULY RISK: WHAT IT IS AND HOW WE GOT HERE

CHAPTER ONE

THE UNRULY
TRIANGLE

O ne morning I received a phone call from a Connecticut number while I was meeting with some colleagues. It might be a hedge fund with an urgent question, so I answered.

"Hey, Sean, can you talk?" I immediately recognized the voice on the other line, a well-known global macro investor. I had logged more than 900 interactions with this client that year including no less than five emails that morning. But he had never called my cell phone.

"I'm actually in the middle of a meeting right now. Can I call you back in 20 minutes?" I asked, knowing there's no way that would be good enough.

"Sure, Sean. I just have one question for you, it will only take a minute. WHAT THE F—K IS GOING ON IN WASHINGTON?!"

Of course, that was not a one-minute conversation.

This type of interaction was representative of my life as a geopolitical forecaster, where I honed the ability to rapidly digest any political shift in the world and put it into the context of "the economy" or "markets." Such skills are highly sought after by Wall Street because an early understanding that a new political leader may crush a particular asset class is immediately actionable—investors can sell that asset, perhaps juiced by high leverage, and make a killing. When the political tides look likely to turn, they can buy it back. "Trump Trades"—Election Day bets on industries that would win or lose when the President returned to office—provide one such example.

The crux of such analysis is to get the trigger prediction correct. What are the odds a government will do a specific negative or positive thing in the next week? In the next month? In the next year? If you can consistently predict policy shocks, investors can make a lot of money expressing that thesis in the market.

In stable political environments, such prediction is possible. But world politics is becoming too complex to model and predict with any high degree of likelihood. As one artificial intelligence (AI) pioneer told me when I suggested using tech to model politics a decade ago: the smartest minds in the world had not figured out how to predict if you want to stream a tenth cat video after you watch nine of them. So predicting what an unstable and complex political system will do next feels somewhere between an educated guess and a fool's errand.

The good news is that, for corporations, the probability of an event is less important than anticipating or rapidly understanding impact. If you mine in South Africa and an antibusiness leader may come to power, you don't really have a choice about whether to stay or go—you're fixed there for a while. Thus, your real focus is not predicting who will win but understanding the impact and extent of such policy shifts so you can respond. This is more than figuring out what is being discussed so that the corporation can lobby against it. This is about figuring out what growth opportunities will be open or closed for that company in South Africa in the future with some level of specificity.

To do that, you need to bring political risk down to a much more concrete level. From my vantage point, the law provides grounding that suddenly makes such analysis much more actionable.

When a policy idea or a political promise meets the administrative state, it becomes a law or a regulation. It becomes something that the government could or will enforce in the courts. It becomes grounds for a commercial competitor to launch a legal challenge. It can create avenues for success in a place, or it can shut them down completely. With the exception of security risk—which is often conflated with political risk—most other politics is just noise.

The trick here is to realize that this is not just politics or law raising risk, but it is the intersection between the two. Throw in the way technology intersects with politics and law, and then the risk landscape become much more complex.

This is the essence of what I call "unruliness," which is the concept that underlies this book. Unruliness results from the dynamic interplay of politics, technology, and law to create risks that don't fit neatly in any corporate silo. Crucially, it creates risks that change shape in real time and require agility to counter.

To conceptualize unruliness, I rely on a simple schematic called the "Unruly Triangle." The core insight of the triangle is that each of the vertices—geopolitics, law, and technology—are connected to each other generating new risks that are constantly in flux.

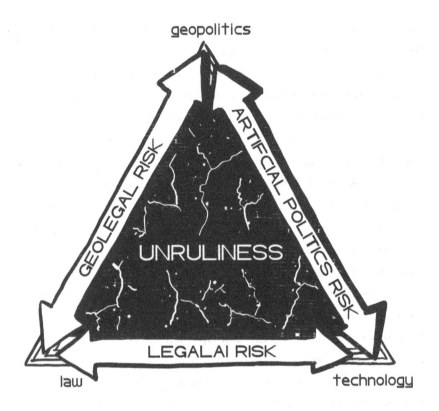

Traditional risk frameworks tend to view the three vertices either as separate factors for risk analysis or as somewhat static such that an analysis of these factors can be done at a single moment of time and assumed to hold. To be clear, the world does present traditional political, legal, and technological risks. But the real source of anxiety for corporate leaders in the years ahead will be the way these intersections manifest.

Thus, we need to think about risk flowing up and down each leg of the triangle from the interactions of these factors. Politics determines not just what the law is but how, when, where, and even if it is applied. Stable politics allows for rule of law and rule of law supports stable politics. The law defines the conditions under which political contestation is permitted, proceeds, and is ultimately settled.

The law does the same for the arenas and pace of technological advancement. Technology transforms the broad social and economic conditions that influence how politics is played at home and abroad and can be used to determine narrow political outcomes. It is also an instrument that can revolutionize all modalities of law for better or for worse—surveillance, enforcement, representation, adjudication, and punishment. New technologies require new legal frameworks, and those frameworks ensure technology remains appropriately regulated.

Rather than being separate risks, for each of these three factors, there is a push and pull that's largely imperfect and rarely stable. But historically a rough equilibrium is achieved and populations, businesses, and lawmakers understand and may even respect the parameters.

This book is sounding the alarm that we are in an extended moment of flux where the process of getting to a new equilibrium will be nasty, risky, and long. This generates three novel risks—Geolegal Risk, Artificial Politics Risk, and LegalAI Risk.

Politics and law intersect into what I refer to as "Geolegal Risk." Geolegal Risk is the manifestation of politics through the legal channel or vice versa. For instance, losing in court because a politically appointed judge favors a given political interest is much different than losing on the merits. But Geolegal Risk is also about the breakdown of international institutions that uphold international law or expansive sanctions driven by politics. There are many other examples where politics and law intersect to shift the landscape of business.

Politics and technology intersect into what I call "Artificial Politics Risk," buttressed by advances in AI. Artificial Politics is when an election outcome has been fundamentally altered by fake news generated by a foreign or malicious actor, causing irreparable damage. It is also when technological advancement is constrained by nonexpert regulators wielding blunt instruments for political gain, to serve entrenched interests or simply out of fear. It is when technology is used to change political systems once and for all; for instance, when an authoritarian government implements surveillance to achieve a decisive advantage over its political opposition. Most importantly, it is when technological advancement so fundamentally shifts the economic landscape—for instance, through technological unemployment—that political systems fundamentally realign either in the domestic political economy or among geopolitical rivals.

The third leg of the triangle is what I call "LegalAI Risk." LegalAI the automation of the law, which brings with it novel risks. It gives the potential to overwhelm governments or competitors with automated lawsuits or to fight back against legal injustices using new AI-assisted tools. Crucially, it raises the specter that technology may shift what the law means at the most fundamental level.

I'll walk through each of these synthetic risks in turn.

GEOLEGAL RISK

As political cooperation erodes, so do rules and laws, presenting the intersectional challenge of Geolegal Risk. Limits on impunity and arbitrariness are established via political codification into laws and norms—and when political convergence no longer exists within a country or across countries, there is often a rise in arbitrary exercises of power through the legal system or despite the legal rights one may have in a particular legal system. Thus, if I can convince you that political convergence at national and international levels is evaporating—which may not be particularly hard to do—you will start to grasp the risk that the rules of a particular country or of international trade will be more open to interpretation than they have been before. When the rules are gray, there is more space for actors to use the legal system against you. Combine that gray area with the advent of technology that makes it easy to exploit targets using the legal system, and you have an unruly world of new challenges.

Geolegal Fragmentation

A world that is increasingly fragmented is a world of greater Geolegal Risk. A politically converging world establishes rules and laws that make it easier for businesses to operate. Think about the European Union. France and Germany went from fighting two world wars to having the same monetary policy. Free movement of people between them. The same body of human rights law. And so on. That meant goods, services, and people could move freely. That convergence was only 30 years ago, yet it is impossible to think of a project like that in the Western world today—and the durability of the European Union itself is clearly in question as it recently said goodbye to its first former member, the United Kingdom.

Today's world is one that is fracturing considerably. Where the United States once believed that economic interdependence between the West and China would bring China into a global system dominated by U.S. norms ranging from free trade to democracy, both sides now believe such interdependence is a risk to their national security. As countries feel worse off, they are starting to use economic and financial weapons like tariffs, sanctions, export controls, and investment controls and interrupting supply chains at unthinkably high rates—attempting to carve the world up into tiny economic pockets of permissiveness and restriction that can be redrawn at any moment.

My former boss and mentor Ian Bremmer has called this world the "G-Zero world" in contrast to a world where decisions are made by the G8 or G20 group of nations, or in contrast to a collaborative G2 of the United States and China trying to solve the world's problems.[1] A G-Zero world is a world without global leadership—it is a world that has few political guardrails and every nation is working only to its own ends.

Where institutions like the United Nations, World Trade Organization, and International Monetary Fund once drove the global development agenda, increasingly countries are charting their own paths under the patronage of their favorite large power (or perhaps being persuaded to choose one over the other). Poor countries are left to find a sponsor, and middle-income countries are stuck trying to navigate between the United States and China.

That type of world is much riskier from a geolegal perspective. Because of global supply chains and global consumer bases, companies of any scale have exposure to a whole host of different legal systems and frameworks. The erosion of supranational rules, laws, and institutions implies increasing compliance complexity as the primacy of the state reasserts itself. It also implies (potentially contradictory) legal exposures across countries that can very quickly turn into concrete risks as political dynamics change.

Legal Unruling

The world is filled with lots of laws on the books. The problem is that the legal system in so many jurisdictions is being undermined, unwound, and weaponized capriciously. This undermines the concept that there is any rule to the laws. Such "unruling" increases the chance that the next decade is particularly unruly.

First, most of the world has never had access to the law or justice. The World Justice Project (WJP) estimates 5.1 billion people—two-thirds of the world—have no access to justice, meaning they cannot access their justice system, are excluded from economic opportunities because they lack legal tools, or live in exceptional circumstances of injustice. In writing about a "rule of law recession," WJP estimates 76% of the global population live in countries where the rule of law declined—a negative direction charted for the seventh straight year.[2]

So, we live in a world where most of the population has no access to justice and it is getting worse for those of us that do. For those who lack access to justice, the law provides a convenient veneer for those with power to deprive them of opportunities or assets. This is not just a developing country phenomenon. A tenant in Los Angeles who is wrongfully evicted by a slumlord experiences this the same way a citizen in Beijing might when their property is seized to build a new military base, with no recourse.

Second, we should recognize a rise in impunity and a decline in democratization. Former U.K. Foreign Secretary David Milliband captured this in a compelling 2023 piece for the *New York Times* where he defines impunity as "the exercise of power without accountability, which becomes, in starkest form, the commission of crimes without punishment" or, more bluntly "the mind-set that laws and norms are for suckers."[3] The rise of impunity is tied in with a backsliding of democratic norms in many places in the world. Political candidates from countries that once valued free and fair elections now might value elections that are free and fair only so long as they win. Critics are increasingly silenced by laws that are adjacent to the political process—for instance, being banned from running in certain elections by being accused of corruption.

Yet, this is not a book about the end of democracy—that book has been written by others.[4] Instead, we need to track democratic erosion as a building block on the way to an unruly world. And we need to extend this concept of impunity to note that this is much more than a national phenomenon. It is happening at the international level where borders or the laws of war don't really tell us what actions are likely to come next from spoiler countries with respect for neither and decreasing fear of punishment for ignoring both. It is happening at the local level where urban crime is simply not punished, for a variety of reasons I will outline.

Third, we need to recognize that legal systems themselves are being weaponized. This is different from impunity, which implies those with power simply bypass the law. Instead, this is about using the law when it is convenient to fight political or business challenges because the legal system is captured by politics and business. This is a sense that every Western election might need to be litigated before, during, and after. This is a sense that every body of settled law should be repeatedly tested at the highest court until the political constellation of appointments enables the extraction of maximum policy change. This is a sense that rounding up foreign citizens or issuing Interpol red notices for arrest is more preferable to making enemies disappear because use of the legal system gives a veneer of righteousness—even when it is just a craven power play.

All of those factors are combining to shift the role the law plays in society. A world where there is no rule of law—either because the law is no longer seen as legitimate or because the law is not enforced—is an unruly world. It is a world where anything can happen next.

In that world, it becomes much harder to answer the following questions: What is the law? Will it change? Will it be enforced fairly? And, is it compatible in every jurisdiction in which you are present?

And if you can't answer those questions, you can't actually make decisions on market entry or exit. Or long-term investment. Or even what the next quarter might bring for you. These are the rules required to do business. And they are eroding.

While we may agree these questions are becoming murkier due to this politically induced bout of rule of law starvation, what most have failed to note is the role that technology will play over the next 10 years to cement this environment.

ARTIFICIAL POLITICS RISK

Just like the Internet brought a democratization of information to global populations, innovation in AI holds the promise to solve the justice gap I described once and for all. Unfortunately, it also has the potential to cement it for good. If we don't understand how technology is changing politics, we will sleepwalk into a permanently unruly world.

First, AI has the potential to transform and reorganize economies. When most jobs can be automated, much of the population loses its reason for putting on clothes and leaving the house every day. In the best-case scenario, a broader portion of the population lives happily ever after off the AI-generated fat of the land redistributed through basic incomes and government benefits. In the worst-case scenario, society splinters as many citizens feel no agency over the direction of their lives and turn into a permanent protest class.

Second, the sheer power of new technologies in a geopolitically fractious world has set off a scramble to constrain or contain sharing of the most novel innovations between geopolitical rivals. One of the most important drivers of risk in the unruly world is the tension between the United States and China over access to the full supply chain underlying AI. These fears create new paradigms of national security control over businesses and new expectations for businesses to be patriotic.

Third, technology allows for the consolidation of power in the hands of those who already have it today. One percent of the world's population owns roughly half of global wealth, while the poorest half of the population owns less than 1% of the world's wealth.[5] Technology has the potential to freeze such economic and power structures in place forever—not that different from the decisive advantages that nuclear countries have versus those that lack nukes. This is because technology can be used to implement surveillance states that may never actually be able to be broken because they are so ruthlessly efficient. If populations can't fight back, the "haves" of today may be the "haves" of the future. That opens up the possibility that such states can act with permanent impunity.

LEGALAI RISK

When I speak of LegalAI, I am not talking about the billions of dollars floating into applying AI to productivity solutions for lawyers. I am talking about the fundamental way that technology will shift the law in the years ahead.

A milder scenario is that technology will simply allow governments to have full visibility over rule-breaking and rule-compliance. I was recently in Singapore and saw a police camera attached to a sign showing how many people had been fined for littering, presumably caught by the monitoring camera. No doubt one can argue that this is more rule of law than ever before—the law says you can't litter and if you do, you'll be automatically fined. When your car prints you a speeding ticket automatically at some point in the future, it will have the same effect.

The problem is that a fundamental tenet of justice is empathy and discretion. Did you litter because you are disabled and lost control of something you were carrying? Were you speeding because you were carrying a stabbing victim to the hospital? When the law becomes automatic, it is no longer the law. The law, then, is simply a punitive system or one to be gamed. It no longer signals norms built on top of the values of society but instead focuses the population on how to avoid getting caught for infractions. It is the equivalent of encouraging drivers to slow down only for the instant they are crossing a speed camera—not to drive at a safe speed because society values a reduction in the loss of life from car accidents.

As the law becomes automated, it has the potential to be more readily accessed. This may increase access to justice, but it also increases access to the legal system writ large. As all goods become digitized, their cost falls considerably. Today I can carry around a playlist made from all the world's music because, as music became a digital product, its cost fell considerably. Soon, I'll carry a playlist of my favorite legal attacks and defenses in my pocket too. Where I might not have been able to flood my commercial or personal enemies with lawsuits in the past because it was prohibitively expensive, now I can. This means citizens are more likely to fight than ever before. This also changes the law from a set of rules guiding society to a game to be played. That lends itself to a type of legal anarchy of increasing weaponization, presenting new risks to anyone with legal exposure.

Finally, AI may open the door to radically new conceptions of how the law works. I'll later describe work by law professors who suggest that someday every citizen may have slightly different laws depending on their circumstances. For instance, a driver who got a bad night's sleep is told their speed limit is lower than someone who had a better night's sleep. There are other researchers who suggest rules and laws be drafted by for-profit regulators who compete to earn money by making the best rules. These are all possibilities that are opened up by technological advancement and would be a sea change for society and business.

FIGHTING BACK

One goal of this book is to elucidate that risk in today's unruly world does not come in neat buckets of political, legal, and technological. Instead, risk is messy and cross-cutting, manifesting in many novel ways we need to work hard to understand and anticipate.

But you are not just a taker in a world of new synthetic risks. You can fight back. My second goal with this book is to show you how to do so.

As you read through the rest of the book, each chapter will take on a novel issue in Geolegal, Artificial Politics, or LegalAI Risk. It will then end with a technique you can use to proactively gain advantage over the forces and competitors that otherwise risk overwhelming you.

CHAPTER TWO

AN UNRULY WORLD IS BORN

To graduate from my university, I needed to be fluent in a foreign language. I was heading to school smack in the middle of the globalization era, and the world was opening up. China was months away from being welcomed into the World Trade Organization (WTO), and I was fascinated by economic and political opportunities in Asia. So, I enrolled in an intensive Chinese course.

It turns out I wasn't very good at Chinese. At all. I'm a fairly monotone guy with a slight California uptick at the end of my sentences. Learning a tonal language was not my strong suit.

Toward the end of the year, after determining I wouldn't continue with Chinese, my Dad sent me an email with a tour itinerary of China and asked if I wanted to go. I thought it was a bad joke.

But he was actually serious. He had taken me to Europe as a child to show me another part of the world and wanted me to see the future of the global economy. So we booked our tickets, and I told my Chinese professor I was headed to China in the summer.

She looked at me in mild disbelief. She said to me, "Speak Chinese to Chinese people. If they speak Chinese back, your Chinese is good. If they tell you in English how good your Chinese is, then it is terrible."

We booked our flights, and a few weeks later touched down in Beijing. I had some free time, so I looked for a music store. I went into a store on one of Beijing's main shopping streets and started talking to a kid who worked in the shop with the 300 words of Chinese I knew.

"Your Chinese is very good," he said to me in English. I swallowed my chuckle.

Genie, as his name tag read, asked me if I was American, and I nodded yes. He told me about how excited China was to join the WTO, which the United States had recently supported. I asked him if he could recommend some Chinese rap to me and he immediately smiled.

"Better," he said. "Follow me."

We walked through a door in the back of the shop into a windowless storage room set up like a second store. In it was a collection of wall-to-wall counterfeits of every major American rap artist. There was Jay-Z, Tupac, Snoop Dogg, the Notorious BIG, and many others all displayed for sale at five times the price of a legitimate Chinese album.

I was surprised that Chinese youth would be so interested in U.S. hip-hop, but I shouldn't have been. It was the heyday of globalization and Web 1.0. The world was getting smaller.

THE ROARING 90s

Globalization, which led to tremendous geolegal convergence, had its heyday from the fall of the Berlin Wall in 1989 until the fall of storied investment bank Bear Stearns in 2008.

This is a sweeping period of time to lump together in one block. The Soviet Union collapsed. China became the workshop of the world and the costs of everything from T-shirts to televisions plummeted. The Internet spread to all corners of the earth, dropping the cost of communication to negligible and opening the door for a global offshore service market. The Global War on Terror reframed international relations. The global economy seized up in panic because of distributed financial exposure to U.S. mortgages.

While the story of the economic drivers of globalization has been told by many others, what's often missed is that the world needed a whole new legal infrastructure to keep the party going. The convergence in rules with new referees was not a simple byproduct of globalization but rather a core driver of it. That's because this convergence de-risked the exposures that came from global trade, begetting more trade and investment. And just as geolegal convergence had a heavier hand in fueling globalization than most realize, the geolegal fragmentation we are experiencing now is more threatening than most appreciate.

We don't have to rewind too far to find a time when a scenario like my Chinese CD shop trip would have been harder to imagine. Through the 1970s, countries largely traded with their physical or ideological neighbors, and the vast bulk of the global economy was centered around the North Atlantic Basin, with an outpost in Japan. The world was effectively split into different orbits, with Soviet and Eastern European society cut off from the West and hermetic China while India lumbered along. Even as the threat of nuclear war cast an existential shadow, this type of world was less risky for day-to-day business—it was simply a set of separate ecosystems of rules. Companies did not have to manage dozens of conflicting regimes. The legal frameworks for their operations were relatively stable.

Everything started to change at the end of 1989. From the fall of the Berlin Wall until the global financial crisis (GFC), the world economy was characterized by one big, simultaneous rush to get rich. Countries that had been inward facing like China or India became economic juggernauts. Sophisticated financial engineering promised the measured sharing of risks.

The 1990s brought a number of political shifts that dramatically changed the global economy. By expanding the potential for collaborative economic opportunity, the shifts also created a logic for legal coherence within and across countries. As countries started to integrate more deeply, businesses began to set up sprawling supply chains that have fueled decades of economic growth. As they encountered complicated, arcane, and inward-looking domestic rules, they pushed for global integration at an institutional level. International organizations like the WTO emerged not just to liberalize trade but to adjudicate it.

Countries and companies started to throw their lot in with the concept that trade liberalization was a one-way street, global supply chains were the future, and compliance complexity was a barrier to growth. The idea that harmonized rules and laws were a goal in and of themselves for business was a common theme—even if having a single set of rules meant accepting harsher constraints in some jurisdictions than they might have otherwise.

Alongside this rush for harmonization came pressure on aligning the rules of global trade through new institutions and configurations like the WTO, North American Free Trade Agreement (NAFTA), and the Eurozone. Most importantly, there was an emerging consensus in much of the West that moving production to cheaper countries in Asia through aligned legal, economic, and business cultures would mean massive global supply chains could not only increase corporate profits and efficiencies but also benefit populations. The belief was that citizens of poor countries would enjoy better living standards and also that economic growth would create a middle class that would push governments in a less oppressive direction. The realization that growth and technological change might serve to legitimize autocracies was still far away.

All of this worked for a few reasons at a particular point in time. Western businesses benefited from the lower production costs, new markets, and easier regulatory environments, which meant they championed further expansion. China, following the disaster of Tiananmen Square in 1989, found a vector to join the post-Cold War globalization boom without undertaking political reform. Western governments oversaw booming stock markets while not having to yet deal with the downside of deindustrialization. Globalization was seen as a way to consolidate the Cold War victory: bring Russia and China into the global economy, and they will not need to slip back into the cycle of rising powers challenging established ones. Everyone can get rich—and more naively—everyone will accept the geopolitical status quo.

This geolegal convergence was unique because it truly was the culmination of political, legal, and technological factors coming together to reduce risk.

GEOLEGAL CONVERGENCE THROUGH ECONOMICS

All of these shifts conspired to bring about a global economy that was very different than only a decade prior. Businesses boomed as they produced goods cheaply in one place and sold them elsewhere, even as they gained consumers in the developing countries they had invested in. As countries like China and India took larger shares of the economic pie, they reinvested in building infrastructure that would further bolster their advantages (hard infrastructure in China, knowledge infrastructure in India.). Other emerging market countries looked to either be part of their growth story or model it themselves.

As the world became more integrated, different business models became possible. Just-in-time manufacturing techniques suddenly made a ton of sense, with personal computers being built to spec hours after customers ordered them. Sprawling chains of suppliers, markets, and revenues increased exposure to both political and legal risk that companies are feeling in today's unruly world.

Companies also started to realize they were vulnerable to disruption via legal means in every country in which they operated both due to the domestic laws and possible legal incompatibility between where they operated and where they were headquartered. This furthered legal evolution through bilateral and multilateral trade and investment treaties and the strengthening of supranational institutions.

The WTO grew from a mainly Western club into a truly global organization with rules, disciplines, and legal structures that cover 98% of global gross domestic product (GDP) today.[1] World Bank loans and grants to developing countries had social, environmental, and anticorruption criteria for projects the bank financed and subsequently monitored. When countries fell into debt service problems, the International Monetary Fund would provide concessional financing to countries facing a balance of payments crisis—conditioned on deep interventions in the domestic political, legal, and economic institutions of countries.

The European Union went from an economic pact designed to keep Germany and France from having another war into a sprawling supranational institution of more than two dozen countries, complete with policymaking primacy on important issues like economic regulation. NAFTA integrated the United States, Canada, and Mexico albeit in a much shallower way than European integration.

GEOLEGAL CONVERGENCE THROUGH SECURITY

While economic motivations had fueled the geolegal convergence of the 1990s, it would be security concerns that would power it in the first half of the 2000s. When planes crashed into the World Trade Center and the Pentagon on September 11, 2001, the North Atlantic Treaty Organization (NATO) invoked its mutual defense clause for the first time in history. America used North Atlantic unity to launch an invasion of Afghanistan amid global sympathy, including from countries like Iran. It squandered that sympathy when it extended its Global War on Terror to Iraq in 2003.

By demanding countries line up with it or against it on Iraq, the United States splintered the world into those that wanted to follow its lead from a national security perspective and those that didn't. There is much to be said about how the Iraq invasion, and treatment of prisoners and detainees, shattered any sense of convergence on the role of the United Nations (UN) or human rights law. But a similarly sized impact was that 9/11 dramatically deepened the role of the state in people's lives. The PATRIOT Act gave the government license to pretty much do what it wanted to keep people secure, and while there was debate and hand wringing, there was no successful effort to keep government powers at bay.

The post-9/11 environment led to intensive scrutiny of business dealings at a level never before seen. This gave rise to integrated data flowing across borders about financial criminals or radical groups as well as individuals who might be trying to book flights or cross borders. It led to calls for scanning 100% of all cargo entering the United States, which could dramatically slow down trade and impose major costs. The net effect of this was the export of America's own security crisis via the legal channel to all corners of the globe. To this day, almost everyone who engages with a bank account anywhere in the world has been vetted according to anti-money laundering and know-your-customer rules that were turbocharged after 9/11. The role of government in the bank accounts of average citizens would later give rise to some of the logic underpinning the cryptocurrency movement.

In addition, Congressional opinion about inbound investment became hypersensitive to perceived national-security risks. In 2006, the House pushed back strongly against an attempt by a Dubai firm to take over six U.S. ports, though the White House was in favor. This dynamic is echoed in the recent saga of Nippon Steel's attempt to purchase a U.S. steel firm, which I'll discuss later.

It was the hegemonic military power of the United States that back-stopped this global system, as it shouldered the bulk of the burden of root-ing out terrorism and patrolling global sea lanes. But ultimately, the United States' ability to project power through its control of the legal levers of a dollar-centric global financial system was even more significant than its weaponry.

While the arc of this story is one of convergence, the countries that rejected the Washington Consensus and U.S.-led global leadership suffered. Iraq, Iran, Syria, Venezuela, North Korea, Cuba, Myanmar, Zimbabwe, and Libya—to name a few—were sanctioned, and many were bombed. The incentives were so great to join the one directional movement toward con-vergence that now had not just economic but had a security logic to it that only those places with deep ideological or religious conviction to resist remained outside.

Backlash to U.S. Overreach

While the number of genuine pariah states was relatively small, a perception of increasing U.S. overreach took its toll on alliances even as worries about national security fueled misgivings about "excessive" supply-chain integra-tion. Although the immediate aftermath of 9/11 meant that security-based legal convergence (at least among the Western powers) was seen as both desirable and essential, as time wore on such convergence fueled resentment.

The United States legally sought and gained extraordinary surveillance access to global telecommunications networks. The hardware might in some instances belong to non-American companies that had acquired it from bankrupt American entities after the 2000 tech crash. But as noted in a 2013 article in the *Washington Post*, approval for such takeovers was made conditional on maintaining a "Network Operations Center" on U.S. soil that would be open to visits by National Security Agency (NSA) personnel at 30 minutes notice. And whatever the hardware, U.S.-based companies dominated the software portals for Internet traffic like email systems, social media, and the like.[2]

Many of these U.S. surveillance powers dated back to the security crisis after 9/11, but they remained relatively obscure (and uncontroversial). Things changed with the revelations by national security contractor turned leaker Edward Snowden in 2013. It turned out that legal authorities assumed to be used mostly against pariah states and nonstate actors operated in a much more expansive universe, including not just adversaries but even allies. A stunning revelation at the time was that even Angela Merkel, the Chancellor of Germany, had had her cell phone tapped by the NSA.[3]

Even as the United States maintained extraordinary powers of surveillance, it was growing increasingly concerned that the growing technological prowess of China would allow it to counter and rival U.S. efforts. And the dominant concern was China's telecommunications champion, Huawei, which was engaged in a buildout of fifth-generation wireless infrastructure not just at home but also across large parts of the world (including in Western Europe). Already in 2012, the U.S. Congress had begun to worry that Huawei's capacities threatened U.S. security interests, and the battle escalated from there as the company's cheap 5G infrastructure began to be deployed around the world. And the process of targeting Huawei depended on the nexus of law, politics, and technology.

HSBC, another bank facing the wrath of U.S. authorities for insufficient scrutiny of its customers in other matters, discovered Huawei's links to Iran while it was trying to have criminal charges against itself dismissed. It reportedly tendered this information to the U.S. Department of Justice "pursuant to formal demand, including grand jury subpoena or other obligation to provide information pursuant to a Deferred Prosecution

Agreement or similar legal obligation."[4] This then led to the extradition (while in Canada) and subsequent imprisonment—for violating U.S. sanctions law—of Huawei's CFO, the daughter of the company's founder. This is just a reminder of the ways in which firms can be drafted through legal means into participation in national security operations, as I'll go into more depth about later.

FINANCIAL INTEGRATION AND COLLAPSE

As the world gradually got a handle on the terrorist threat, the economy continued to hum along to the tune of geolegal integration. By 2006, I was working with the Federal Reserve Bank, and my job was to research why it was hard to get loans for manufactured houses—prefabricated structures that rolled off assembly lines and could promise the least-well-off a chance to get on the property ladder. I ultimately drew the conclusion that it was hard to finance them because they were not actually valuable—a conclusion that would become more acute when the entire global economy started melting down in 2007 as other housing asset prices began to collapse in unison.[5]

While the GFC would wreak havoc on geolegal convergence, the coordinated response across the world's major economies was possible only because all the structures that had been built during the prior era served as venues and vehicles for global cooperation to stem the bleeding. The G20 group of nations became a key avenue for cooperation among developed and high-growth economies to come together and pledge coordinated stimulus as well as to ward off protectionism. In the United States, the American Recovery and Reinvestment Act of 2009 led to increased government spending and tax cuts on the order of $800 billion. China launched a fiscal stimulus program of almost $600 billion (about 13% of its GDP at the time, compared to the U.S. stimulus of 5% of GDP).[6] To stanch the financial bloodletting, the Federal Reserve engaged in three rounds of Quantitative Easing and extended dollar swap lines to many troubled countries. And the coffers of the global development banks and international financial institutions were deepened with capital increases of about $300 billion.[7] Absent such coordinated crisis response, the depth of the crisis would have been much worse. It is hard to imagine the world mustering such a coordinated response in today's environment.

Yet, even though global coordination saved the economy, the GFC sowed the seeds for the reversal of many of the factors that drove geolegal convergence. As the crisis unfolded, and in its wake, the United States and Europe were no longer seen as political economy models for emerging markets to emulate. Countries vied for tighter regulation to protect their economies. Trade barriers loomed as a potentially attractive method to maintain jobs. And a raft of knock-on economic shocks ensued.

The United States retreated inward as partisanship markedly increased. Democrats were pulled to the left by the Occupy Wall Street movement and its fellow traveler Bernie Sanders. Conservatives fostered the Tea Party—a proto-Make America Great Again political movement—in response to President Barack Obama's dramatic expansion of government via the bailouts and his contemporaneous healthcare overhaul. These two movements reshaped politics on both sides into a force for emotion and outrage. But the impact on the right would be much more powerful, turning the politics of anger into a movement willing to shut government down to prove a point. To some extent, it was this moment that most encapsulated the transition to the politics of today. Predominantly white working-class voters from rural areas and conservative states who had been left behind by technological progress and globalization now had a new vehicle to express their anger. And other constituencies would follow them.

The financial crisis in Europe manifested through possible country-level defaults that led the continent into a half-decade of economic chaos and fragility. The economic crisis was especially pronounced in the Eurozone where the imposition of austerity was made a condition of support for troubled countries. One result was an outpouring of left and right populisms in multiple European countries that continues to today. The United Kingdom's exit from the European Union started here.

China suffered much less than either the United States or the European Union from the 2008 financial crisis. This in turn gave it considerably more prestige in international finance as well as in geopolitical terms. As the North Atlantic Basin turned inward grappling with the political and economic aftermath of the crisis, China became more confident overseas. A new economic focus on infrastructure gave it shiny new projects to show off and material capacity and project expertise that could be exported to other developing countries. China saw turmoil in the West as an opportunity to begin building alternate infrastructure that would further split the global economy. Its Belt and Road Initiative and Asia Infrastructure Investment Bank for the first time since the decade after World War II marked new economic arrangements with Beijing, rather than London, Washington, Brussels, or New York as a center.

The perception of a distracted and troubled West also led to China's new leader Xi Jinping pushing harder to catch up with it in economic and geopolitical terms, which in turn allowed him to argue that China required a stronger leader at home. Xi struck against domestic enemies, corruption, ideological backsliding, and restive minorities through a mix of political, legal, and technological means that resulted in censorship, surveillance, and ultimately a split in the global Internet.

A whole host of political crosscurrents unfolded as a result or at least in some way influenced by the crisis. The Middle East went through the "Arab Spring," which toppled authoritarian governments and left war, uncertainty, and democratic reform (in some cases) in its wake. India, Saudi Arabia, the United Arab Emirates, Turkey, and other rising economic powers increasingly looked to chart their own path rather than slot into the established U.S.-led economic order. And though Russia's expansionism began just before the financial crisis with its summer 2008 invasion of Georgia, it became increasingly clear between then and the 2022 invasion of Ukraine that Moscow did not intend to accept the U.S.-defined post–Cold War security order.

2016: TWO LEGS OF THE UNRULY TRIANGLE EMERGE

Artificial Politics

Most analysts overemphasize a rise in populism as the reason the United Kingdom left the European Union and U.S. voters ultimately elected President Trump in 2016. However, while it may not have been obvious at the time, 2016 was the genesis of the Artificial Politics leg of the Unruly Triangle as politics and technology began to intersect to sway the Brexit referendum and the U.S. presidential election. These results were a surprise to business leaders and financial market players, who were positioned the other way—underscoring how the unseen hand of tech-driven political interference can leave nearly every player in the economy wrong-footed.

At the time, I was working on integrating technology into geopolitical forecasting and a mutual acquaintance introduced me to the CEO of a company called Cambridge Analytica, then an in-demand politics–meets-data science outfit. When I suggested they might be interested in our election forecasts, he told me that the only thing he'd be interested in was making election outcomes a sure thing. That was not something I was interested in. Instead, it set off alarm bells about the murky world of technology-based manipulation.

It turns out that Cambridge Analytica was harvesting Facebook data of tens of millions of voters in order to build psychological profiles of them and voters like them such that political advertising was more likely to persuade—or manipulate—them.[8] The company embedded with Donald Trump's presidential campaign. The same CEO would go on to declare in an undercover video, "We did all the research, all the data, all the analytics, all the targeting, ran all the digital campaign, the television campaign, and our data informed all the strategy" for Trump's 2016 presidential campaign.[9] A whistleblower told the U.K. Parliament while testifying that the firm swayed the Brexit referendum, "data is the electricity of our new economy ... We enjoy the benefits of electricity, despite the fact that it can literally kill you."[10]

The extent to which Cambridge Analytica swayed Brexit and the 2016 U.S. election remains a topic of debate but a less controversial element of the 2016 Artificial Politics story was the fact that Russia intervened to help Trump. For instance, Russian hackers broke into Democratic computer systems, leaked sensitive documents, ran troll farms amplifying racist material, and much more all in pursuit of supporting Trump's election bid.[11] The U.K. government also found Russian disinformation played a role in the Brexit referendum, though just how much is open to debate.[12]

Geolegal Risk

Those elections gave rise to a tremendous amount of Geolegal Risk, as decades of international institution building started to be picked apart. The shock result of the United Kingdom's Brexit referendum and Trump's election gave conclusive proof from two leading democratic countries that much of the electorate's support for globalization and geolegal convergence had worn thin.

Brexit itself began the actual dismantling of international infrastructure that seems commonplace today. A narrow, unexpected majority of

U.K. voters opted to leave the European Union in 2016. To some extent, the politics of growth and social policy were subjugated to the politics of legal negotiations of exiting the European Union for the next half-decade. And in a sign of how populist politics on the right had changed the institutional backdrop that businesses had come to count on, it was Boris Johnson (then foreign minister of the United Kingdom) who responded "f—k business" to corporate concerns about a "hard Brexit" exit from the European Union without an agreement.

Trumpism presented a roughly simultaneous force in global politics as the campaign and ultimate victory of Donald Trump led to a new politics of bare-knuckled institutional renegotiation. Trump simultaneously threatened to cripple NATO, the United Nations, the World Health Organization (WHO), the WTO, and many others. In effect, he forced the question for Americans of whether they wanted to participate in the structures that America had led in the post–Cold War era, and the answer for many voters was that they no longer did. His argument—and one that resonated with enough American voters that it won him the presidency via the Electoral College and 46% of the popular vote—was that the way to "Make America Great Again" was to put "America First." In other words, the United States was tired of providing global public goods to an ungrateful world—whether this took the form of a commitment to lend military support to its allies, to keep its markets for goods open, to accept flows of immigrants and refugees with a pathway toward citizenship, or otherwise.

Trump's tenure in office saw a full-fledged assault on many tenets of globalization that firms had come to depend on. He not only imposed big tariffs on China but also imposed them on steel imports from NATO allies including Canada, claiming that this was necessary for U.S. national security. In so doing, he invoked the WTO's Article XXI National Security Exemption, pushing to a new limit the rationale that a country is the only judge of what it considers to be a national security interest. His administration also effectively dismantled the WTO's apex judicial mechanism, the Appellate Body, by blocking the appointment of new judges to it.

The crucial takeaway, however, was that voters had started to realign on these issues. The administration of Trump's successor, Joseph Biden, would maintain many of his anti-trade policies albeit with a different tone of voice. Trump was elected again in 2024 on similar promises of even bigger, unapologetic tariffs and the implementation of a new isolationism.

The obverse of such U.S. disengagement from other parts of the world was an increasing focus on pure national self-interest among other countries. As noted, China had already begun to set up alternative mechanisms to increase its influence in the world, and it alternated aggressive "Wolf-Warrior" Diplomacy against countries with which it had territorial or other disputes with ham-fisted attempts to use both the carrots and sticks that came with its growing economic heft. Over the course of the decade, China overtook the European Union to become the world's second-largest economy, its largest importer of commodities, and its leading exporter of manufactures. Over the same period, the shale revolution more than doubled U.S. domestic energy production, turning it into a small exporter and reducing its reliance on the Middle East. This led to warmer relations between the Gulf monarchies and China and deepened the latter's cooperation with a Russia growing ever more distant from the West. The countries of Southeast Asia began increasingly to hedge their relationships with both powers, and Indian foreign policy moved away from "nonalignment" to a hardheaded transactionalism.[13]

What this all translated into was a much more volatile geopolitical backdrop for corporations. The "one-world" utopianism of the post–Cold War era had faded, but the bitter ideological divide between rival economic systems had not returned. Instead, the world was once again fragmenting geopolitically but with far deeper economic linkages between countries than had ever been the case. This also meant that patterns of alliances between (and even within) countries could no longer be taken for granted. International economic and security relationships became not just more transactional but also more instrumental. Vietnam could have Comprehensive Strategic Partnerships with Russia, China, and the United States; Saudi Arabia could cooperate with Russia in the Organization of the Petroleum Exporting Countries (OPEC+) but buy its weapons from the United States; India could become a key member of the anti-China Quad but continue its long-standing friendship with Russia. The world of economic and security diplomacy was fragmenting to be sure in some respects, but also coming together for particular outcomes, like the pieces in a kaleidoscope, before shifting once again ahead of the next turn. And corporations were expected to negotiate all this.

But the geolegal order was yet to face its biggest challenge—a virus.

***

COVID AND A LEGAL LOCKDOWN

"Why don't you just go set up in Ukraine?" asked the potential investor on the other side of the phone.

The question threw me off. It was 2019, and I had just explained that I was in the process of building a start-up with talent largely based in Rwanda. The country had no corruption, top universities, and the fastest Internet in Africa. The government was making technology a priority and had just collaborated with Silicon Valley drone unicorn Zipline.

My political risk experience taught me that Ukraine had great talent but was a risky place. Russia had already annexed Crimea in 2014 and would likely come back for more. Organized crime, corruption, and the risk of cyberattacks from the East all loomed large. Rwanda was so obviously a better choice.

I couldn't hold back my contempt. "Are you asking me why I don't take a worse business environment and real geopolitical risk so I can work with Europeans instead of Africans?"

The line went silent. We didn't get the deal.

By 2019, I saw a world filled with opportunity, even amid geopolitical fragmentation. I was Deputy CEO of the top geopolitical risk firm, spending my days briefing CEOs and sounding off on TV about politics. It was a great job, but I couldn't shake a feeling I had from a sabbatical a couple of years prior.

In 2017, I went to an elite business school program where I was surrounded by CEOs and would-be CEOs of household-name businesses. All of them were telling stories of integrating technology into their enterprises. Courses emphasized how disruptive new technologies—artificial intelligence (AI), 3D printing, robotic process automation, and the like—would reshape business. I realized there was a real chance the political advisory world—and the advisory world more broadly—would be disrupted too.

I wanted to be the disrupter rather than the disrupted. So, I did the rational thing for a millennial: I left my stable job to set up a start-up. After all, we had just had our second child. What could be smarter than going to zero income?

I began to develop the initial business plan for Hence Technologies with my friend and co-founder Stephen Heitkamp. The world was becoming increasingly remote capable, but jobs were not geographically distributed. When Steve got the chance to move to Rwanda, we realized we had a unique opportunity to build a globally distributed software company with a hub in East Africa.

Our thought process at the time reflected a whole host of systemic assumptions about the world.

We assumed that the cost of financing would remain cheap such that building a software start-up was plausible and potentially worthwhile despite high failure rates. We assumed that raising money in British pounds, earning dollars and euros from global clients, and paying staff in Rwandan francs presented manageable risks. We assumed that air travel between the United Kingdom and Rwanda would remain seamless.

In short, we assumed the world would not become unruly.

In January and February 2020, we received a number of investor commitments, so we proceeded to incorporate the business in March.

On March 11, 2020, our company, Hence Technologies, became officially registered. On the same day, the WHO declared COVID-19 a pandemic.

COVID Emerges

In late 2019, a virus emerged in Wuhan, China, that spread easily, leaving sickness and death in its wake. At first, it seemed localized with limited cases outside China. Westerners watched in disbelief as China shut down full cities, and localities in Italy wrestled with doing the same. Yet even at the beginning of March 2020, U.K. Prime Minister Boris Johnson bragged of shaking hands with constituents, and U.S. President Donald Trump claimed the virus would simply disappear.[14]

Just days later, however, it was clear that the virus was spreading around the world at an alarming rate. The WHO was under pressure for failing to contain the virus to China. With its back against the wall, it finally declared a pandemic. Within weeks, the global economy ground to a halt. It would take nearly 10 months of on-and-off lockdowns before the world would have access to vaccines.

Law and Order Overload

COVID was a crucial milestone. The international collaboration that had stemmed GFC bleeding was out of reach due to fracturing global politics. Yet, when the pandemic hit, goods and people stopped moving in a way that could never have been coordinated. At first, this was to stop the virus, but it actually laid the groundwork for a new protectionism. The use of legal tools to mandate this sets the stage for the Geolegal Risk, Artificial Politics Risk, and LegalAI Risk I will unpack across the rest of the book.

COVID and Geolegal Risk

From a Geolegal Risk perspective, governments created new legal authorities. In some cases, this was the more benign updating of economic authorities to respond to crises, like in the European Union. But in nearly every case, this was about creating authorities to deprive citizens of their most basic rights in pursuit of the greater good. Leaving your house or eating out with your family were now suddenly government choices. Requirements to work from home hit the less-well-off harder than elites who had access to nannies or bigger living spaces to manage the time.

Governments with authoritarian tendencies were able to expand control of the state in ways they would not have to undo after COVID-19, leading to an enduring decline in the rule of law. In Iran, for instance, the government fired live bullets and tear gas against prison protests at the start of the pandemic, killing 36 prisoners. This no doubt cast a shadow on anyone thinking of protesting for other reasons.[15] In Egypt, the government enlarged the military's role in politics via emergency rules.[16]

In China, hardline zero-COVID policies drastically curtailed both inbound and outbound foreign travel, with flights between the United States and China dropping 95% between 2019 and late 2022, when the policy was lifted.[17] Meanwhile, within China, urban neighborhoods that had even a single case of COVID were subject to dramatic lockdowns.

The measures sparked widespread speculation that the pandemic was just an alibi to curtail foreign ideological and cultural influences, while simultaneously allowing a dramatic increase in domestic surveillance.

The pandemic also undermined geolegal convergence logic and created new rationales for managing emerging Geolegal Risks. The pandemic added the rationales of self-sufficiency, resiliency, and redundancy to existing arguments against offshoring and just-in-time inventory management. It empowered bipartisan coalitions pushing subsidies and tariffs for reshoring critical parts of supply chains. But it also fanned the flames of racism and xenophobia as populations used country of origin as a reason to discriminate. Grotesque examples of anti-Chinese and anti-Asian discrimination stemmed from the perception that COVID was a "Chinese virus." The president of the United States referring to COVID as "kung flu" reinforced such perceptions and seemed to provide air cover for such racism.[18]

The biggest effect, however, was with respect to the politics of vaccines, which intersected with law in two ways. First, could governments actually force citizens to take them? Legally they could, but there would be political backlash fomented by disinformation, as discussed later in the chapter. Second, how would governments prioritize receipt of vaccines? Most took a risk-based approach, giving vaccines to the most vulnerable and asking others to wait in line, which caused its own backlash from citizens who wanted to jump the queue.

Artificial Politics

Dramatic expansions of power laid the groundwork for today's Artificial Politics Risk with respect to surveillance. Citizens had to consent to tracking through location and contact tracing if they wanted to earn back their right to leave the house. Governments amassed huge amounts of citizen data just waiting to be exploited by politicians who so desire.

The crisis undermined the role of elites in society. Few governments "got it right," and many were shown to have fumbled in their responses.

Governments literally took away the most basic rights of citizens and were accused of doing so too late, for too long, and in unacceptably draconian ways. This opened the door for persuasion via social media by all types of actors.

Moreover, in a COVID-specific version of Artificial Politics, a rise in virus-related disinformation poisoned normal channels of news to the population. The race to develop vaccines proved to be ground zero. The United States and China developed vaccines by the end of 2020, but China's, based on older technology, would be more quickly available for export. The United States reportedly ran disinformation campaigns against the Chinese product to prevent its rival from scoring a diplomatic victory.[19]

U.S. and European mRNA vaccines used new technology that drew skepticism from corners of their populations. The assertions ranged from traditional libertarian concerns about bodily autonomy to farfetched claims that the vaccines would insert tracking chips into recipients' bodies. Anger about vaccine mandates coincided with political exhaustion with government control, leading citizens to backlash against wearing masks as well.

The underlying questions around vaccines ultimately often came down to trust—did one trust often-distant technocratic elites to identify problems and offer solutions while respecting local conditions, traditions, preferences, and constraints? The answer to that question in turn often determined the answer to the broadest of political questions—not even whether one stood on the left or right but rather whether one believed the actions of the state were legitimate.

Black Lives Matter

As Americans were largely stuck at home, many turned to social media to pass the time. On May 25, 2020, a man named George Floyd was murdered by a police officer who kneeled on his neck for nine minutes during his arrest on suspicion of using counterfeit money at a convenience store. Video spread widely stoking anger that had been building among many Americans.

First, they were angry about the persistent perceived impunity with which the police could dispose of the lives of people of color and rarely face the consequences. The officer in question was tried and convicted of murder, but the incident raised larger questions about a legal doctrine seen as overly protective of local police forces. The doctrine—qualified immunity—protects a government official from lawsuits alleging that the official violated a plaintiff's rights, only allowing suits where officials violated a "clearly established" statutory or constitutional right.[20] Second, they were angry at the Trump administration more broadly—its pandemic response, its broader politics, and its dismissive reaction to anger about George Floyd.

Protests started to build in cities across America not just about the way police treated Black people and others of color but also how society was systemically unjust. Many companies performed self-flagellation in an attempt to atone for just how little they had valued diversity over time, as they tried (and failed) to straddle a divide between increasingly outraged partisans on either side of social issues. As I'll unpack later, this turbo-charged corporate action on values-based issues was setting future traps in which companies are currently ensnared.

The protests themselves became fodder for other divisions. They typically took the form of large mass gatherings and marches outside that were permitted or denied by authorities, in turn leading to resentments that COVID-era public health rules were being selectively enforced. Criminal justice has long been a racially divisive issue in American politics, but the confluence of COVID and the George Floyd protests made questions of policing and selective enforcement especially polarizing.

Stop the Steal

As the 2020 U.S. election season got underway, President Donald Trump started to hedge in case of a loss. As Democratic states pushed through electoral rules that prioritized mail-in ballots in the face of the pandemic, Trump started planting seeds that the election itself could no longer be fair. He stoked public concern that Democrats were trying to steal the election by enabling their voters to vote more than once.

On November 3, 2020, Trump lost to Joseph Biden. Almost immediately Trump swung into action to undermine the election. As the *New York Times* recounts, he engaged in a full-court press to ask states to substitute electors in his favor and to help him "find" the votes he needed to win. He leaned on the Justice Department to launch investigations that would imply or claim the election was fraudulently won. He pressured Vice President Mike Pence not to certify the election on January 6, 2021, as was his constitutional duty.[21]

Pence failed to do Trump's bidding and ultimately certified Biden as president early in the morning the following day, but not before Trump had whipped up support among his followers to protest Pence's decision to go ahead. That protest turned violent and ultimately led his followers to storm the U.S. Capitol Building. Biden became president, and a number of legal cases would be brought against Trump. But these actions did not prevent Trump from becoming the Republican nominee for the 2024 election, an election he would go on to win. His path there involved not just a rout of internal opposition within the Republican Party but also very significant decisions by the U.S. Supreme Court on the powers of the presidency. The legacy of the 2020 election and its aftermath was a full reversal from U.S. preaching on election integrity and democracy overseas. U.S. politics had turned unruly.

ENTER LEGALAI

To some extent, little happened in the first couple of years of the Biden administration. The economy recovered from COVID, with inflation staying too high for too long and urban streets showcasing a COVID hangover of tent cities and open-air drug use. The United States pulled out of Afghanistan with disastrous consequences. The idea of metaverses and digital assets, which had gotten a boost from the stay-at-home COVID years, took hold, even leading Facebook to rebrand itself as Meta. But on November 30, 2022, as Andy Bird mentions in the foreword, everything changed.

On that day, a start-up called OpenAI released its large-language model ChatGPT, and the generative AI tool scaled to one million users in less than a week and 100 million users in just two months. The Internet went wild pushing its boundaries and tasking the system everything from difficult knowledge work to drafting driving directions in the form of limericks. While technology can often take time to sink in, ChatGPT captured the imagination of business and society alike.

Artificial intelligence shows up as a key character in this book, affecting politics at its most foundational levels. But what is less appreciated is the impact that AI has on the law. This intersection serves as the third legal of the Unruly Triangle—LegalAI.

Applying technology to the law is nothing new. Great minds like Richard Susskind have been working at this intersection for decades, and my own company, Hence Technologies, has spent the last half-decade working on AI solutions for law departments. But most of the efforts have focused on helping companies become more productive through automation rather than true disruption. With generative AI, technology was now smart enough to pass the bar yet still dumb enough to invent case citations when lawyers sought its advice. This raises some interesting possibilities—and risks.

First, it raises the specter that lawyers—long known for resisting technology—might have finally met their match in the form of ruthlessly efficient systems for collecting and analyzing data as well as developing reasoning modeled on the world's best minds. Second, it brings forth the prospect that citizens who had fallen out of the justice system because they can't afford lawyers might now get legal advice from computers. Third, it raises the chance that attacks using the legal system might be automated. Fourth, it challenges regulators to figure out if they can properly control AI—leading many localities to ban the application of AI to law in the first instance. Finally, it raises the chance that AI-powered law may look nothing like the law of today—whether that means AI is used for maximum law enforcement or whether it means we'll all have individual law tailored just for us at every moment.

Over the course of the book, I'll make clear just how fundamental these considerations are to the work of modern businesses.

TOWARD AN UNRULY WORLD

Globalization was the process by which Chinese kids learned about U.S. hip-hop and then logged on to download bootleg albums they could sell. Today we live in a world where U.S. kids find out about new hip-hop artists on Chinese platform TikTok—so long as the politics of suspicion don't ban that platform in the United States.

Globalization sprang from each of the vertices of the Unruly Triangle. Political shifts toppled governments and opened up new economic relationships. Technology made it easier than ever to trade anything anywhere in the world and also for information to flow freely. The law was used as a vehicle to codify such progress rapidly and expansively, especially through the growth of new institutions.

This led to a new playbook for companies seeking to grow as big as possible: globalize everything. Capture as much global market share as possible. Globalize supply chains to the extent traditional political and legal risks could be managed. Push for continued legal convergence to reduce regulatory and compliance friction.

The economic opportunities were so powerful that pretty much every company—no matter how small—became globalized in some way, from production to communication to distributed teams.

This level of interconnectedness fuels the global economy but makes us more brittle than we realize. Traditional supply chain analysis might focus on where goods are coming from. But we increasingly have to focus on where our ideas and our supply of talent are coming from. For instance, companies rely on pipelines of ongoing talent at a time when the politics of immigration has become increasingly restrictive. They rely on foreign markets not just for revenues but also to test products against competitors in a global proving ground. In today's world, both goods and knowledge supply chains are exposed to increasing political and legal risk—with such risks rising as technology plays more and more of a role in the functioning of the supply chain itself.

Each side of the Unruly Triangle is shifting in ways that are disrupting the status quo of globalization. Since the financial crisis, there has been a steady building drumbeat against free trade, offshoring, and outsourcing. Legal institutions that were built during the globalization era are collapsing. Fear over how technology will be used by geopolitical competitors is splintering the world rather than connecting it. Alliances are fraying, and both the law and the financial system are being weaponized. War and conflict are completely unrestrained by international law.

Today, we hear debates about whether the world is deglobalizing. There is scant evidence in the data that trade flows are shifting much, which should be comforting but actually means that most companies have more risk exposure than they realize. That's because there is a lot of evidence we have reached the end of geolegal convergence and it is giving way to geolegal fragmentation. Firms now face a persistent erosion of rules and norms and increasing uncertainty about not just when and how the laws might change but even about whether current laws will be enforced. And this is happening in many countries. Compounding matters, firms face a world of conflicting legal demands across the various jurisdictions in which they are present, as well as an ever-increasing effort by countries to extend the reach of their laws beyond their borders.

Part II of this book will grapple with the core elements of geolegal fragmentation. War and conflict are evolving to be fought with new weapons against a backdrop of fewer guardrails, no global police force, and fraying alliances. The law is being weaponized to fight domestic political battles undermining the rule of law in many jurisdictions, or as a tool of extraterritorial reach to hobble economic or geopolitical competitors. Technology is changing the nature of rules and laws themselves both by automating the law and by undermining it. Corporations are facing a period of increasing claustrophobia as political and technology shifts implore them to be patriotic and woke—or the exact opposite—at the drop of a dime.

PART II

GEOLEGAL RISK: WHEN POLITICS AND LAW COLLIDE

CHAPTER THREE

UNRULING
AMERICA:
THE EYE
OF THE STORM

I n 2024, the United States seemed to avoid an unruly hurricane. A dramatic presidential campaign featuring assassination attempts, felony convictions, foreign interference, and a late-stage switch of Democratic candidates drew to a close with contenders Donald Trump and Kamala Harris polling within the margin of error nationally and in all the important Electoral College states. America seemed to be spiraling toward a disputed election that might reprise acts of political violence, like the storming of Congress on January 6, 2021.

And then none of that happened. President Trump was returned to office having won every swing state, the popular vote, and unified control of Congress. Whether they were licking their wounds, respecting the Constitution, trying to look magnanimous, or simply trolling Trump,

Democrats immediately acknowledged the victory and committed to a peaceful transfer of power. Politicians and business leaders alike congratulated America on the apparently miraculous feat of a painless handover, as if the United States were some sort of emerging market demonstrating to the world that its political process could be trusted, when actually America is a country governed under the world's most enduring written constitution, guarantor of the world's safe haven assets, and home to the world's most powerful military.

America's evolution is emblematic of a "rule of law recession" taking hold around the world, as the World Justice Project calls it. For the better part of a decade, more countries have seen a decline in rule of law than an increase.[1] That means it's becoming more dangerous to do business in each of these locations than ever before because you cannot count on a predictable political process safeguarded by the courts or a fair judicial process in the event the company or one of its executives ends up in front of one of them. When it comes to America, that a peaceful transition was even in question underscores the point.

But something deeper is happening. Just like China and Russia have looked out at the world globalization created and rejected the existing international infrastructure, Americans swept Trump back to the White House on plans to dramatically remake domestic institutions and America's role in the world because the current approach doesn't work for them.

Writing about current affairs raises the risk of being immediately out of date by the time of publication. And publishing at the start of the second Trump administration raises the prospect that what I think is happening today could be terribly wrong. But I'm blissfully aware of that risk and taking it wholeheartedly because I think there's a seismic shift in American politics for which Trump is both a channel and an accelerant rather than thinking the movement supporting Trump exists only because of him.

That movement represents a desire among voters to shrug off the status quo—to leave behind precedents and norms—and to rethink government more broadly. Whether what a majority of voters want is exactly what Trump promises to deliver or whether they are just looking for some sort of change remains unclear. Regardless, this raises the prospect not just of substantial policy volatility but of the literal "unruling" of the United States—unwinding the rules that have governed politics and business for the lifetime of most senior executives.

Combine that with the way technology will shift politics and society over the medium-run, and it is obvious the 2024 election didn't dodge the unruly hurricane: it clarified that we are in the calm eye of the storm.

UNRULING

When the world is unruly, it is easy to miss fundamental changes in the rules of the game because we mistake them for temporary volatility. Trump's return to power was not an aberration. It was not a fluke. It was not a surprise. It reflected the deep desires of those whom globalization left behind—and technology will leave further behind—to fight back by shifting the rules of the game before it's too late.

That intersection of political and legal change—of Geolegal Risk— presents a dangerous environment for businesses that prefer policy stability and are optimized for the world as they find it today. It's a tough place to be when competitors may be better positioned for a world of new and different rules. It's an awkward moment for companies that are comfortable lobbying on policy changes but less so when it comes to normatively prescribing the architecture of government.

Before we can fight back, we must understand what is actually underway. In effect, the Trump administration has vowed to rethink the rules and norms of governance—many of them all at once. The vision is potentially unbounded and will be characterized by big swings to reshape the role of the national government.

That reconsideration is taking place on both international and domestic policy. It is taking place not just about policy but about the actual structure of government. And rather than expecting the typical legal institutions that stabilize in favor of the status quo to do so, those institutions themselves will be further changed in the process.

On some issues, like social policy and business regulation, the effort will be to reduce the consolidation of power at the federal level that has taken place over the last 100 years, devolving authority back to state governments by eliminating federal oversight and regulation. This could involve eliminating whole departments of government or at least fundamentally paring back regulatory authority and rules in place. This risks amplifying the patchwork of state rules that business already must comply with by eliminating areas of national harmonization.

There will be an emphasis on "starving the beast"—cutting taxes to justify cutting federal government spending. This may well be a short-term boon to companies as their tax bills go down. But blunt, large-scale cuts in federal spending risk eliminating all the individual subsidies, tax breaks, and regulatory carveouts companies have accumulated and optimized for over decades of lobbying and, in some cases, regulatory capture. For angry voters, that may be the point. For companies, that will be a headache even if the net amount they owe the government drops.

In other cases, the federal government will become even more proactive. On economic statecraft, the government will move tariffs from the technical and legal channels into the political by advocating for applying them at significant levels across the board. While that will be booed by economists, it's what 56% of voters want—which is a number that may go up over time as technology eats more jobs while voters think foreign trade is responsible.[2]

On immigration policy, the only way to achieve Trump's aims will be to significantly expand the powers and activity of government. Fifty-eight percent of Americans support his aims of mass deportation of undocumented immigrants, with similar support for building border walls and reducing immigration more broadly.[3] Again, this may be the low point for such sentiments as voters look for scapegoats to blame the downside of AI-led productivity growth in the future.

While no doubt Trump's success or failure will fill in the texture of unruliness, it's not actually critical whether Trump passes any of these policies to prove the point. The fact is that voters roundly support status quo destruction and will have more reasons to do so in the future. And the roadblocks to executing these policies now or in the next 5–10 years are receding.

A BIAS FOR SOMETHING

The U.S. Constitution has a status quo bias built in through checks and balances created by a separation of government powers. It has generally been hard to shift U.S. policy because the odds that Congress and the President agree are not particularly high. And when they do, such alignment is often ephemeral as after two years of unified government, voters typically flip control of one chamber of Congress.

But today, checks and balances are less clear. Presidential power has expanded dramatically due to an erosion of legislative and judicial oversight. The White House under most recent presidents has been willing to use executive orders and agency power to go around Congress whenever it disagrees, which subsequent presidents then use to justify going further.

While there is a myth of impartiality in the U.S. courts, the political nomination and appointment process can have political outcomes. Many federal judges and Supreme Court Justices seem increasingly willing to rule in favor of policies supported by the Republican Party or in favor of its government officials. This may be because they agree with the

Republicans, because they were appointed by Republicans, or both. While the first Trump administration lost in front of its own appointees numerous times, even a small increase in partisanship in the courts is significant. Partisan courts reduce the role of Congress and are already leading to seismic decisions that overturn decades of precedent.[4] Some would even say it amounts to judicial legislation—judges effectively making their own laws through pronouncements and decisions. The Supreme Court's 2024 ruling that presidents have immunity from prosecution for official acts both supports the prior point and separately erodes judicial oversight of the executive branch.[5]

With the status quo guardrails damaged, the gates are open to seismic policy change. And voters are in the mood for change.

The U.S. two-party system has also long-been held to be a stabilizer but today makes voters more dogmatic and tribal than ever before. While the parties in power have flipped repeatedly over the last decade and a half, a clear partisan divide has made elections more pugnacious including the use of weaponized prosecution of political enemies. Personal animosity combined with an erosion of norms has led to the repeated charade of impeachments for sport, in addition to those that are for real. An uptick in foreign digital interference litters the information universe with further reasons for each side to hate each other, as does the ownership of media by the country's richest individuals—whether that be digital media like X (formerly Twitter) or traditional media like the *Washington Post* and *Los Angeles Times*.

As a result, when parties shift in power, as has occurred in the last three elections, they go for broke, fearing a very narrow window to effect change. And their adherents show up with digital bullhorns to amplify their messages. This time, the accumulated erosion of guardrails and a shift in the mood of the country has opened up the possibility of systemic change rather than simply policy change.

AMERICAN EXCEPTIONALISM?

Imagine I asked you to invest in the sovereign debt of a country like the one I described. The country managed to deliver a peaceful transfer of power in only one of the last two elections, while the previous party in power pursued a number of politically motivated prosecutions against the now-President. The ruling political party has successfully entrenched itself in the court system and has swept to power by channeling voter anger into populist support on the back of xenophobic and isolationist views as well as dismantling the national regulatory infrastructure. The President has suggested he shouldn't have relinquished power the last time he lost and that voters may never need to vote again given his re-election, which was aided by the world's richest person pointing one of the most powerful social media platforms in his favor.

You'd probably worry that these were not idiosyncratic realities but instead signs of creeping authoritarianism. You might worry the country could turn into Hungary or perhaps Russia. To the extent you'd want to invest, you probably wouldn't want do it at the risk-free rate of return.

But the United States is different from other countries. It prints the reserve currency. It has the only military that can project power in all corners of the globe. It is home to some of the world's most innovative companies driving the technologies the rest of the world will be dependent on in the future. And it has a long tradition of moderating disruptive forces and finding its way forward through democratic change.

Whether you believe the United States is headed toward authoritarianism from a geolegal perspective really comes down to the judgement call of whether you think the United States is exceptional. I continue to think it is—that citizens and, perhaps the military, have a breaking point at which they would fight back and reject true authoritarianism—which is why this chapter has focused on the risk of sweeping change enabled by institutional erosion rather than the risk of systemic collapse.

That's in the short term though. The direction of travel is more worrying when combined with the way technology will enable authoritarianism, as I'll discuss in Part III about Artificial Politics Risk.

FIGHTING BACK: THE GEOLEGAL LINE OF DEFENSE

To fight back against the implications of unruling in America, business will need to mobilize the full power of their legal and government affairs capabilities. That increasingly means integrating the two more deeply than they ever have been before.

There has been a trend of consolidating government affairs and risk teams under general counsel (GC) who have a growing strategic role in the organization. This is a wise move because the sheer amount of regulatory and policy change that is going to be unleashed in the United States will trigger untold legal implications that must be anticipated and fought upstream.

Setting the agenda for what your company must lobby against versus what you must be prepared to accept now requires both a legal and a political lens which must be combined into a geolegal perspective. The means not fighting legal with legal and politics with government affairs but rather fighting Geolegal Risk with a combined tool kit.

While beefing up the authority and capability of legal and the functions that report to it are a critical way to fight back, there are two challenges with this approach. First, many GCs are career lawyers or non-U.S. specialists who will fail to grasp the gravity and nuance of what's in play from the open window for sweeping change. Issue spotting and horizon scanning will be critical to distinguish signal from noise, and this must come from the top in order to mobilize proactive resources in the business when risks are identified. Companies that appoint "political" GCs, with deep careers straddling the law and policymaking, are likely to be better prepared to fight back.

But the second challenge is that fighting back and winning policy concessions is going to require a new mindset that treats the United States as if it is not exceptional—as if it is actually the emerging market that its behavior implies. This is because the real policy action is actually happening at a political level, led by a manifestation of the Republican party that is fueled by populist support and that values allegiance and loyalty more than its predecessors. This is not the way traditional lobbying works because it implies elevating your presence above the tactical fray and into the strategic conversations about the shape of government in the decades ahead.

The good news is that companies know how to run these playbooks, if only they recognize its necessary. Treat politics in the United States like you would treat it in Hungary or maybe Turkey, and you will have more success than if you treat it like you would in France. This implies making real, serious investments in bringing on board political influencers who can get the attention of those in power. But it also means realigning business priorities to those of the administration rather than expecting to shift it. And, remember, the president's sherpas can come and go, so you need to remain flexible as political appointees will likely be discarded like they are in other personalistic regimes.

It goes without saying that there is a risk companies get too good at this influence game. As politics becomes a transactional deal of loyalty for concessions, companies may be asked to carry water for the administration that crosses tripwires or redlines. This is why, despite the emphasis on political heavy hitters, it remains critical to have legal in the lead to make sure that cozying up to government doesn't cause public relations nightmares or legal liability down the line. Failure to do so may simply trade one risk for another.

CHAPTER FOUR

UNRULY CONFLICT: WAR WITHOUT GUARDRAILS

"Y ou better shower with your bathing suit when you're in China."

That's what one China expert told me when we were both invited to speak at a major Chinese think tank about U.S. and Asia trade policy a few years ago.

I knew the dynamic between the United States and China had changed much from where it had been in the heady days of globalization, when the secret universe of counterfeit rap CDs seemed like a central challenge of a more integrated world. But this was still unnerving.

It had become increasingly standard practice to travel to China digitally naked—meaning without your everyday phone and computer for fear they would be hacked by Chinese intelligence. But I had never considered the risks of being physically naked.

The Chinese intelligence sponge would no doubt suck up as much information as possible from my devices when I connected to the Internet or perhaps left my device unattended in a "secure" hotel safe. And it was possible I'd bring home an implanted gift to keep my IT colleagues fully employed for many weeks. So I'd listen to a handful of albums on a non-networked iPod Shuffle, and I'd work only on a laptop I could dispose of, which would stay by my side for the whole trip.

But why on Earth would I need to shower with a bathing suit on?

It turns out that the congressional staffers and academics I was traveling with were being invited for more than just our policy comments. As influential voices in the policy debate, the long-term planning organisms of the Chinese government had identified us as people to get to know.

Even though most of us were not in positions of significant power nor privy to information that Beijing might place great value on, China would still look to gain leverage over us in some form. Why? The U.S.-China relationship was growing adversarial, and it was becoming cheaper and easier to engage in low-level conflict. So the number of combatants was expanding.

China could try to surreptitiously implant backdoor access into my phone when I passed through a hotel metal detector, perhaps with a distraction to cause a minor delay. And I would have no idea.

Or it could be more frontal. Imagine getting an email 10 years later that asked whether I'd like pictures of me naked in the shower finding their way onto the Internet? If not, I better do what they say. Again. And again.

How did I become a potential combatant in U.S.-China tensions? Well, nearly everyone is. Perhaps I was more valuable because I had frequent communications with policymakers and businesses leaders. But a lot of other people of very much average importance in this U.S.-China fight get caught up in it.

In this environment, individuals, companies, governments, and militaries will carry much more exposure in their global footprints than they realize. This exposure is not just geopolitical. Technology and legal systems present frontline risks that everyone will come into contact with.

This world of unruly wars is not war as usual. Governments, militaries, companies, and individuals all have playbooks on how to deal with conflict. Some work, some don't—but the first strategy for nearly all companies and individuals (and many governments and militaries too) is to avoid conflict. Don't want to deal with the North Korea conflict? Then be careful not to make a film that spoofs Kim Jong Un. Want to stay out of U.S.-China competition? Don't develop and save the plans for any new valuable technologies on your network. Don't want to run afoul of U.S. anti-money laundering laws? Then probably don't run a bank that takes deposits from people with money. Want to run your business efficiently with just-in-time inventory management? Don't source from China or ship things through the Red Sea or buy any raw materials from Russia.

The world is going through a time of systemic change, and companies face more risk exposure to widening conflict than they ever have before. We could easily wake up to North Korea crossing the border into South Korea, knocking that country's semiconductor, smartphone, and other technology production offline in one fell swoop. The same could be said with respect to China and Taiwan—although the bigger risk is that China takes a step so dramatic that it's not just Taiwan's market that is taken offline but also the mainland cut out by sanctions. No doubt companies feel greater exposure to the world's oil supply as missiles fly in the Middle East.

The world has seen such risks before, but it had legal guardrails to keep things in line. The United Nations would debate collective security. NATO would act decisively with one voice. The U.S. military patrolled global shipping lanes and was willing to act as the world's police force. None of that can be taken for granted in a world where relative U.S. power is declining and the second Trump administration has little appetite for military adventures to enforce a global political order. Moreover, countries increasingly act outside the structure of international organizations, laws, and norms. This is a radically changed environment from just a decade ago.

Knowing how to thrive in this environment will determine what countries become the next great powers and what companies survive. To paraphrase Warren Buffet, it's only when the tide goes out that you get to see who's been swimming naked. Or showering, as the case may be.

The way in which companies and individuals like me are being pulled into state conflict points toward a broader and more dangerous trend. Conflict itself—even war—is becoming more dispersed and complex. The Cold War featured a diverse set of actors engaged in complex conflict and politics. But Washington and Moscow were directing client states, rebels, and paramilitary groups—all combatants consciously supporting their superpower benefactor—to act in ways that advanced their respective global causes. They spied heavily on each other's scientists and political elite and possibly even some highly placed business leaders. But the game was bounded. Average civilians were generally not targeted, kidnapped, or blackmailed. Noncombatants were just that.

The USSR and United States might not have always followed the rules of international law, but they supported in principle ideas around Westphalian sovereignty and made sure to claim to be fighting for the true wishes of the people in whatever state they were intervening in, be it Vietnam, Afghanistan, most of Central America, and assorted countries in Central Africa.

Today borders appear less sacrosanct, laws of war are more politicized, and the battlefield has widened to include noncombatants—and not just those showering but also those playing basketball or advocating for political change from afar. This is the changing political vector of war and conflict.

What makes this new political vector especially dangerous, though, is that it is augmented by a technology vector that opens a new space for offensive operations. Advanced kinetic warfare is becoming available to more actors thanks to cheaper, highly capable drones. Cyber has become essentially a new theater of combat, but one that goes further and deeper into an adversary than all but the most destructive kinetic weapons. I'll get to that in Part III when I look at war through an Artificial Politics lens.

Last, if noncombatants get unwillingly pulled into conflict through the political and technology vector in ways that are mostly negative, the emerging legal vector puts nominally noncombatant companies and individuals squarely in the battlefield not only with risks but with some opportunities—and lots of complicated choices to make.

War today is very different from the country-based armed conflicts of the even recent past. Typically war would originate from a state or from a militant group. Today, it may be declared or undeclared. It may be fought by proxies funded from afar, keeping battle far from the homeland. War may embroil citizens who have rights to be protected. But increasingly today war may also pull companies and individual noncombatants into the fray.

War today is blurry and unbounded. The political vector of risk is enhanced because major global powers are acting or threatening to act in an expansionary fashion. The technology vector of risk emerges from the fact that war is being fought with traditional weapons as well as cyber weapons capable of incredible sabotage—and soon, it will be amplified by artificial intelligence–powered weapons capable of precise catastrophic kinetic and cyber damage. The legal vector of conflict is of increased importance because regulatory and judicial systems are being weaponized against companies and individuals that are not combatants but still are part of adversarial struggles.

THE POLITICAL VECTOR: UNBOUNDED WAR

Navigating the unbounded nature of the new war is significantly more complicated than in the past. Previously, two strategies did most of the heavy lifting. First, you could avoid countries that were prone to war—or have plans to get out of them if everything went haywire. Second, you could buy insurance products that would compensate you if there was a conflict.

For entrenched national and corporate interests, this geopolitical moment is one of extreme risk. The world is unlikely to become more conducive to those interests in the coming decade; probably the best the United States and its Washington Consensus allies can maintain is 90% of the status quo in terms of the global balance of power. But for Russia, China, North Korea, Iran, and even less belligerent states that are looking to remake their place in the world like India, South Africa, Turkey, perhaps Brazil, Nigeria, and Indonesia, the coming years are a once-in-a-century opportunity. For the first time perhaps since the end of World War I, the fundamental balance of power in the world is being negotiated. In the waning days of World War II, the United States and USSR essentially sucked all the oxygen out of any broader global discussion about what the post-war world would be. At the end of the Cold War, the United States triumphed, and a shockingly large majority of the world embraced capitalism, democracy, and a U.S.-defined international order. What will the balance of power look like a decade from now? For the first time in a long time, it is hard to foresee. Exactly how the second Trump administration affects this dynamic is uncertain, but in all likelihood it will accelerate the process toward a fragmenting world order.

Borders

From a political point of view, war is evolving largely through power struggle. In effect, governments like Russia under Vladimir Putin are willing to start wars of aggression with countries like Ukraine and someday, perhaps, Poland, the Baltics, or others. Governments like China are no longer willing to accept a Western-led world and are willing to project power regionally and beyond through both diplomatic and military channels. Countries like the United States and the United Kingdom are fatigued by war and have no appetite to put boots on the ground to stop China or Russia but will act aggressively with sanctions and with their checkbook.

This revisionist approach to international borders is a key symptom of the global rule of law recession. On the day Putin walked across the border, companies doing business in the region effectively lost both Ukraine and Russia as markets. They lost the former because of rising security risks that disrupted operations and decimated the local economy. They lost the latter because the unified sanctions response from Western countries made it illegal, impractical, or embarrassing for them to continue to operate there.

There is little evidence that Vladimir Putin ever respected the borders of post-Soviet states with Russia. From Georgia to Crimea to the Donbass to the entire Ukrainian state, it has been close to two decades since the 2008 initial Russian incursion into a separatist region of Georgia. But for much of the world—politically and legally—the notion of borders being sacrosanct has been a guiding principle, if not always a reality. The invasion of one country by another required specific justification. While the justification for the U.S. invasions of Iraq, Afghanistan, or numerous other states can be (heavily) debated, the United States went to great effort post-2001 to claim authority under international law and UN resolutions that it had the right to use military force against another sovereign state, saying that it was facing a threat to its own sovereignty. The Bush administration may have preferred to ignore international law, but even at the height of rhetoric around the United States taking on the so-called burden of global empire, it knew engagement on the question of international law and justification for violating the sovereignty of other countries required attention.

For Putin, Russia's military adventures in its near abroad required essentially zero serious engagement on why its annexation of Crimea or later full-scale invasion of Ukraine were justified under international law (though Russia made a very half-hearted attempt to claim it was acting in self-defense and in response to some sort of imagined genocide against Russians in Ukraine). Because they are grounded in such a pointed rejection of an international order based on sovereign borders that can trace its origins back centuries to the Treaty of Westphalia, Russia probably presents the most acute threat to the global order. The threat of a broader war in Europe is higher than at any time since World War II, and the threat of nuclear exchange is higher than at any time since at least the Yom Kippur War in 1973 and probably since the Cuban Missile Crisis. This is understandable because the bar to violating national sovereignty and borders is rapidly lowering. The direct implication for the national security of various other Eastern European states is massive, but there are broader implications for countries around the world and for businesses that operate globally and likely have some basic assumptions about the sovereignty of the states in which they are present.

While the Russian invasion of Ukraine probably did more to undermine norms around respect for borders, the United States and Europeans responded much more forcefully to support Ukraine than most observers expected, including and perhaps most of all Vladimir Putin. This lessens the chance of the rapid undoing of the security order. But while the list of countries countering the Russian military action in Ukraine is surprisingly robust, there are significant countries also either remaining neutral or passively supporting Russia. India assesses little upside to defending an order it had little role in creating and instead sees a bargain to buy Russian energy exports. States across Africa and the Middle East argue the West is being hypocritical in aiding Ukraine while supporting Israel's large-scale military operations in Palestinian-ruled Gaza and Lebanon.

It appears the notion that norms around borders should be preserved despite the high financial and human cost—and risk of frightening escalation—is not widely shared across this world. While Europe is likely to continue to support the sacrosanct nature of borders, whether the Trump administration preserves, weakens, or overturns the similar U.S. position on global borders remains uncertain. This has consequences for the trajectory of geopolitics and the environment in which countries and companies will operate. NATO's united opposition to Russia's invasion of Ukraine likely gives hawks in Beijing pause that say China cannot become a great power until it takes its erstwhile province of Taiwan. But the precedent for great powers (which for these purposes, Russia is) exercising unilateral power in their near abroad is nonetheless set. Even before the Ukraine war, the chances of an eventual military action by China to annex Taiwan was a key regional risk. While NATO's response to Russia complicates China's tactical military approach to Taiwan, Russia's actions enlarge the strategic space for China to increase pressure on the island.

All of this is happening at a time when the United States is losing both relative power and desire to act—for better or worse—as the world's policeman, a development that is likely to be reinforced by the isolationist instincts of the Trump administration. For decades the United States took it upon itself to provide global public goods in the form of international security. Since 9/11, the United States was proactive in providing aid to partners to fight terrorism. The U.S. Navy patrols sea lanes to keep commerce flowing. In many places where democracy seemed at risk, the United States would consider operations to restore it.

The U.S. military no longer has the capability to project sustained power to address acute or looming crises in Iran, North Korea, Taiwan,

Ukraine, and Gaza. More interestingly, the American public and elected officials appear to increasingly reject that sort of role for the United States. The second Trump administration will revert to a more isolationist foreign policy, as it did in his first term. For all of Trump's tough talk, he engaged in the fewest military actions of any U.S. president in decades. A drone strike Trump ordered on Qasem Sulaimani, the head of Iranian intelligence on a visit to Baghdad, was the only action that could have reasonably led to conflict. This likely says less about Trump and more about the politics of the moment that he correctly read.

International Law

The nature of hot war and cold war are both changing. It was not long ago that the United Nations authorized forces to keep peace and de-escalate hostilities. Or authorized forces to repel belligerent countries. But in today's world, getting Russia, China, the United States, the United Kingdom, and France to agree, which is a prerequisite, is almost impossible.

The International Criminal Court is a case in point. A court derives its legitimacy from those it governs, who rely on it for impartial judgment and bolster an infrastructure of law enforcement and political support to ensure it can serve its function. The problem with international courts is that the "governed" are nation-states that tend to support the institution when it is favorable to them and undermine its support when it is not.

Cases are pending against Israel at the International Criminal Court (ICC) and the International Court of Justice for its conduct in the war in Gaza. It wasn't long ago that Slobodan Milosovic was convicted at the ICC of crimes against humanity, among other charges. It was even more recently that the United States applauded the ICC for issuing arrest warrants for Russian President Vladimir Putin. A few weeks after Israel was indicted at the ICC, Congress invited the Israeli Prime Minister to Washington for a formal address.

The power of international shame and condemnation—or even the threat of individual or country-level sanction—seems to no longer provide much of a disincentive during today's unruly conflict. In fact, the more these institutions are proactive, the more they damage themselves in the current environment by even those countries who are members bypassing rulings that flout power politics. In 2024, Putin, for instance, traveled to Mongolia, an ICC country, which declined to arrest him.

Although key countries like China, India, Israel, Russia, and the United States refused to join the International Criminal Court when it was established in 2002, the new global justice body represented a symbolic apex of the international legal order. War crimes and crimes against humanity could be tried in a permanent court in front of the world. Since then, several dozen individuals have been indicted for crimes in wars in central Africa and Sudan, and more recently in Myanmar, Venezuela, and of course Russia/Ukraine. But has the ICC genuinely made would-be war criminals more reticent to commit the sorts of horrors that could lead to them being indicted? Not particularly.

It is not only U.S. adversaries that are becoming more adventurous in this environment. U.S. allies appear more willing to pursue policies that would have raised objections from the United States and international organizations. Israel has long sought to project deterrence by responding to threats with decisive force but would generally not act beyond the West Bank and Gaza and certain types of Hezbollah targets in southern Lebanon, the Bekaa, and, with yet greater caution, Syria. But Israel's strike on the Iranian Embassy in Damascus in April 2024 and its even bolder hit on Hamas' political leader in Tehran itself marked a growing comfort among the Israeli leadership to hit Iran directly. In response, Iran launched unprecedented drone and missile strikes on Israel, marking the first but not the only meaningful direct exchange of fire between the two. Then in October 2024, all taboos against direct confrontation were broken as Iran fired ballistic missiles at Israel and Israel responded with air strikes against key military targets inside Iran.

To many in the West, the war in Gaza and the war in Ukraine fall under very different categories of international law—for political rather than legal reasons. The West funneled billions of dollars of high-tech weapons to Ukraine to defend itself from Russian invasion, and the West also sent billions of dollars of high-tech weapons to Israel to support its military action in Gaza. The differentiator for the West is that the brutal Hamas attacks and mass kidnappings on October 7, 2023, necessitated the yearlong military retaliation that has leveled Gaza and killed more than 50,000 people, whereas Ukraine did nothing except begin to reorient itself toward Europe and away from Russia. In response, Russia occupied Ukrainian land and killed more than 10,000 civilians. This is a meaningful and important distinction, but it is also so clearly aligned with the West's geopolitical interests and diplomatic strategy that it feels like even with different Ukrainian and Palestinian behavior, the West would align itself in the same fashion. For much of the world that has come to identify with the plight of the Palestinian people, it points toward the end of international law and the ICC being meaningful.

Citizens as Leverage

The world has always been a perilous place. News stories of Americans getting arrested for accidentally wandering into Iran cropped up from time to time but often raised quizzical thoughts of "why were they messing around there anyway?" Most people abroad did not have to worry about being wrongfully detained. Unless they were former military, a dissident, or maybe an oil company worker, the odds of being arrested on trumped-up charges were quite low. In the rare cases when it happened, it was in unsurprising places: mostly Iran, but also in places where militant groups held sway like in Lebanon, Iraq, Yemen, Afghanistan, the Niger Delta, North Korea, and so on. Most places gave foreign visitors the benefit of the doubt. Even in places that had zero tolerance for any misbehaving, like Saudi Arabia, expulsion was vastly more likely than detention.

But that's changing now as conflict is democratized. The global order is shifting, and conflicts between countries are now multidimensional. Diplomatic spats, cyber fights, and armed conflict traditionally had an escalation pattern to them. It was usually only terrorists who looked for "soft targets." That's no longer the case.

What we have now are citizens on vacation, working abroad, or living in exile who are being targeted by states to gain leverage or extract vengeance. In many cases, these are "normal" people who have done something nominally wrong and find themselves suddenly embroiled in ghastly affairs. In other cases, they are journalists or past government officials getting the book thrown at them—or worse. On some level, this is an evolution of my visit to China in this chapter's opening except instead of worrying about the government trying to gain leverage over me, I'd have to worry if I'd be a pawn in a geopolitical game perhaps via conjured-up evidence that I was a spy.

Citizens know they are subject to foreign law when they travel overseas, but what they don't often consider is that places with a weak tradition of rule of law may decide to turn their sights on a foreign national for other reasons. Increasingly, normal citizens and business executives are getting tied up in geopolitical spats. More often than not, Western countries eventually make concessions to rescue their citizens. For Donald Trump, who is both comfortable dealing with regimes with weak rule of law and keen to make "deals," this phenomenon of detaining Americans for geopolitical gain could increase.

There are cases where regular people find themselves embroiled in international spats, with sentences that are intricately tied to international relations. In 2016, U.K.-Iranian national Nazanin Zaghari-Ratcliffe, who had worked with the BBC and Thomson Reuters, was arrested by Iran on seemingly trumped-up charges. She spent nearly eight years in and out of detention until the United Kingdom paid off a historic debt of approximately GBP400mn contemporaneously with her release.[1] In 2016, American college student Otto Warmbier was arrested in North Korea for allegedly stealing a propaganda sign. He contracted an illness that was ultimately terminal while in North Korean custody.[2]

In 2022, as Russia was hours away from invading Ukraine, it arrested American Brittney Griner, a basketball player carrying a small amount of cannabis oil. As relations between the United States and Russia moved to the worst place in post–Cold War history, she was sentenced to nine years of hard labor. She was released only when the United States traded a global weapons dealer to free her.[3] Evan Gershkovich, a journalist held in Russia on dubious espionage charges, was sentenced to 16 years in jail. He was released in the summer of 2024 as part of a major multicountry trade. Most of the Russians freed from Western jails were actual criminals and spies; those freed by Russia, like Gershkovich, had generally not committed any actual crimes.[4]

Countries do not even need to wait for individuals to visit as they are reaching out across borders to target perceived enemies. In the past, those in exile were largely protected by the fact that their former governments were afraid of the downside of operating on foreign territory. Sovereignty matters; remember, it was even controversial for America to target Osama Bin Laden in Pakistan. But in a world of murkier international law and cross-cutting geopolitics, penalties are never straightforward, often not forthcoming, and sometimes simply worth the price.

Jamal Khashoggi, a Saudi dissident, was dismembered in a foreign consulate—perhaps the most notorious example.[5] Russia has conducted increasingly brazen international assassination attempts at dissidents and former spies.[6] The use and abuse of Interpol Red Notices is a well-known subcategory here, whereby law enforcement requests from countries seeking to quiet dissidents or political enemies can result in their isolation or arrest abroad. Bill Browder stands out as the most well-known example of such targeting, but there are many more.[7]

Chinese operatives have been charged in the United States with stalking, harassing, and threatening dissidents in order to achieve their repatriation.[8] China dispatched counter-protesters in San Francisco to rough up and silence protesters during a visit from Xi Jinping.[9]

Hardeep Singh Nijjar, a Sikh activist, was killed in Canada allegedly with some involvement of the Indian state.[10] Belarussian opposition figure Roman Protasevich's flight from Greece to Lithuania was diverted to Belarus under the pretext of a bomb threat. He was hauled off the plane and subsequently sentenced to an eight-year jail term (though later pardoned).[11]

Among apolitical targets, business leaders deserve to be arrested when they have committed crimes; there's no argument about that. What we are seeing increasingly, however, is the arrest and refusal to repatriate foreign business leaders—often without compelling evidence of the crimes they have committed. This is jeopardizing the ability of companies to staff their foreign outposts, which is an early warning sign about a potential decline in trade and economic cooperation.

Meng Wanzhou, CFO of Huawei and daughter of its founder, was arrested in Canada as part of an extradition request by the United States for sanctions violations. No doubt this was tied up with broader U.S. concerns about Huawei. After more than 1,000 days under house arrest, she reached a deal with the U.S. Department of Justice that ultimately freed her. Related to the case of Meng, China arrested "two Michaels" who were charged with espionage—Canadians Michael Kovrig and Michael Spavor. They were held for nearly the same amount of time as Meng and released when she was. There are many other examples.

While I've spent time documenting foreigners being targeted, there are political crackdowns regularly on local business leaders who don't fall in line in many countries. These could be your partners or companies in which you have investments. While you might respect a China-based business partner who refuses to turn over sensitive data to the government in Beijing, they are unlikely to be in business much longer.

FROM LAW TO LAWFARE

"Lawfare," a portmanteau of law and warfare, was coined in the 1970s, though Google Ngram shows that the term was all but unknown until the early 2000s.[12] At that point its use grew along with the United States' ever-growing "war on terror."

Lawfare was an offensive tool during the Global War on Terror, as legal moves were used to hinder adversaries, for example, by freezing or limiting their access to resources. Civil rights lawyers were concerned about how legal maneuvers might impact individuals and minority communities. In this era, anti-money laundering (AML) and know-your-customer (KYC) laws were important sources of state power; it was easier to limit Osama bin Laden's money flow than it was to find him. Those laws and others enabled the National Security Division of the Department of Justice, in coordination with the Department of Defense, to carry out lawfare against drug cartels, terrorist groups, and rogue states.

This kind of thing can be very effective, but like any new weapon, it can inflict collateral damage. For example, global AML rules—as any bank lawyer or compliance officer will tell you—are complex, and their enforcement is intense and detailed. Banks in Manhattan and the City of London have hired thousands of staff to do the work, and by all accounts they have been up to the task. But not every node of the global financial system has those kinds of resources, and there are whole countries—small ones, naturally—that are periodically at risk of being cut off from the global financial system not because they are state sponsors of terrorism or chummy with cartel kingpins but because their banks don't have the where-withal to compete in the bureaucratic modern pentathlon that global anti-money laundering regimes require. A global nongovernmental organization (NGO) called the Financial Action Task Force monitors the capabilities of country financial systems that strike them as wobbly; if a nation's bank controls aren't up to the task, the penalty is to be cast into outer darkness.[13] Or at least, cut off from the global financial system—which isn't much different.

If lawfare is any effort to hinder an adversary using legal means, then its legacy is long because the technique is so intuitive. The idea of hiring a lawyer to kick your enemies in the shins was presumably born about five minutes after the first lawyer hung up their shingle. So when two countries go to war, one of them will surely try to figure out how to tie up the sovereign assets of the other with lawsuits. If this works, it is only natural to ask how one defines "sovereign assets," since a broader definition might allow more assets to be frozen. Perhaps oligarchs are moving money on behalf of the government, or perhaps they are proxies for it. Perhaps their activities just keep their adversary's economy alive. One way or another, it will be time to seize their yachts sooner or later. In this way, litigation and regulation may degrade the adversary's military strength as much as bombing an oil supply depot or taking out a few bridges.

This sort of lawfare has been hot since Russia invaded Ukraine in early 2022, but the business of freezing enemy assets, or at least tying them up in legal wrangles, apparently goes back at least as far as the prelude to the 100 Years War, when French partisans had good success tying up Plantagenet resources in French courts. Perhaps lawfare goes back to the Book of Ezra, when adversaries of the Jews appealed to legal authorities to resist the rebuilding of the Temple and the restoration of Jerusalem.[14] In that case, Darius the Great had other ideas—but it seems to have at least delayed work on the Temple, which is the most reliable effect of lawfare.

Not nearly as ancient history, back in 2014, Karthik Sankaran (who has collaborated with me on parts of this book) and I started highlighting increasing U.S. efforts to use the dollar's central role in the global financial system as a law-based method of political suasion—really a weaponization of finance. In short, a deep technological and legal networking of the world economy made it easy for powerful states to use such interconnectedness for their own security interests, which in turn helped unleash some of the forces of geolegal fragmentation we see today.

And while what we had was little more than an idea in 2014, a decade later Henry Farrell and Abraham Newman would write that "The United States was no longer just the world's remaining superpower. It was a state with superpowers. Like a spider at the heart of a global web, it could detect the subtle percussion of what friends and enemies were saying to each other from thousands of miles away. And when it thought it necessary, it could tightly wrap an adversary's economy in smother strands that were stronger than steel."[15]

As to what allowed the United States to do that (even to allies)—it was the triangle of law, politics, and technology. For instance, French bank BNP Paribas was hit with an $8 billion fine in 2014 for violating U.S. sanctions because some of its U.S. dollar transactions with sanctioned countries momentarily cleared through a U.S.-based correspondent bank. This led to countries like Russia reducing exposure to the dollar in favor of the euro but when it invaded Ukraine in 2022, the Atlantic alliance came together with sweeping sanctions. Major Russian banks were banned from SWIFT, the dominant international interbank-messaging system headquartered in Belgium. But the really big move was a joint freeze of Russia's enormous sovereign reserve pile in excess of $600 billion (much of which had actually been moved into euros), denying it access to those to fund the war.[16] Reserves had been frozen before but never on such a scale.

Two points about lawfare are important when we survey the evolving geolegal landscape. First, lawfare works only to the extent nations are inclined to observe and enforce the law. Much lawfare relating to the Global War on Terror took place in U.S. courts—it was possible only because the U.S. judicial branch was willing to entertain litigation opposing the actions of the executive branch, and the U.S. executive branch was willing to follow the orders of the judicial branch even when it lost. Those orders were based on domestic U.S. laws relating to treatment of prisoners and international treaties related to extradition. Even though the United States suffered embarrassing scandals around gross human rights violations during the Global War on Terror, it generally allowed courts to police the military. It is hardly a universal practice to give your adversaries lawyers who will advocate for their interests in front of judges who frequently rule in their favor. But it happens in some countries—that's the rule of law.

The second point is that lawfare happens at a greater scale when countries are at greater economic and military parity. In a world with one uncontested superpower, there is little occasion for countries to engage in a complicated contest of wills through the courts. But in the world as it is developing, the relative balance of power points to an era in which law is used creatively and extensively to project power. The previous example of Huawei's CFO and the arrest of the "two Michaels" is a useful reference. Given the rising national security importance of economic power and cutting-edge technology, it stands to reason that the Meng Wanzhou affair was just a foretaste of a great lawfare feast to come.

FIGHTING BACK: GEOLEGAL STRATEGIC PLANNING

In a world that is changing so rapidly and across so many dimensions, the most important way you can prepare to fight back is to learn to do geolegal scenario planning. While companies range in their scenario planning capabilities, even narrow exercises to contemplate geolegal implications of world events can give you an edge. Rather than come up with all of the mutually exclusive scenarios that could characterize future states of the world, you can start by thinking of material exposures you have and how a central plausible representative scenario can guide your preparation for a host of geolegal factors at play today.

As a representative scenario, let's say we woke up tomorrow and China declared that Taiwan must begin to follow mainland Chinese law, leveraged potentially by a blockade to get the island to submit and companies to follow suit. This is more of a risk than in the past as the United States recedes from global leadership and other powers test its resolve to defend its allies. The United States would almost certainly first respond with increased sanctions. The impact of carving China out of the global economy would make Russian sanctions look like child's play.

The United States already has sanctions on lots of Chinese firms—whether because they are believed to be arming Russia, engaging in human rights violations, dealing with other sanctioned entities such as Iran, committing intellectual property (IP) theft in either civilian or dual-use technologies, and so on. But thus far, the major nodes of China's connections with the rest of the world have remained untouched—its biggest banks, its central bank and the repositories of its foreign reserves (State Administration of Foreign Exchange, China Investment Corporation), and its broad access to the dollar payment system.

These are all vehicles and networks similar to those that the United States and European Union have incrementally but decisively targeted over the course of the Russia-Ukraine war. The incremental approach was likely chosen because Russia was much more enmeshed in global financial networks than other sanctioned countries like Iran, Libya, Sudan, or North Korea. And China is much more connected to the world's financial and real economies than even Russia is, meaning that the financial disruptions from sanctions (or even speculation that these might be in the works) could add to the economic hit from the interruption of goods supply chains. There could be second- and third-order consequences here as markets fret about known and unknown unknowns.

While you can certainly build scenarios for the different eventualities that might come to pass from such an event, the most insightful element of strategic planning from a geolegal perspective really is to develop a set of legal and political questions you might need to answer in the event you saw signs something this seismic was playing out. Such questions are challenging to develop because they intersect politics and law but collaboration between internal and external experts in both disciplines can help you generate something similar, as can intelligent software that is fed information about your exposure and about history.

Starting first at the highest level of abstraction, I'd ask questions about the breadth of oncoming sanctions based on (and extrapolating from) the Russian example:

- What will happen to China-linked assets held by investors in the United States (or in the West more broadly)?
- Will those assets be tradeable and, if so, with which counterparties?
- What will the price impact of trading restrictions be, and will it affect leveraged players?
- Will Chinese entities be allowed to withdraw money from Western financial vehicles?
- Will they try to front-run potential asset freezes?
- Will this have an impact on the liquidity or solvency of key intermediaries or counterparties?
- Will they appeal in Western courts against such measures?
- Is there an adequate resolution regime that can deal with these questions?

Having a feel for these general questions—much of which can be anticipated in advance—will allow you to narrow your focus further to your exposure. One way we typically think about controlling such exposures is through insurance, and this would be a first stop on the risk management path.

In this case, however, it's not clear whether fallout between China and Taiwan would be covered under general force majeure clauses in JVs and supply contracts. Insurers are already tightening up policies and raising costs against directly ensuring Taiwan exposures.[17] Indirect exposures for organizations, and those who insure them, is a real consideration. Business interruption and contingent business interruption insurance policies could respond to the knock-on impacts of a conflict. This raises questions both about stress-testing existing policies for how they would respond in such scenarios and also preparing for the broader economic shock to your market and the resilience of your insurers in the event that a China scenario swamped insurers with outsized claims.

Finally, there's a whole host of questions companies would need to ask in the event they woke up to China declaring that mainland law would apply to Taiwan and third-party companies would be held liable for any violations. Beyond the fact that the United States would respond with sanctions, companies would need to consider at least the following questions:

1. **Jurisdictional context**
   a. Do we have a China/Taiwan legal entity?
   b. Are we doing business in China/Taiwan under local law?
   c. Do we have real property in China/Taiwan?
   d. Do we have employees or contractors in China/Taiwan?
   e. Are we doing business with suppliers or customers in a way sufficiently integrated to constructively qualify as doing business in China/Taiwan?
   f. Do we sell or buy sensitive technologies or export-restricted goods to either Taiwanese or Chinese entities, or entities that sell into or buy from China/Taiwan?
   g. Do we have data that resides in China/Taiwan—on servers or otherwise?

   h. Do we have the personally identifiable information (PII) of China/Taiwan residents?

   i. Do we have loans from China/Taiwan-based banks and financial institutions?

   j. Are we (or our subcontractors or major contractors) listed on the public markets in China/Taiwan?

2. **Contracts**

   a. Do any contracts bar us from doing business in China? At what point does Taiwan become part of China for those purposes? (Also see "Export Restrictions.")

   b. Do we have integrated suppliers or customers who will require or request that we *not* attest that we are following Chinese law in Taiwan?

   c. Could following Taiwanese requirements put us in breach of any contract provisions?

   d. Will this drop the valuation of our Taiwanese business in a way that will impact viability provisions in our contracts?

3. **Data Privacy/Security**

   a. Is our Taiwan-domiciled data treated differently under the national data security/privacy law of China?

   b. Is the PII we have related to Chinese nationals (employees, customers, contractors, etc.) held in a way that complies with Chinese law?

4. **Advertising/Marketing Law**

   a. Are our advertisements and communications in Taiwan compatible with Chinese law?

   b. Would changing our ads/communications violate Taiwan's laws?

5. **Employment**

   a. Do we have labor contracts in Taiwan that would be violated by applying Chinese labor law?

   b. Do we have material suppliers or customers who would have the same problem?

   c. Would Chinese law regard any of our contractor relationships in Taiwan to be employment relationships?

   d. Are there labor standards that conflict between Taiwan and China—i.e., where standard practice in Taiwan would put us in violation of Chinese rules/law?

   e. Are there obligatory employee benefits in China that we would need to offer to Taiwanese employees?

6. **Finance and Securities**

   a. Could following Chinese mandates put us in breach of any loan/financing covenants?

   b. Do we do business with Taiwan-based banks/financial institutions that might be vulnerable/shaky because of China's actions?

   c. Will this drop the valuation of our Taiwanese business in a way that will impact covenants in our financing arrangements?

   d. What risks do we need to disclose in our next securities filing (assuming publicly traded)?

   e. Should we consider changes to our capital structure to reduce exposure to this volatility?

7. **Export Restrictions**

   a. When does Taiwan become China for purposes of export restrictions—i.e., selling products into Taiwan?

   b. If China's export restrictions now apply to Taiwan, are we exporting from Taiwan anything that wouldn't be allowed to sell out of China? Are our suppliers? Are our customers?

8. **Tax and Tariffs**
   a. Does compliance with Chinese and Taiwanese law at the same time obligate us to pay double tariffs/double taxes?
   b. Does paying Taiwanese taxes violate Chinese law?
   c. Does paying Taiwanese tariffs violate Chinese law?

9. **Environmental**
   a. Does Chinese law have a higher environmental standard (e.g., emissions, waste, etc.) than Taiwan, and can we realistically meet it?
   b. Are product regulations (GMO, carcinogens, etc.) different in China than Taiwan?

10. **Political (Domestic to China)**
    a. China's law requires companies of a certain size to have a Chinese Communist Party committee—do we need to create one in our Taiwanese entity?

These are not that different from the questions companies had to answer when they fled Russia. But the point is, you don't want to have to flee. Planning in advance by working up not just the geopolitical scenarios but the geolegal questions that arise can position you far better to weather the storm.

CHAPTER FIVE

UNRULY SECURITY: YOU'VE BEEN DRAFTED FOR BATTLE

During globalization, companies and their governments were fundamentally separate entities pointed in similar directions. Companies wanted borders and trade restrictions broken down and lobbied governments to harmonize rules globally to help them grow. Governments wanted their businesses to thrive but often also wanted to export their values to the world through closer ties. The symbiotic relationship between corporations and governments became one of pushing for openness globally while lobbying for narrowly targeted benefits like tax breaks at home.

The world is much more complicated now. Governments are using populism to curry favor, which means smacking entire industries if it helps them get re-elected. Corporate innovation is faster than government regulation, so rules can have unintended consequences as governments fail to keep up. Public pressure can force companies to take political stands, only to get smacked by other segments of the population for doing so. As the United States and China gradually diverge, companies are being caught in the middle with governments leaning on them to be patriotic and, in some cases, operate as national champions. National security reviews are becoming more politicized and companies are losing markets because of consumers who want to boycott the politics of their headquarters.

In this chapter, I'll lay out the geolegal crosscurrents at play with respect to national security and end by considering corporate diplomacy as central strategy to fight back.

PATRIOTS AND NATIONAL CHAMPIONS

While companies are facing a host of pressures, the newest is the need to be patriotic. Job creation features in elections across the Western world, and a key vector of the jobs debate is "built here" versus "built there." Western politicians often don't just blur the line between public and private—they actively disregard it, particularly when running for office. Perhaps more predictably, Xi Jinping openly calls upon China's businesses—banks,[1] private firms,[2] scientists,[3] entrepreneurs,[4] and of course state-owned enterprises—to be patriotic and "join the fight" against the United States.[5] Multinationals doing business in either country are in an awkward spot.

This is a rude awakening for corporations that benefited from post-1989 globalization, a phenomenon that made them multinational in a way very different from prior periods. Production processes—plus technological and managerial know-how—were spread around the globe through physical and service supply chains. Ownership was diffused through widespread cross-border shareholding, cross-border revenues became larger, and senior management personnel were drawn from around the globe. Today, those activities are both politically suspect, creating potential reputation risk. And such practices are subject to increasing legal and regulatory scrutiny—and often outright prohibition.

Second, multinationals with far-flung supply chains—many of them in Western countries—are still smarting from the supply chain shocks of COVID-19 and also are looking at live wars in Eastern Europe and the Middle East, which make them worry more about resilience. Western governments know that keeping their key corporations onside is important.

Third, the Russian invasion of Ukraine in 2022 has exposed the material fragility—in terms of both defense and energy—underlying European talk of "strategic autonomy." It has also gave a new lease of life to the trans-Atlantic alliance. But even this is an unstable equilibrium, given the Trump administration has divergent views from Europe on Russia and NATO specifically.

Above all this, the biggest issue hanging over business is a deepening U.S.-China rivalry across multiple military, technological, economic, and geopolitical planes. And the complexity of that conflict, between the world's largest and second-largest economies (with the latter deeply integrated into Western markets and supply chains), presents a delicate dance for today's Western corporations.

In the United States, for instance, companies looking for official backing to protect them from measures like the European Union's "regulatory superpowers," Chinese export subsidies, SOE competition, and the like are being asked to act like they deserve it. The criteria for "deserving it" are fuzzy but appear to be broadly nationalist. At the same time, many of those companies are trying hard to avoid being drafted into full-fledged inter-state competition that could cause them to lose key markets or suppliers or subject them to retaliation.

Matters are being compounded as the scope of international industrial rivalry goes beyond a delimited arena of military (or even dual-use) technologies. Governments have realized that the logical corollary to supporting their own national champions is hobbling the other side's national champions.

The U.S. government's reported pressure on a deal between Microsoft and technology company G42, which required the latter to give up Chinese equipment and software, is a great example.[6]

Another recent instance is the report of a freeze on formerly permitted sales by U.S. chip manufacturers to Chinese champion Huawei, in the wake of reports that the company had unveiled a surprisingly sophisticated phone in 2024.[7] It is likely that this reflects a broader realization that revenues and profits from purely civilian uses can be plowed into military technology. After all, access to fungible cash-flow in a diversified enterprise that is then pushed back into R&D may be yet another very powerful "dual-use technology."

All of this, however, risks "national security creep," a phenomenon studied by Kristen Eichensehr and Cathy Hwang of the University of Virginia.[8] The "creep" refers not just to the extension of strictures on foreign investment into the United States (under Committee on Foreign Investment in the United States [CFIUS] rules) but to potential restrictions on outbound flows of capital. But beyond this, the strategy combines economic and national security priorities insofar as the goal is not just to bar trade in specific products and technologies but to ensure an adversary is incapable of even developing them.

The authors make the point that National Security Creep might affect not just the scope of U.S. executive restrictions on corporate conduct but also the ability to contest them. This is because the judiciary has been historically deferential to the executive (particularly when backed by bipartisan legislative approval) on national security issues, since the Constitution gives the executive branch-wide latitude on foreign affairs. But this is a challenge because so little of the domestic economy is actually domestic, business is increasingly an international issue, and the courts are more and more political. When combined with lower visibility (and often even secrecy) of the inputs into such executive decisions, corporations could encounter much more uncertainty in "national security" jurisprudence and regulation than in more transparent and settled areas like securities law.

National security creep is likely to increase. Take "know-your-customer" (KYC) rules, legal tools meant to prevent banks from indirectly financing terrorist organizations, drug cartels, or rogue states. The progressive merging of economic and national security policies hints at a future in which multi-national corporations in a broader range of industries will be required legally (or expected politically and reputationally) to apply KYC standards not just to their customers but to their customers' customers, their workers, their suppliers, and their investors to comply with crisscrossing, conflict-driven strictures from each of their jurisdictions.

As lawyers from Hughes Hubbard & Reed argue in *Bloomberg Law*, "Companies are—as the DOJ has warned them—on the front lines of this economic war. Taking lessons from successful warfighting strategies are necessary to anticipate and block the next steps of the highly sophisticated, complex evasion networks [companies] face today."[9] In effect, you can't run and hide—you need to decide your position and get ready for battle.

Some companies will be both eager and able to embrace the designation as patriotic "national champions," but others may prove reluctant to do so. In a July 2023 essay for Foreign Policy Research Institute, Karthik Sankaran (who has collaborated on parts of this book with me) divided America's public and private trade factions into Openers (who want more opportunities around the world); Repatriators (of jobs to the United States); Decouplers (from Chinese markets and sources); and Derailers (of China's rise in toto).[10] Companies that have built out large and complex supply operations around the world, and have increasing numbers of consumers outside the United States, are more likely to join the camp of openers, while companies struggling with foreign competition, labor unions, and the national security community are likely to fall into the other camps. Politicians will presumably respond to a combination of ideology, constituent interest, and donor preferences in making this choice. U.S. President Donald Trump represents some combination of Repatriator, Decoupler, and Derailer depending on the day.

Oddly enough, even the producers of goods in the old-school military-industrial complex may have misgivings about a full-on identification as a U.S. champion. The globalization of both value chains and markets means parts are sourced around the world, and that military aerospace manufacturers may also need to sell airliners or engines elsewhere, something that has made them de facto openers. And being too closely identified with one side engaged in a Great Power Rivalry can paint a bull's-eye on their back for various forms of retaliation by the other side. But the great Chinese firewall, and the rise of a parallel Internet ecosystem behind it, means many of America's software and cloud giants have been "decoupled" almost since their creation. With several of these also in the forefront of the AI revolution, a pivot to "patriotic capital" might be easier for some giants.[11]

But even an Internet firewall did not preclude financial flows across the Pacific between these parallel technological ecosystems, a situation that has aroused the anger of China hawks, and their ire is likely to intensify. The accusation is that capital inflows have fueled the rise of an authoritarian near-peer competitor: China. Such complaints have been levied against investment banks and financial index providers but have gained a particular edge when aimed against the venture capital community. The fear is that those particular flows are about more than just capital—they also carry with them information about advanced processes like AI and quantum computing, pushing China closer to the technological frontier. A famed Silicon Valley VC partnership, Sequoia Capital, split its U.S. and China businesses in the face of such concerns, but this did not mollify the House Select Committee on the Chinese Communist Party. The committee sent a scathing letter last year, noting that "[a]lthough Sequoia's split appears to resolve some of the concerns detailed above by curtailing the flow in some cases of U.S. managerial and technological expertise to problematic PRC companies, significant questions remain—and should be answered by Sequoia."[12]

Corporate lawyers have always been in the business of making things work on paper, for instance, to create documentation to limit liability, reduce taxes, attract investors, and so on. The great innovation of limited liability companies is that the law will respect legal arrangements as long as they are done properly. In the realm of taxes, the canonical rule is that "Any one may so arrange his affairs that his taxes shall be as low as possible; he is not bound to choose that pattern which will best pay the Treasury; there is not even a patriotic duty to increase one's taxes."[13]

But the Sequoia capital story shows that formalities may be disregarded when national interests are at stake. Sequoia's lawyers, reasoning from the law, decided to create a wholly separate entity to carry on its work in China. Members of Congress looked at that and concluded that it was exactly the same arrangement as before, plus some paper asserting that it was different.

The incident also underscores that corporate leaders and their counsel can expect to fight more battles about their patriotism before one of America's toughest courts—a Congressional Committee hearing. Allison Carter, editor-in-chief of PR Daily, outlines a few steps companies can take if they get dragged in front of Congress for a beating.[14] The upshot is that companies need to integrate their legal, government affairs, and communications approaches to have any chance of satisfying the legal, political, and public relations imperatives of a "good" (or at least not terrible) congressional hearing. Such cooperation is likely to become more important as firms come under closer scrutiny on grounds of national security. It is important to recognize that what is at issue is not just the letter of the law but perceptions in Congress as well as in wider public opinion and the ability to anticipate (and perhaps shape) legislation coming down the pike.

The challenges to corporate cross-border behavior are likely to mount, but there may be one partial offset here. As the pressure on firms to behave as national champions rises, so might the official inclination to create and foster them. Under the Biden administration, this came with subsidies coupled with efforts to improve both the standing of labor and labor-management relations (a somewhat more European model). But it is possible that pressures in the United States to create more robust national champions in the global marketplace will lead to a relaxation of antitrust concerns about inter-firm collaboration, mergers, and domestic market concentration (also a somewhat more classically European model).

NATIONAL SECURITY REVIEWS

But one country's national champions are another country's national threat. And the fear that foreigners are coming to buy up national treasures has always mobilized strong emotions.

Still, countries generally love foreign direct investment (FDI)—that is, when a foreign country buys a stake in a firm or project in their territory. FDI can boost domestic companies and create jobs, helping domestic firms challenge competitors and, often, gobble up know-how from new management.

But countries are increasingly concerned that benefits of FDI will flow in reverse. What if foreign companies were seeking to buy British companies in order to learn trade secrets or, worse, national security secrets? The U.K. government wouldn't like that very much and would try to stop it. Indeed, the law firm Dechert notes that there are more than 50 investment screening regimes—from the Philippines to Estonia—all designed to address the fact that not all inbound investment is benign.[15]

The most well-known of these regimes is CFIUS, an inter-agency effort that advises the president whether to block mergers or acquisitions in the

United States on the basis of national security. In 2008, I gave my first presentation on CFIUS to a room full of sovereign wealth funds who were all scared the United States would embarrass them, as it did when Dubai Ports World (DPW) was dragged through the political mud for trying to acquire U.S. port operations in the post 9/11 era. While CFIUS didn't directly block the deal, Congress exerted substantial political pressure that led DPW to hive off the sensitive assets, after significant reputational damage.

Back then, the rules of the game were easier to understand and seemed mainly to be a worry for state actors trying to buy clear national security assets. That is no longer the case. Today, the U.S. CFIUS process can review deals even after they have been completed. Deals in particularly sensitive areas involving data and technology can be reviewed even if a foreign government is not directly involved. The threat of embarrassment often leads firms to abandon deals while CFIUS investigates them. If the president blocks a deal, judicial review is limited or nonexistent.[16]

In fact, the sheer volume of deals that CFIUS reviews—and of companies pulling out of deals or deals being blocked by the president—has increased dramatically. In 2022, for instance, 87 deals were pulled for fear of a negative decision compared to 5 in 2013.[17]

Today, the line between a state-controlled actor and a private actor looks different. ByteDance, the parent of social media powerhouse TikTok, is a Cayman Islands–incorporated company majority-owned by global investors including some of the biggest U.S. investment funds. But it also has Beijing as its headquarters and a number of relationships throughout the Chinese government.

The collection of Americans' data by the Chinese government via TikTok is a concern since the Chinese government can compel Chinese companies to turn over their data. As TikTok has become an influential vehicle for delivering content, including news, to many Americans, the fear is it could become a vehicle for spying on or influencing Americans. TikTok presumably has Global Positioning System (GPS) and app-usage data, beyond simple TikTok usage data, on the general public, members of the military, political leaders, their families, and so on. The platform could also become a vehicle to plant support for whatever the Chinese government wants—whether that's feeding Chinese propaganda or turning the volume up or down on U.S. electoral messages it doesn't like.[18] Companies like Uber have successfully used their customers to apply political pressure to those trying to ban it.[19] TikTok reportedly tried something similar by sending notifications to its users to lobby Congress in its favor, which spooked lawmakers further because it was a sign of the influence U.S. politicians worried about.[20]

U.S. skittishness about an adversarial power, China, having such a large digital footprint is not surprising. In the past, CFIUS forced the divestment of dating app Grindr from a Chinese company over fears of the collection of information about Americans' sexual orientation and other sensitive health data.[21] U.S. President Donald Trump tried to force TikTok to divest its U.S. business in his first term but was gummed up on procedural grounds. There are other examples.

In a striking act of bipartisanship, the U.S. Congress passed a law in early 2024 to ban TikTok from operating in the United States if it was not divested by its Chinese parent on a strict timeline.[22] U.S. law has always barred foreign ownership of TV and radio stations, so the law was perhaps less controversial than it may have seemed. But in light of free speech concerns, the case may still play out in court over a longer time horizon. In the interim, the United States maintains the ability to block many of TikTok's activities via CFIUS.

A more striking example occurred when Japan's Nippon Steel offered a significant share premium to purchase U.S. Steel. Japan is one of America's closest and longest-standing allies and host to significant U.S. military assets. Japan is also the largest source of FDI into the United States.[23] Japan frequently submits to CFIUS review, and no Japanese deals have been formally blocked. Yet, then-President Joe Biden scuttled the deal citing concerns about national security.

All of these examples raise serious questions about rule of law in the United States. There is the legal and regulatory structure called CFIUS that governs sensitive asset purchases in the United States. That structure typically encourages companies to collaborate with the United States to gain a seal of approval that their deal does not harm national security and to mollify any concerns before they become a public issue. However, these deals have jumped from the regulatory apparatus—the CFIUS process—into the political process, which sends a warning sign for companies and countries that seek to avoid scrutiny. The United States is not the only place for global investors to invest their money. And other countries will start to treat American companies the same way.

FIGHTING BACK: CORPORATE DIPLOMACY

It may be tempting to think of your company as just one of many economic players in an increasingly political environment. But this would be the wrong conception. In fact, corporations themselves are political actors—and increasingly so. The odds are higher than ever before that your company has management in one country, suppliers in another, customers in a third, and a headquarters somewhere completely different. Owners (if you are publicly traded) could be all over the world. Or, your company could be virtual and without a true home, but majority owned by one sovereign wealth fund. This means the levers of influence you might need to pull are increasingly dynamic.

Adding a "corporate diplomacy" team is one route to navigate this. The concept here is to develop a more sweeping view of your global corporate interests than you have ever had before. You are not just a manufacturer with a vision to help your customers, but instead you are a total political organism that has its fingers on the pulse of what would be good or not good for your interests. This means having an integrated and global view rather than a country-by-country perspective. For the growing number of companies that are bigger than the GDP of many nations, this may seem second-nature, but it is of growing importance to smaller-scale entities too.

The parallel here is a country-based diplomatic corps: no matter where in the world those diplomats find themselves, they have a clear vision of how to advance the interests of their nation. That vision doesn't always involve lobbying other governments but also shaping public perceptions. It involves robust, ongoing, and technology-enabled data collection. Crucially, a corporate diplomacy team integrates views from across the business; it is not just managing public relations.

To extend the analogy of companies and countries further, to fuel your diplomatic corps you should also consider standing up or enhancing your intelligence function. Many companies already have intelligence teams, but often they are limited to corporate due diligence or cyber threats. Increasingly, some are taking a broader view. As I'm told by Lewis Sage-Passant, global head of intelligence at Novo Nordisk and author of *Beyond States and Spies: The Security Intelligence Services of the Private Sector*, "More and more companies are building strategic intelligence teams to look at geopolitical issues in a broader way, driving the overall geopolitical strategy of the company in cooperation with government affairs."[24] That way, when your frontline corporate diplomats are flying the flag for public influence, they are being powered by deep, real-time insights.

For companies, success at corporate diplomacy involves first very clearly defining your broader interests. While you may be used to speaking to politicians about narrow wins, actually the small-issue/short-term view may run counter to broader influence development. Rather, do you value country- or policy-level stability in a foreign country where you operate? If you do, you can figure out how to align with the government to shape public views in support of stability. That might mean standing with a government even when it is narrowly governing counter to your opinions. Many U.S. companies drew the conclusion in 2024 that the risk of the political and electoral system breaking down was much worse than the risk of the wrong candidate in office, and said as much publicly.

You then must build a clear sense of how you can project your influence. Companies spend tremendous amounts of money on marketing but much less on shaping broader narratives. Consider how you can make your company be viewed as a force for good in your homebase and key countries—which will give you much more license to pursue narrower interests in the future.

Some of this is about charitable work and supporting local causes, but much of this is about telling the story of alignment—and that increasingly means acting patriotic, at least in the United States. When I speak about technology and war later in the book, I cite the example of Apple's refusal to unlock a device at the request of the FBI after a localized terrorist attack. But imagine if FBI counterintelligence needed an iPhone unlocked because a Chinese or Russia spy was carrying details of a major biological attack that was about to take place. Refusal to support in that case is not just a problem with the government; it would be viewed as unpatriotic.

It is perfectly acceptable for companies to be viewed as citizens of nowhere. But that is an active choice, one that needs to be communicated, and one that comes with consequences. Choosing whether and how to align with your home country is much more than just a public affairs exercise—it involves stakeholders across your business and then needs to be articulated.

But aligning with one country can cause challenges with others. So you also need to consider how you can tell the story of cross-cutting political challenges you face across all your geographies. Instead of viewing each geography as a separate battle to be won, think about a broader narrative to educate politicians in one country about how you have no choice but to do business a certain way because of pressure in another place. To the extent you are cultivating a long-term relationship, this will carry more weight.

Finally, think about ways to integrate national security narratives as a defense against other policy challenges. For instance, technology companies arguing that they need a certain scale to help a country stay ahead from an artificial intelligence perspective may resonate when seeking to hold off antitrust attacks based on size and antitrust concerns.

CHAPTER SIX

UNRULY SAFETY: PROTECTING OURSELVES WITH GLASS CASES

A couple years ago, my wife was leaving our house to go to work. "Where did you park the car?" she asked me. The question was odd, as I had left it on the driveway on a decent road in Muswell Hill, a neighborhood consistently rated as one of London's best.[1] I could see through the open door that it wasn't there anymore. So I called the police.

I told them that my car had been parked securely on the driveway and must have been stolen overnight. As soon as I hung up the phone, I received an email from the police closing my case. I called back to tell them it must have been an error and that I'd be available all day if they wanted to talk to me or the neighbors.

"Claim insurance," the officer on the line told me. "We don't have the resources to investigate stuff like that."

Over the course of the next few weeks, there were two more car thefts, three catalytic converters stolen, and a house break-in in our neighborhood. The police were basically unresponsive.

Today, I spend a lot of the year in Santa Monica, a California beach town where the children of celebrities like Ben Affleck play in the same YMCA basketball league as my kids. It's the type of neighborhood where you wouldn't be surprised to see a Kardashian buy some diamond earrings from behind a glass case.

I went to Target recently to buy some toothpaste, and to my surprise it too was in a glass case. So was laundry soap. And over-the-counter allergy medicine. I ring a bell, and I get the Kardashian treatment just to buy my housewares. Why on Earth would toiletries be in a glass case? Because people keep walking out with them, confident there will be no consequences.

My goal in this chapter is to prove that the unruly world is not just happening at the international level due to shifting geopolitics or at the national level due to populism in elections. Rather, it is a feature of everyday life for citizens in many jurisdictions, which creates Geolegal Risks as citizens take actions in their own hands to improve their safety.

The previous examples are local examples of basic government failure— and these local-level erosions affect perceptions of the law more broadly. Insecurity often leads to scapegoating, which catapulted the politics of immigration to the top of voter concerns in the 2024 U.S. Presidential election.

Some businesses will turn to taking power away from the government— for instance by privatizing security, which may help their organization but further deprives the state of a core role it plays in society. Local law erosions can also roll up to national and international effects as voters choose enforcers who will turn to technology to solve the issues. Such enforcers may clean up the mess but may damage business, the economy, or society in the long run. In the future, it is technology that will do the heavy lifting of remedying the underlying issues, though this is not without risk for those who use it.

WHY IS THE LAW NOT ENFORCED AT A LOCAL LEVEL?

With respect to the local level, the problem is certainly not a lack of laws. As California Governor Gavin Newsom puts it, "There are plenty of laws on the books, and it'd be nice to see some of these damn laws enforced for a change."[2] Why does it increasingly feel like shoplifters or "porch pirates" can act with impunity?

In some places, nonenforcement is a remedy to discriminatory laws and enforcement that came before it, and a belief the police act with impunity. In other places, it is because budgets are constrained. Further, many places do not believe the criminal justice system is the right way to address drug use, antisocial behavior, and the like, preferring social and health services to take them on. Regardless, a combination of nonenforcement, an opioid crisis, massive inbound immigration, and tougher economic conditions for the worst-off post-pandemic are all leading to perceptions that crime is up—and, in some cases, tolerated or ignored by the institutions whose job it is to stop it.

Many will draw a line from these dynamics to an immigration crisis that plagues towns across the U.S. border and those where undocumented immigrants or asylum seekers ultimately try to make their homes. The demonization of immigrants as sources of crime and violence, or as exotic "others" who round up and eat pets (per the U.S. President), reinforces a sense of local lawlessness that inspires fear in many for their own safety.[3] There is also an effect on perceptions of the law when many groups of immigrants must wait their turn for admission only to see others bypass formal channels or when the United States shirks its international responsibilities to refugees and asylum seekers or when city mayors send buses of new arrivals across the country to so-called sanctuary cities by subterfuge or force.

The upshot is the same across these examples as it is across drug use or property crime: when citizens feel unsafe and believe the law doesn't matter because it is not enforced, then they become encouraged to take action into their own hands.

Let me be clear: I am not a staunch law-and-order advocate. I believe that law enforcement and the justice system often deliver unfair outcomes on the basis of race, national origin, and socioeconomic class. And I think that politicians who try to pin crime rates on certain racial groups or immigrant populations are often being racist, xenophobic, and/or disingenuous for political gain. But when whole categories of crimes are not enforced, citizens rarely accept that outcome. They will look either to take power away from the government or to bolster leaders that are happy to trample on long-held human rights and civil liberty safeguards with promises of security.

Vote for Enforcers

One solution that citizens take is to vote for candidates calling them with society-splintering dog whistles. U.S. President Donald Trump, while a candidate, once publicly said, "If you rob a store, you can fully expect to be shot as you are leaving that store.... . Shot!"[4] As Trump pointed the finger of responsibility for crimes at immigrant groups, voters who experience unsafety due to the erosion in law enforcement channeled concerns into voting for Trump's proposed remedies of mass deportations and border walls, both physical and digital.

Sometimes this is a pendulum swinging back from a more liberal-leaning administration. In other cases, this is taking conservative approaches and going much further. Or it is an invitation to get tough in a discriminatory way.

In nearly all cases, getting tough is more likely to be a short-term remedy whereby citizens of majority groups feel safe for a while at the expense of less-well-off groups in society only to find they have sowed the seeds for a much fiercer backlash in the future. This is especially true in poorer countries where police truly do lack resources or are prone to corruption.

In El Salvador, for instance, the president has arrested no less than 1% of the population in a bid to quell gang presence and violence. Doing so requires a poor country to invest in things like stadium-capacity mega-jails where up to 70 inmates share a single cell but receive no services to prepare them to re-enter society.[5] Such policies involve leaving a lot of broken families in its policy wake, sowing the seed for future challenges.[6]

Of course, when compared to how the Philippines under Rodrigo Duterte dealt with the problem, it looks light-touch. The administration of "Duterte Harry" simply shot thousands of perceived criminals; he once claimed that "he would be 'happy to slaughter' three million drug addicts in the country."[7] According to Philippine authorities, from 2016 to 2021, 6,201 people were killed by the police.[8] Not all of them were involved in the drug trade—and the sheer magnitude of police killings strongly suggest that many innocents were killed.

Policies like the previous involve trampling on a lot of human rights in the process. On some level, they may provide safety, but that safety comes at the cost of erosion of civil liberties, privacy, or institutions in society more broadly. While this may suit societies on the brink of collapse, it's only likely to create a more polarized society in wealthier countries reacting to real or perceived impunity.

Privatization of Security

When there's a government failure, a natural response is to throw money at the problem. Increasingly, people try to fortify themselves by hiring their own armed guards, perhaps as a pooled resource for the neighborhood. There's been a massive boom in private security spending in recent years as citizens have tried to cope with this government failure.[9] Armed guards will drive up and down their street hoping to deter criminals by knowing that they could face the ultimate consequence if they test anyone in the neighborhood. And, of course, companies are making use of this strategy as well.

One philosophical problem with privatizing a public service is that it lets the government off the hook. One of government's core functions is to provide security through rules and laws. Accepting that the government can't do that is tantamount to rejecting the government's capacity more generally, which offers impunity to those who break the law.

A second philosophical problem with privatizing *this* public service in particular is that it is commonly accepted that part of what constitutes a legitimate government is that it has a monopoly on the use of force—especially deadly force. The universal exception to this is self-defense, but especially outside the United States, it is accepted that I should not run out into my driveway and shoot whoever might be stealing my car. When the government gives up entirely on the project of defending its citizens and their property, the desire (or need, or perhaps even right) for the private use of deadly force may grow.

The practical problem is that there's a fine line between private security and vigilante justice. Private security is often less well trained, not bound by any oath, and may have ethics that diverge from the local police who are ultimately supposed to be doing the arresting. For instance, a security guard at a New York Walgreens claims that police arrested him for assault after he tackled a repeated shoplifter but refused to press charges—which is what the police wanted. Instead the guard wanted the thief to receive social services.[10] It doesn't matter who has the right policy prescription; the police intervention resulted in both the thief and the guard being arrested because of this mismatch.

TECHNOLOGY TO THE RESCUE?

Citizens and companies will increasingly turn to technology to solve this problem. But are they building unbreakable walls or simply glass cases?

Surveillance and Glass Cases

Part and parcel of remedying security failure is a higher tolerance for surveillance. When citizens feel less safe, they are willing to tolerate much more government surveillance. The post-9/11 environment tolerated a huge increase in novel legal powers for governments to surveil in pursuit of safety. This is different from enforcers or rounding up "bad guys" and giving them harsh penalties. This is about using technology to collect small infractions—or, taken to its logical extent, all infractions. This is about letting governments fish, snoop, and control in order to maintain order.

Surveillance cultures vary. A lighter-touch version is to turn to always-on government monitoring systems that automatically issue fines and penalties. Singapore, jokingly known as "a fine city" because of the number of penalties issued for every conceivable type of social violation, uses surveillance to combat petty crime. A more invasive version of this is the always-on techno-authoritarianism in places like China, all designed to promote a harmonious society.

Yet, in trying to protect themselves, citizens and corporations will attempt to build foolproof protection. But often they are simply building their own glass cases, like the one that housed my toothpaste. The problem with glass cases is that they can be smashed so they function somewhere between a placebo and a minor deterrent. When linked with law enforcement, they serve to punish rather than prohibit.

There's a lot we can do and spend money on to make ourselves feel like we are getting safer. After my car was stolen, I felt quite abandoned by my local government—like I was living on the frontier and had to defend my family. So, I spent about £2,000 on a Ring security system and £80 on a wheel lock. The latter was annoying and could have been cut in two by any thief with the right equipment; still it acted as a deterrent.

The alarm system, however, was flashy with all sorts of cool features. For the next two years, I was the first to know if there was a fox in my backyard, particularly in the middle of the night. Any human who wanted to enter could simply have smashed a window. Given my prior experience with the local police, it's not clear to me that my knowledge a crime was in process would have actually led to the crime being stopped. That was my own glass case.

Of course, as everyone builds these barriers, society changes. Neighborhoods become completely surveilled, and people start to become suspicious of anyone who walks by and triggers an alert. Private surveillance expands the public surveillance net. It's costly and controversial for police departments to install surveillance cameras in places other than Singapore, China and the like. However, there has been an explosion in private security systems as cost has come down and perceptions of crime has risen. Collected data is all available for governments to mine. Sometimes this is done overtly, through subpoenas and direct requests for access from security systems. In other cases, this can be through backdoor access when national security or other justifications allow.

Private surveillance cameras also potentially impinge on the privacy of neighbors—for instance, the thought of my neighbor having hours of footage of my children playing in the front yard because of their own wide-lens camera creeps me out. This can bleed into quasi-enforcement as citizens may post footage of crimes online, which can raise issues of privacy or mistaken identity. Enhanced personal and corporate surveillance can also give way to government surveillance because society becomes more accepting of it. And documenting crimes without enforcing them can simply heighten the perception of impunity.

Cashiers on Patrol

Some stores are taking this further by turning their human staff into humanoid robots. Well, not really but many shops are putting their staff on the front lines. Lidl GB has tried to differentiate itself by being the first supermarket to exit trial phases and equip all staff with cameras.[11] There has been a rise in the placement of body cameras on general staff members in retail shops in order to capture crimes in process and step up intervention. The theory is that if people know they are being photographed at close range, they won't steal. This involves staff getting into position to video the crime in process. This is being taken a step further with AI-powered surveillance that is trained on the movements of known shoplifters to identify when shoplifting is likely to be occurring.

But knowing someone is stealing is different from stopping them. These solutions effectively deputize regular staff to intervene, even when there are policies preventing it. For instance, in 2023 Lululemon fired two staff members for intervening in a theft.[12] The company says the employees were fired because employee safety is of paramount concern and they put themselves in harm's way. Many retailers have similar policies due to liability to the employer if either the thief or the employee gets hurt in the process. The problem is that technological identification of more thefts is only going to thrust employees into the middle of a hostile situation that they will potentially escalate. And when that technology reveals it has its own biases (i.e., if it flags someone as a shoplifter because it was trained that many shoplifters wear medical face masks or adjust their sagging pants), those companies will not enjoy the PR spotlight.

FIGHTING BACK: STAY OR GO?

In many places in this book I am a fierce advocate for the use of technology to solve problems. That is not the case when it comes to urban impunity. Technology is a risky and short-term solution—the building of a glass case—and it further erodes government and the law. Instead, I think the solutions are more analog.

For some businesses, a holistic assessment of whether they want to actually stay in the affected market is telling. As the costs of theft, security, and PR disasters stack up, it may make sense to simply leave and focus on other markets. But leaving isn't costless: any goodwill built in a community you then abandon goes away overnight. When the pendulum swings back and the law is enforced again, you may not be welcome for re-entry. And, of course, exodus also reduces the chances that a city gets back on its feet.

For companies that want to stay, there are no easy solutions. But one strategy for fighting back is to build coalitions with adjacent businesses that also suffer from existing conditions and would suffer further if there is an exodus. Landlords suffer when companies exit or are simply unwilling to pay high rents. Hotels and restaurants suffer when open-air drug use scares away potential visitors or when guests don't feel comfortable going to local shops. Where before companies might just work with law enforcement, today they must build coalitions of stakeholders who will give law enforcement backing to enforce the law if done in a fairer way. Finding those partners is crucial to a successful strategy, alongside deepening reporting and collaboration with law enforcement.

Of course, this type of change takes time as its only from deeper investment in remedying societal ills that one can begin to address local impunity and the perceptions of citizens being in danger. Supporting longer-term community efforts for drug treatment, housing, and social services will bear fruit over time. The politics of doing so openly, however, vary by jurisdiction.

PART III

ARTIFICIAL POLITICS: WHEN POLITICS AND TECHNOLOGY COLLIDE

CHAPTER SEVEN

UNRULY FUTURE: WHEN AI EATS DEMOCRATIC CAPITALISM

give a lot of speeches. When I was an analyst, I'd have dense slides that could tell you the whole story even if you missed my presentation. Today, I favor a much more lightweight slide deck, which has a simple sentence and a provocative image next to it.

My current deck runs about 60 slides. I'll get on stage and present the first 30 slides before I get to the one about technology and jobs. When I do, I'll mention that every single image in my deck was generated by artificial intelligence (AI). Now, that may come as no surprise to readers of this book who surely are dabbling in the technology themselves. But when I get to this slide, I usually point out that because I've used AI to generate the slides, I didn't have to pay a designer to design the images. I didn't have to pay a photography company to license their photos. I don't have an intern running between me and my graphic designer learning the art of storytelling via apprenticeship. I didn't pay taxes on the wages of any of those people.

Nope, it's just me and my $20 per month large language model (LLM) doing work that would have required dozens of hours of a human's time. It's just me and my AI quietly, almost undetectably, eating jobs.

What may be less clear is that, in doing so, we could be eating democracy itself. While it's easiest to make the case that there will be pressure toward authoritarianism from a rise of tech-led political change, there's simultaneous pressure toward socialism in some corners. What I hope to achieve in the third part of this book is impress upon leaders the need to realize that the status quo of democratic capitalism will be under severe stress from tech-led change in the near future as the contract between workers, citizens, and governments frays. Welcome to the unruly age of Artificial Politics.

TECH AND JOBS

There's been a lot of technological progress in recent years. Generative AI may be all the rage, but robots, autonomous and electric vehicles, document processing systems, 3D printing, and so much more are changing the world economy in irreversible ways. Such technology brings the prospect of much higher productivity per employee—which implies also that few(er) employees may be needed in those endeavors. The question is whether other jobs doing other things will be created—when, where, and at what wage—and will it be enough to give those losing their jobs some relief.

Here the precedents from prior regionally concentrated job losses, whether due to trade or technological change, are not too promising. Studies of the "China shock," which hit concentrated pockets of U.S. low-to-middle tech manufacturing hard, have found virtually one-for-one increases from job losses to long-term unemployment, falling household incomes, and increased reliance on government handouts.[1] Meanwhile, even the relative success stories about regional revivals are often driven by a very different mix of technologies and industries than what existed prior to the shock and are over a multiyear or even multi-decade time period. Pittsburgh is an often-touted example of a resurgence after the decline of its steel industry, but the bounce back took a long time and was accompanied by net population losses. And with the leading sectors now concentrated in advanced technology, education, and medicine, it is unlikely that many middle-aged steel workers made that employment transition.[2]

Depending on which study you choose, there's ample evidence that one-third to half of the economic activity in major economies could be automated. Research from McKinsey shows that around 12 million workers will be displaced by technology in the next half a decade alone.[3] Expanding the scope beyond America, investment bank Goldman Sachs warns that 300 million jobs could be replaced.[4]

It's not hard to figure out which jobs are at the highest risk. Cashiers, customer service, and office clerical work have already been automated. Hotels are increasingly rolling out self-check-in similar to airlines. Interacting with a human will be a luxury for five stars or first class. Those whose job it was to serve other humans will only be pampering the rich as the rest will be served by technology.

Generally, there has been an expectation that knowledge work is at less risk—that bosses and decision-makers will probably be people rather than robots for a long time. As smart as IBM Watson is at diagnosing tumors, humans still want to talk to another person about their cancer outlook.

This is true to a point, but less true in a world of generative AI. For instance, it's easy to understand how travel agents were upended in the first wave of the Internet by online travel booking systems that handled the execution of travel. However, getting robust, personalized intelligence about your travel still required hours of searching and synthesizing or talking to an expert concierge, which protected certain forms of the business. Now, ChatGPT and other models can spit out helpful tailored travel itineraries instantly and at no marginal cost if you have a subscription.

Thus, a whole broader range of work is at risk. Lawyers in particular are an instructive case. It's not that a person given a choice wants an AI representing them in a child custody battle any more than they want an AI fully taking on their cancer diagnosis. But the reality is that so much of the work that precedes a day in court is the type of repetitive work that intelligent software is good at. And when interacting with the technology feels like interacting with a real person, the leap to using it in the same way is not so far.

In fact, the Pew Research Center finds lawyers to be the second highest concentration of male jobs exposed to AI across all jobs.[5] Tasks like making sure you have all the right documentation are table stakes. Doing legal research so you can automatically generate much of the documentation is here today, albeit with hallucinations. Shadow boxing your best arguments using an LLM is right here right now. At the end of the day, the human lawyer will be the editor and conductor, not necessarily the entire orchestra.

While the law and lawyers serve a special place in this book, they are not the only knowledge workers on the line. Ask the journalists who used to write about sports scores or stock prices, which AI can now do as well or better. Or how about that less creative but often lucrative corporate work done by photographers and graphic designers? Now that generative

AI can conjure up decent images and videos in a few seconds, many will forgo their services, as I realized I've been doing without taking an active choice to do so.

In fact, there's a whole universe of highly skilled and, often, highly paid workers who will no longer have work. Many of them, however, will still have debt from their education.

POWER DYNAMICS

It goes without saying that the biggest group of winners from this type of technological innovation are the owners of capital and the companies that create these new technologies. That isn't just their charismatic founders, but it's the data scientists and engineers who will increasingly be paid seven figures for their contributions to automating the universe and own equity in the upside. Because such roles favor the more highly educated, these technological breakthroughs will accrue to those who already have some amount of power and social capital.

One of the more interesting wrinkles of technological innovation, however, is that while computers are good at some things, they are poor at others. They can perform computations that no human could and not break a sweat. But it's taken years of research to make progress teaching robots to fold a towel.[6]

The implication, here, is that traditional power dynamics in society may soon be upended.

Corporate workers, who have long had higher salaries and jet-setting lifestyles, may soon be unemployed, while manual workers may find themselves with steady income. Carpenters, electricians, pipe fitters, and the like will still be humans for a long time.

Human-executed creative work will similarly be prioritized. ChatGPT is impressive at writing a song (or a lawsuit, for that matter) in the style of the late rapper Tupac Shakur, but it is much worse at generating its own compositions that resonate with music listeners or art critics.

So what happens to the army of individuals who no longer have jobs in this unruly world? First, they try to organize to slow down technological progress. Hollywood spent most of summer 2023 protesting the potential use of AI in movies and production.[7] The Trades Union Congress in the United Kingdom held conferences focused on raising awareness of corporate use of AI in hopes of fending off full automation.[8] The Pause AI movement attempts to do this through greater regulation and oversight.[9]

The problem is that such strategies will fail. There is so much momentum toward harnessing AI in business that it's impossible to imagine slowing down. Besides, governments barely understand the technology, so intelligent brakes on it are not easy to develop.

AI is a one-way street—the jobs that go away are never coming back. As a result, those who land out of work may well be out of work for life.

That's not to say that AI as a technology couldn't lead to net job growth in society as human work takes on new forms—it certainly may. Many will cite Jevons' paradox, which posits that when resources are used more efficiently and their prices fall, people actually use more of that same resource; a February 2024 *New York Times* op-ed gave the example of the energy-saving uses of LED lights resulting in mega-projects like the Las Vegas Sphere.[10] The logic, then, goes that as lawyers and other knowledge-providers become more efficient, people will demand more legal service or consulting advice or whatever the good is.

The problem, as I see it, is that real people don't live long enough for net effects nor do they care about aggregates when they are personally suffering. That is to say that over a long enough time horizon, sure, Jevons' paradox could take hold, and there will be many more things for humans to do assisted by AI. For instance, there is evidence to suggest that, over the long term, AI could lead to the displacement of the professional class and redistribute wealth, by rebuilding the middle class. Some argue that AI could create an economy where the work and skills that have traditionally been associated with the professional class, such as consolidating arguments, performing medical analyses, designing products, or flying planes, could now be performed by a larger number of workers, since lower-skilled workers could use machines to help them perform these tasks.[11] This type of labor shift would require a more tailored education system that teaches students how to use these technologies effectively. If successful, it would make "elite expertise cheaper and more accessible," while also increasing the variety of potential career paths for lower-skilled workers.[12]

The problem is that the distributional impacts on today's workforce imply many, many losers—and that's a big challenge. Soon, companies will replace workers with AI to cut costs and the structural changes required to make this transition successful, such as improvements in education, will take decades to yield results. Many educated individuals, who are now often part of the upper-middle class, will likely revolt in a fashion like how the working class glommed on to protectionism when they thought their jobs went overseas.[13]

The fates of the AI losers won't be sealed via a single decision point. Frequent mass layoffs will upend any sense of stability and security for future workers, creating general anxiety among the population. The population will more broadly lament identity loss as well as their own obsolescence and alienation, while simultaneously fearing machines that have a mind of their own.[14] They will fight back when they live near nuclear power plants that are restarted to fuel AI's insatiable power demand, or when their water supplies are redirected or contaminated in pursuit of the same.[15] And because populations will experience this in different ways, resentment and division will rise as their anger is channeled through different interest groups and political parties.

BUY THEM OFF ... OR ELSE

So what's a loser from AI to do? They tried to slow things down and failed. Next, they will turn to government support. The problem is that no social safety net—no matter how large—will be able to make up the lost wages of the professional class who are not looking to government to help them pay rent but instead to help them pay their nannies and luxury car notes.

Governments have been experimenting with Universal Basic Income (UBI) structures in recent years, which engages with a shift in welfare philosophy from benefits being a short-term effort to paper over temporary dislocations to, instead, providing ongoing support to all citizens. The concept of an unrestricted UBI was first developed in the 16th century and later promoted by Milton Friedman and Martin Luther King, Jr., post-1950.[16] Support for UBI has surged in popularity in the twenty-first century, especially during the COVID-19 pandemic, with supporters ranging from Facebook founder Mark Zuckerberg and one-time presidential hopeful Andrew Yang.[17] Most recently, Sam Altman, CEO of OpenAI, contributed $24 million to conduct a three-year-long study on UBI, which was released in 2024.

There is no singular definition or model of UBI that is recognized as the "standard," since countries have attempted a variety of models with differing eligibility criteria, forms of distribution, regularity, and levels of exclusivity in recent years.[18] But the general idea is that UBI gives money to the whole population really without any requirements to earn it. According to the Stanford Basic Income Lab, in its most ideal form, the UBI payment is unique in that it is periodic, paid in cash, universal, paid to individuals, and unconditional.[19]

Given recent AI advancements and related job market disruptions, many governments have shown an interest in UBI programs to support those citizens most negatively affected by the technological revolution. In theory, UBI could support the "losers" of this AI transition and act as a safety net, providing stability and support for every citizen so that they can cover their basic needs.

Proponents of UBI argue that since it is universal by nature, it would be more accessible to lower-income households and individuals than means-tested programs, whose effectiveness is often limited by overburdened administrations, negative stereotypes, and high costs.[20] On the other hand, opponents argue that UBI would reduce people's incentive to work, reducing labor force productivity.[21]

In varying formats, UBI experiments have been carried out in the United States, Canada, England, India, Iran, Kenya, and Finland, among others.[22] Only a small number of governments have actually introduced unconditional UBI at a nationwide or province-wide level; many of the experiments regarding UBI are funded by nonprofit organizations, philanthropies, or research groups.

From 2017 to 2018, the Finnish government unconditionally provided unemployed Finns with a payment of $635, with benefits continuing regardless of whether the participants got a job. The trial did not directly help the participants find work, but it did improve their mental well-being and increased their trust in social institutions, including in the justice system, the police, and political parties and figures.[23] Starting in 1982, Alaska's state government also provided citizens with an unconditional annual payment ranging from $1,000 to $3,000, pulled from the state's investment fund, the Alaska Permanent Fund, which generates money from oil sales and mining contracts.[24] In 2011, the Iranian government funded UBI when it phased out food, water, and fuel subsidies.[25]

The Brazilian government has experimented with a more conditional basic income, which requires participants to keep their children enrolled in school and visit doctors regularly.[26]

The evidence that UBI "works" is mixed; some studies show that UBI often improves recipients' well-being, ability to access education, and trust in institutions, and in some trials, recipients worked more than those on unemployment benefits.[27] Other studies, often conducted over longer time periods, found that UBI payments improved participants' health and mental health, but only in the first year of the study, and that UBI payments eventually did lead individuals to choose to work fewer hours and earn less income.[28]

With the COVID-19 pandemic in 2020, the U.S. population became increasingly open to implementing UBI, with research showing that in April 2020 88% of liberals and 45% of conservatives supported some form of UBI payments.[29] However, in the United States and in other countries, the question of how governments will pay for UBI remains. In Finland or Alaska, the UBI programs were so successful because the governments had the means to establish such programs. In Finland the personal tax rates are very high and the social welfare programs, which UBI complements, are already well established. In Alaska, UBI programs were financed by the state's oil and mining revenue.

So what's not to like? Well, there are three main problems with UBI. First, those programs are blindingly expensive. The UBI proposal that presidential candidate Andrew Yang promoted in 2020 would have cost $2.8 trillion annually, which is basically the cost of America's entire health and retirement safety net.[30] And as knowledge workers lose their jobs and want the government to maintain their lifestyle, not just their basics, the price would go up. Therefore, for the United States to introduce similar UBI programs, it would need to raise taxes, discontinue current programs, or seek out new revenue sources, such as by introducing a carbon tax, to generate the necessary funds.[31] It is hard to write a less attractive policy prescription from the perspective of the current administration in

Washington, but they wouldn't be alone. Only small population countries or natural resource producers could make an orderly transition in that direction.

Second, I suspect UBI means the death of social mobility. The ability to work one's way up the food chain to create a better life for oneself and their families is a critical component of democracy. If one believes their station in life is set, then their focus turns more toward stability than anything aspirational.

But the biggest factor is that programs like UBI require a dramatic shift of business culture away from democratic capitalism and to something more socialist in nature. In the United States, Democrats are more open to UBI while Republicans are often concerned that UBI would "transfer money away from those who need it most, change the distinctly American relationship between citizens and government, and sharply raise taxes or the national debt."[32]

While the balance of this chapter talks about the risks of rising authoritarianism as a result of new technologies, it's also easy to see how countries slide deeper into socialism. That won't happen in the United States, but it will be attractive elsewhere, which can also create burdens on business that may bear some of the cost.

It is not hard to imagine scenarios that are worse than implementing UBI to deal with technology-led displacement. Large portions of the population could be cut out of opportunities for work and growth, with little recourse to benefits that help them sustain their lifestyles. With a sense of permanent decline, such populations could become a permanent protest class. If you have no stake in the outcome of the economy, there's little risk to you becoming a spoiler. The emergence of new labor movements and political parties designed to slow down economic growth and implement technological protectionism is not hard to imagine. And this is coming at a moment when political trust is so low that the additional pressure could break the political system itself.

Job displacement has always resulted in anxiety among workers, which has manifested itself in peaceful strikes, violent riots, or changing political preferences. In 1811, workers responded to the Industrial Revolution by organizing the Luddite riots, which violently attacked factories, textile workshops, mills, and the machinery inside.[33] As technology displaces all economic classes of workers, they will protest differently. There are fears that a protest class could increasingly resort to violence to achieve their goals. "Neo-Luddites," or modern-day technophobes, became obsessed with 5G wireless towers and attacked them in the United Kingdom, Canada, and the United States. AI will have a similar affect.[34] There are growing fears that given enough time and funding, this backlash against technology could create a global movement and a violent protest class, who might use terrorism to stop the rapid expansion of technology in society.[35] This follows evidence that loss in manufacturing jobs is linked to an uptick in right-wing extremism and recruitment into such groups.[36] When we start to talk about nuclear power plants fueling the use of AI, we can get into some scary scenarios of sabotage.

There are a couple of other issues. If, as noted, AI is as likely to affect white-collar than blue-collar labor, then this will mean a loss in relative status and relative absolute income. Further, it is unlikely that even a UBI, should one ever come about, would be enough to replicate the quality of life of a junior professional living in an urban or inner suburban area. Throughout history, when professionals lose status or incomes, they have tended to project their migration toward a more radical right, but this is not a hard-and-fast rule. Richer displaced workers may use their resources to slow down technology growth by leaning heavily on politicians to regulate AI and new technologies more aggressively. The big point is that a society that is already polarized politically could see it exacerbated as ever more groups that thought themselves safe from "economic anxiety" come to experience it.

SHOULD MORE TECHNOLOGY MEAN MORE DEMOCRACY?

When the commercial Internet spread like wildfire in the 1990s, there was a sense that it would create conditions for democracy to also spread, with the Internet acting as a space where individuals from all over the world could come together and trade ideas, information, and opinions.[37] The Internet's success was a testament to the triumph of democracy in the 1990s, especially during a time where dictatorships were falling left and right, a vast number of democracies were being newly established across the globe, and in which Francis Fukuyama famously argued that the success of liberal democracy had resulted in "the end of history."[38] In the face of this unabashedly positive view of democratization, many believed that this expanse of emerging technology and the Internet would undoubtedly strengthen existing democracies and expand democracy across the globe and that it was impossible to even attempt to censor the Internet.

The logic behind this argument was that since one of the prime features of successful democracy is the free and reliable flow of information, the accessibility of information on the Internet meant that citizens would have better access to information to make informed voting decisions, which, in turn, would allow the government to better respond to citizens' needs. The same logic was applied for social media platforms; many believed that social media would give people more voice and help them connect, organize, and protest more effectively, all of which was expected to reduce polarization and aid democracy's ascent.[39]

No doubt there have been some democratic benefits from the Internet. But this idealized vision of democratization has begun to crumble in the last decade as we see technology weaponized, often by authoritarians who want to undermine existing democracies and close down their own internal debates and discontent. But we should also reflect on what happens when a platform for public discourse in a democracy is purchased by someone who wants to turn it into a political weapon: changes in X (formerly Twitter's) algorithm to amplify Elon Musk's pro-Trump content is a case in point.

The most successful example of domestic Internet censorship is arguably China, where the Communist Party has made controlling the Chinese information environment one of its highest priorities. To do so, it has developed the Great Firewall, which routinely spreads pro-government propaganda and "fake news" stories, often about Taiwan, on government-owned social media platforms. But it also tracks who says what and enacts serious punishments for veering too far from the party line.

This type of technological surveillance is not an isolated phenomenon; other countries, including Russia, Pakistan, Iran, Turkmenistan, and more, have also attempted to restrict their population's access to reliable information and their ability to organize against the government by blocking virtual private networks (VPNs), ordering Internet shutdowns, or forcing citizens to use government-controlled and monitored social media apps.[40] Essentially, autocracies are creating surveillance states that suppress dissent, censor online platforms, and deepen their control over citizens.

Later, I'll go in depth about deepfakes, but it's worth noting that associated risks come about in part because democracies generally are connected through technology and tolerate free speech with little emphasis on fact checking and control.[41] Anyone who uses a social media platform today knows that the line between what is allowed, what is annotated, and what is disallowed is fine in order to not trample free speech. This opens up opportunities for autocracies to infiltrate democratic media sites and spread false narratives, as occurred through the 2024 U.S. presidential election and many other elections around the world. This type of attack on a core principle of democracy—access to free and accurate flow of information—will then likely lead to an erosion of trust in democratic institutions among the population.

SURVEILLANCE

Happening in parallel is the fact that technology will enable governments to control populations more than ever before. So as society splinters due to the political ramifications of technological unemployment, governments are likely to hold on by using more and more automated tactics of control. This is a risk in both existing authoritarian countries and in countries we think of today as democracies.

It's easy to spot classical authoritarians using technology to their benefit. Instances of surveillance tech being used to repress protests, free speech, and racial profiling by police groups have been reported globally, but particularly in Kazakhstan, Russia, Iran, Azerbaijan, China, and others. In Iran, for example, facial recognition software has been employed to identify and punish women who don't wear headscarves in public.[42] In China, there's evidence the government uses facial recognition to profile Uyghurs and other Muslims.[43]

What's less easy to identify is unintentional digital authoritarianism, such as the use of surveillance for public health monitoring and contact-tracing apps, which can still pose big risks to citizen's rights.[44] James S. Pearson at the University of Amsterdam advances this argument by outlining how public health surveillance makes it easier for people to be exploited should leaders with authoritarian leanings come to power. The risk of surveillance in the future leads people to self-censor today because they know the government may be watching them and fellow citizens now or in the future.[45]

It's as if the government is building a data lake of surveillance that it can use once its intentions change. As prior chapters outlined a disturbing trend of authoritarian flirtation in many Western countries, the consolidation of data and means of control is particularly startling. But it's more than that: These Western countries are actually the source of many technology platforms that are used for conducting surveillance and implementing social control around the world.[46] This creates a perverse incentive for notionally democratic leaning countries to continue to build up stakeholders who support the development and deployment of such technologies.

The use of AI and emerging technologies, whether intentionally or unintentionally repressive, also fundamentally alters the level of trust that exists between a state and its citizens, and thus alters the shared social contract between state and citizens, national political culture, citizens' expectations of democracy, the right to privacy, and value of human rights.

Technology also has the potential to create surveillance states and entrench digital autocracies because it fundamentally alters a citizenry's expectation of the right to digital privacy. The right to privacy is an undeniable feature of a well-functioning democracy, a right protected under Article 12 of the Universal Declaration of Human Rights. Digital privacy has "become fundamental to preserving our understanding of freedom, autonomy, and human dignity—the values underpinning democracy itself."[47] As such, privacy allows for "free expression and assembly, laying the groundwork for democratic activism free from tracking, intimidation, and censorship" and is "considered a gateway right in liberal democratic institutions that undergirds the exercise of every other right."[48] Furthermore, there is an agreement "between democratic governments and their citizens for privacy and civil liberty protections" in democracies, which can be eroded through a government's use of surveillance technology over a longer period of time.[49] Surveillance technology can inherently change how populations view their own right to privacy, which they generate from "cultural, social, and individual norms," ultimately resulting in a change in view of their own political culture.[50,51] As a result, the longer privacy is disregarded and the surveillance state exists, the less citizens will expect privacy and challenge the state or the social contract to demand it.

Furthermore, surveillance tech is especially useful for authoritarians because of self-censorship once citizens know they are being watched.[52] Therefore, the misuse of technology by leaders is especially influential in "swing states," states that are in between democracy and authoritarianism, since the use of technology for surveillance or exploitation purposes can stifle dissent and discourage activism, potentially accelerating democratic backsliding and entrenching an autocratic regime.[53] Technology's ability to surveil and control populations gives national leaders the ability to change national political culture and the demands of a citizenry, a phenomenon we have seen play out worldwide.

This abuse of technology has immense implications for the rule of law.[54] In China, for example, authorities have begun using a "rule by law" rather than a "rule of law" strategy. In using this strategy, the Chinese Communist Party "uses law as a tool to wield power, not constrain it," which directly juxtaposes the "accountability" and "just law" component of "rule of law."[55] Rule by law combined with highly effective surveillance makes protesting difficult and risky, potentially changing Chinese citizens' expectations of privacy, which in turn makes democratization in China very unlikely.[56,57] Those supporting Chinese democratization might argue that China's authoritarian structure will prevent it from advancing innovation and will thus have to begin incorporating democratic features. However, reports have found that AI and autocracy can often be self-reinforcing. One such report in the *Quarterly Journal of Economics*, studying China's use of facial recognition software and Internet surveillance technology, has supported "the possibility of sustained AI innovation under the Chinese regime," in which "AI innovation entrenches the regime, and the regime's investment in

AI for political control stimulates further frontier innovation"—also known as an "AI-tocracy."[58]

Thus, the broader fear here is twofold. First, traditionally authoritarian regimes may gleefully implement new technologies to establish permanent control over populations that cannot fight back. Second, traditionally democratic countries may begin to deploy such technologies to counter societal ills while sleepwalking into softer forms of authoritarianism they claim to loathe.

For instance, I previously covered how urban crime laws are not being enforced in the United State and the United Kingdom but that companies have begun to use AI to predict shoplifting. What about governments using surveillance to predict if a person carrying a blanket is likely to lay down and go to sleep in conflict with local ordinances or just out for a picnic? That could be both efficient and effective—but also startlingly in contrast to most conceptions of privacy and rights.

Of course, as governments begin to fuel themselves on surveillance data, they will lean on the technology platforms that collect this data for private purposes to turn it over. These platforms have immense information. While anyone can game their technology to keep secrets, my wife and I have pretty much perfect knowledge of where each other is and what we are doing based on each other's social media feeds where we share our activities voluntarily. That means that all of the social media apps we use have the same, as do the mapping apps and other software we use that keep track of us in the real world to deliver digital experiences. There will be a host of legal evolutions as governments reckon with how they can mandate companies make that data accessible using different legal tools or technological backdoors. Where companies comply, they supercharge the state. Where they decline, they may need to leave.

In recent years, there has been a dramatic increase in the number of U.S. government requests for tech and social media companies to turn over data to aid in investigations. Before 2013, there were very few solid estimates of the number of U.S. government data demands, but after Edward Snowden's leaks, tech companies became significantly more transparent about the number of and nature of government requests received. Facebook, for example, published its first report on the number of government requests for data access in 2013 and promised to continue publishing regular reports on the topic to improve transparency.[59] Around this time, Google, Twitter, and Microsoft also began publishing such transparency reports, and today it is common practice to do so.[60]

In 2020, the U.S. government was the top requester of user data compared to any other country and generally, the U.S. requests double the amount of data from companies that the European Union does.[61,62] In the first half of 2023, Google was approached by U.S. federal agencies and courts for data access 63,666 times.[63]

However, companies don't always approve the government's requests for data. A notable example is the Apple-FBI encryption dispute in 2015 and 2016. Following a terrorist attack in San Bernardino, California, the FBI requested both data from Apple, which it was granted access to, and a backdoor to the iPhone, which would essentially eliminate crucial security and privacy features, which it was not granted access to. Apple argued that such a backdoor would "have the potential to unlock any iPhone in someone's physical possession" and would set a dangerous precedent for the government to "demand that Apple build surveillance software to intercept your messages, access your health records or financial data, track your location, or even access your phone's microphone or camera without your knowledge."[64] The FBI hired a number of companies including Australia-based Azimuth Security and Israeli software company Cellebrite to gain access to the shooters' iPhones, circumventing the need for Apple's assistance.[65] In 2020, Apple was once again approached by the FBI to decrypt the phone of the suspect in the Naval Air Station Pensacola terrorist attack, which it refused to do.[66]

These requests put companies in a tricky spot, forcing them to choose between defying law enforcement and disregarding user privacy. However, privacy concerns arising from government data requests are not just domestic concerns. In 2023, U.S. Senator Ron Wyden claimed that foreign governments were requesting data from Apple and Google, specifically for access to push notifications, which often automatically generate data that is stored by Google and Apple.[67]

The big challenge is that in a world of political polarization and erosion of rule and law, one way governments can maintain control is to infringe on rights. The problem is this can bring the whole democratic system down, particularly because such countries are unlikely to go far enough to use technology to maintain total control, as an authoritarian government would.

CRYPTO

A final point to note is that decentralized finance risks creating opacity where there was once transparency. Advocates see anonymity of the use of private electronic money—like Bitcoin—as a feature, not a bug. And there are many scenarios where that may reinforce freedoms, for instance, when used to anonymize fundraising for pro-democracy causes. But the development of alternative financial structures also risks undermining the existing plumbing of capitalist democracies. Countries, like the United States and those in Western Europe, can't tax what they can't see, so financial flows that are invisible cut out their ability to fund the government. The invisible flows can also mask illegal activity conducted by bad actors who may be criminal or geopolitically nefarious. While I've discussed in prior chapters how a rise of insecurity has led to private security that deprives the state of its monopoly of force, private money also deprives the state of its monopoly on regulating the economy. Cryptocurrency is much more nascent in its adoption than the automation and surveillance described earlier, but its impact will be as important over time.

RISKS TO DEMOCRACY

Many books have been written about the end of democracy, but few of them integrate the political, technology, and legal factors that give us real leverage over the question itself. Having touched on how technology may move the United States and other Western countries toward authoritarianism, we can at least be thankful for a fully functioning court system to restrain government and private actors that want to infringe on democratic freedoms. Except we can't, because court systems are being politicized, which is often the first sign of a drift toward autocracy.

In *How Democracies Die*, Daniel Ziblatt and Steven Levitsky make a compelling case that democracies die through incremental restrictions rather than bloody coups.[68] As wealth inequality grows—and will continue to grow, due to technological displacement—citizens will increasingly be enticed by populist politicians. History has shown populists often attempt to seize the legal system directly or indirectly. While I've spilled plenty of ink on Donald Trump's return to office, his promises during the 2024 campaign that if he was elected voters "won't have to vote again" raised concerns that he'd use the levers of power to cut back constitutional protections and fundamental freedoms.[69] That's just a taste of what's coming.

Such efforts may be in the form of court-packing or of "reform" like efforts in Mexico to turn the justice system over to direct elections. Or it may be more direct, as has occurred in Hungary. Viktor Orban and his Fidesz party began packing the Constitutional Court with loyalists in 2010 after changing the number of judges from 11 to 15, and in 2011 creating a new constitution, the Fundamental Law, through which they were able to lower the retirement age for judges, resulting in the immediate firing of hundreds of judges.[70] Since then, "the judges have never contradicted the government in any case politically important, but rather rubber stamped all requests addressed to them."[71]

Other examples abound. Venezuela's election in 2024 resulted in well-substantiated claims that an opposition candidate won, only for that candidate to run out of the country under threat of arrest.[72] In Turkey, a number of potential candidates have been arrested on charges like "insulting members of Turkey's Supreme Electoral Council."[73] India has seen its own share of similar events with opposition leader Rahul Gandhi arrested for defamation in 2022, but his sentence was suspended by the Supreme Court.[74] Another leading opposition figure, Arvind Kejriwal, who ran the national capital of Delhi, was arrested for bribery and campaign finance violations—a multipartisan crime in India by all accounts—and resigned his post.[75]

FIGHTING BACK: YOUR AI MANIFESTO

The upshot of all of this is that traditionally democratic societies are going to come under increasing pressure from a confluence of factors. Technology will shift the job market in fundamental ways that will shift the politics of many countries more toward conflict than collegiality. Technology will make it easier to erode rights via surveillance and the questioning of truth. The legal systems that are meant to defend against such backsliding are already fraying.

I don't raise this because I think democratic capitalism is perfect and we should all weep for its potential demise. I raise it because pretty much anyone doing business in the Western world wakes up expecting it to exist as their home backdrop and that may not be the case in the future.

Populations may resolve this with more utopian policy proposals like basic incomes. Or they may move more fully toward authoritarianism. The point is that democratic systems are coming under increasing stresses, which means fundamental assumptions businesses hold about their operating environment no longer apply.

Assumptions like swift clarity about who is in charge after an election or expectations of a fair hearing in court need to be tested constantly. As will expectations of privacy for businesses and individuals. There are gains to be captured for businesses that can maneuver during this transition. But only those that have their eyes open will have the chance.

What can you actually do now when you see a world like this ahead? Some would say to make as much money as you can before the music stops—to be "short-term greedy." But the businesses that will really succeed will be those that realize today they need to shift to being "long-term greedy." Of course, it's hard to be long-term greedy if the political economy in which you operate collapses.

Gus Levy, Goldman Sachs' managing partner in the 1970s, coined long-term greedy to underscore the fact that success and financial returns should be measured over decades rather than days.[76] Breaking out of your quarterly earnings cycle mindset is tough, but that's just what the prescription requires.

When you know the world will look radically different from how it does today, you want to measure yourself on progress toward long-term evolution rather than on how profitable you are as all these shocks and dislocations unfold. To get the space to do that, you need to articulate your vision for how your company will evolve.

One example might be articulating an AI jobs manifesto, built with the key leaders of your strategic team and communicated to reassure staff and position your company politically and to the markets.

Start with the core challenge: investors are anxious to know you are implementing new technologies and your employees are anxious that you plan to replace them with AI. Do you?

If you don't plan to replace staff with AI, you can articulate the principles you will use to assess how and why AI will be used in your business. Perhaps you are fully committed to rolling out AI tools that amplify the skills of your staff, while committing to keep them employed as you do. You might consider making a pledge that no employee will be let go due to implementation of AI over the next five years, or some reasonable timeline. This may make you a magnet for human talent. It will probably ward off strikes and protests about automation at your business. It will help Wall Street understand that you are not slow to roll out technology but you are doing it with a strategic perspective and for tactical advantage.

If you do plan to roll out AI for efficiency gains that include job reduction, you can proactively articulate a commitment to retraining staff for new roles within your enterprise. AT&T faced a similar challenge when it went through digital transformation almost a decade ago. The company committed $1 billion to "reskill" as many as 100,000 employees for the types of jobs it anticipated it would need in the future. It partnered with online platforms and traditional universities to deliver education. By doing this, the company was able to retain the firm-specific knowledge those employees had, increase employee loyalty, and provide an education service that government and traditional providers would not have otherwise made available to geographically concentrated populations.[77] While they might not realize they were being long-term greedy, they certainly laid the groundwork for it.

Of course, not every company can afford a massive reskilling program. In that case, try to carve out a public position that places yourself on the side of workers by asking government proactively to prepare for what's coming. Communicate to government that you want the social consequences of technological advancement to be managed so such advances continue and aren't disrupted by backlash. While you don't need to advocate for a New Deal–style Works Progress Administration, getting government to think proactively about what lies ahead from the perspective of business will help stabilize tendencies toward socialism or authoritarianism. It will help guide government toward new forms of education and support that can be paid for by aggregate gains in efficiency in order to stabilize communities and politics more broadly. And workers will be more likely to accept your application of cutting-edge technology if they feel you are trying to help them land on their feet for the future even if the company can't fund it alone.

CHAPTER EIGHT

UNRULY TECH: A SECTOR YOU CAN'T REGULATE

Elon Musk, founder of technology companies like Tesla and SpaceX, waded into the 2024 U.S. presidential election late in the game. With a few weeks left, the world's richest person could have just donated to President Trump's campaign to return to office, helping him win the money game against his opponent Kamala Harris. Instead, Musk also used tricks from the tech-titan handbook and ultimately made a material impact on Trump's ability to win swing states.

Software is built on consumer psychology, with many of the most popular apps giving rise to addiction through user manipulation. Instead of simply rewarding me for buying coffee, Starbucks' award-winning app creates personally tailored game-like challenges designed to get me to spend more money. I might earn 50 units of virtual currency redeemable for free drinks if I buy seven Pumpkin Spice Lattes in two days, or some other sequence I might not otherwise do.[1]

Musk embarked on similar gamification to encourage citizens to register to vote and ultimately support Trump. He promised to pay registered voters in swing states to refer their friends to sign his online petition, while also putting $1 million per day up as a sweepstakes prize for one signer every day until the election.

This plan was brilliant for two reasons. First, if he had simply offered to pay people to register to vote, he would have been directly violating the law. So, he did what many tech companies do and invented a pathway that might or might not be legal and exploited it long enough to achieve his goals. When he was taken to court by Democrats trying to stop the giveaway, he argued that it was not an illegal lottery but instead was effectively paying to hire "the best spokespeople for [the] pro-Trump agenda."[2] It doesn't really matter what it was—the impact on the election is irreversible, even if a fine would be triggered down the line.

But less well understood was the second element, which was that a simple payment to voters would prove far less effective than a combination of network effects through referrals and gamification through a sweepstakes. What he did was entice Trump supporters, the Trump-curious, or simply the transactional to take a good look at his nominee of choice.

When it was all said and done, Musk hacked the election with a Silicon Valley mindset, "FU" tech money, and the virality of an online petition.

A GAME YOU CAN'T WIN

As Musk's gambit demonstrated, tech leaders and their companies aren't just gamifying software. They are gamifying politics and their own regulation in a version of cat-and-mouse the government can't win because it can barely afford to play. The sense that some of the most innovative and well-funded businesses in the world are able to act however they like reinforces a sense of an unruly world.

First, it reveals the fact that tech companies are effectively self-regulating, often limited only by what their internal teams decide are the limits of innovation—not what government says.

Second, this form of Artificial Politics—where tech and politics collide to undermine traditional regulation—breaks down rule of law and it permits other sectors to run fast and pay penalties later. Third, technology presents an opportunity to reinterpret all laws in society through a techno-logical lens. For instance, free speech in the United States is a fairly settled body of law—until it comes to the roles and responsibilities of social media platforms for enforcing it.

And this technology is moving fast. As tech and legal expert Jae Um, founder and executive director of Six Parsecs, told me, one of the biggest challenges we are seeing is that technology incumbents are using their sizable war chests and existing go-to market channels to get new AI products into the market at an incredible speed. While there will be low-end disruption of existing business models by smaller, more nimble upstarts, the general thrust of AI is that the biggest companies in the world are falling over each other to bring complex, disruptive technology to the market through the world's most established sales and product channels. Thus, we are facing a lot of unknown unknowns as technology businesses are largely unconstrained and in a risk-taking position. When billions of people start talking to AI without understanding the risks—as is already happening—it will be tremendously challenging to put in place safeguards that undo or limit harm. Look at social media and the chal-lenge of misinformation. The dangers are now obvious. But doing any-thing retrospectively to stop them without trampling on free speech and consumer choice is less so.[3]

Governments are very slow to appropriately regulate new technologies. They are often competing with the private sector for the best talent and have trouble recruiting experts who can help them get ahead of the curve when they can spend only a fraction of the compensation. As the *Wall Street Journal* reported, million-dollar pay packages for engineers are more and more common in the private sector while government pay packages rarely exceed 20% of that amount.[4] As a result, government regulation of new technologies often trails very far behind the regulation that might be desirable or necessary.

This leads to private-sector companies pushing the boundaries of existing law. The argument "I'm just a technology platform" rather than a taxi company or a real estate company or a media company is a common strategy for bypassing rules while scaling. Ride-hailing companies outcompeted preexisting taxi cartels by defining themselves out of the existing regulatory framework and then activating their customers for political pressure when incumbents tried to shift regulation to encapsulate them.[5] Airbnb played a similar game by choosing not to adhere to traditional real estate laws as it outcompeted hotels and landlords. Social media networks like Facebook and X (formerly Twitter) faced analogous situations where they bypassed the strictures of being a media company by asserting that they may look and smell like one, but they are not one. When companies like OpenAI face legal and regulatory challenges that accuse them of building their foundational models on top of the intellectual property of others, we're effectively looking at the same thing: once you scale to hundreds of millions of users, you have a lot more options than if you're waiting for approval at the starting line.

The reality is that, however elastic the law may be, it does not contemplate the complexity of emerging technology. However, attempts to regulate those new innovations create their own complexity. This is particularly painful when regulators don't fully understand the core technologies they are regulating, in part because the innovators themselves are still trying to make sense of why tools like AI work the way they do. In that case, you have added regulatory complexity without the benefit of safeguards that regulations usually provide the economy and its participants. This will be an even bigger challenge in the coming years as we seek to regulate not just AI but digital assets, space technology, metaverses, quantum computing, and the next wave of biotechnology.

As legal technology expert Casey Flaherty, co-founder and chief strategy officer at LexFusion, told me:

"There are an estimated 5 million public regulatory bodies worldwide. That doesn't count private regulators, like homeowners' associations. Regulators regulate. Their MO is to propagate new regulations. Regulations not only accrete but overlap, intersect, and, frequently, conflict. Net new human activities often birth net new regulations. The digital world emerges. Eventually, we have the heretofore alien concept data privacy, and the regulations to support it. Social media explodes, for better and for worse. We introduce regulations to curb the worst of the worse. We're currently experiencing the same dynamic around AI with a seeming bias towards pre-emptive action due to prior lessons learned. We are trapped in a complexity flywheel. The world itself becomes more complex. Regulations become more complex in reaction thereto. Regulatory complexity adds to the complexity of the world."[6]

Europe is in the process of implementing a comprehensive AI act, which takes a risk-based approach to AI—ratcheting up rules governing different types of AI systems based on anticipated risks. Stiff fines—as high as 7% of global revenue—could be imposed for failure to comply.

Given that the Venn diagram of businesses operating in Europe and using AI in some form covers most multinational companies, the law is effectively the first shot fired in global AI regulation. Other countries—or states, like California—will follow with their own rules, creating a complex web of obligations.

And in that web lies enforcement, which is never clear cut. Companies will have to weigh the commercial challenges of slowing down because of notional or potential regulation and enforcement with the risks of simply barreling through new rules to win market share—and pay the price later. Knowing that it may take half a decade before these rules are in force will no doubt encourage many companies to simply push ahead.

WHOSE LAW IS IT ANYWAY?

When government gets behind the curve it tends to overreact. This leads to risks from the overreaction as well as risk of further erosion of the law.

On July 29, 2024, three girls between the ages of six and nine were stabbed to death at a Taylor Swift–themed dance class in Southport, a town in the north of England. Eight other children and two adults were also hurt in the attack.[7] The murderer was a 17-year-old born in Britain to African parents, but false rumors that the attacker was a Muslim who arrived illegally to the United Kingdom in a boat began to spread on social media.

By the next day, online conspiracy theories morphed into something more sinister. These rumors are thought to have originated or been amplified by foreign countries like Russia that wanted to sow unrest.[8] U.K. Prime Minister Keir Starmer, who had arrived in Southport to lay flowers and pay his respects, was met by an angry crowd who shouted to "get the truth out."[9] The protests grew uglier as the day went on, with rioters throwing bricks at Muslims who had come to pray and at the police officers who were protecting them. A police van was torched, and 27 officers were taken to hospital.[10] In the days that followed, more than 20 cities and towns around the United Kingdom saw riots that targeted migrants and Muslims, police officers and their equipment, and mosques and Asian-owned shops. A hotel housing migrants was attacked in Rotherham. Lists began to circle with the personal details of immigration lawyers so they could be targeted by protesters. Police told lawyers to stop meeting their clients and to brace for firebombs in their mailboxes.

More than 400 people were arrested in the following weeks.[11] While that may seem like a story of bringing those who were violent to justice, it's actually just the beginning. The British government shortly after announced it would bring to justice anyone it could track down on social media who had spread false information. Were it just Brits—like a woman from Chester arrested for doing so—that would be less interesting.[12] But the government announced it would be going after people regardless of where they live. Pakistan then arrested a web designer who had posted questionable information related to the event.[13] Social media companies in the United States came into the crosshairs. Elon Musk clashed with the U.K. government over his role in amplifying content around the attack, with the implication that he could be somehow liable for posts he made about a potential U.K. civil war.[14]

This type of reaction is typical for governments that have lost control of technology within their borders. After all, the U.K. government is not wrong that foreign technology platforms like Facebook and X amplify content that can lead to unrest, and there is little it can do about it. As a result, the response from government is to overreact when it needs to catch up.

The world is moving toward geolegal fragmentation yet the world is more connected than it has ever been. The Southport example is a particularly striking one because it ties together a number of themes from the unruly world—anti-immigrant sentiment, violent protest, restrictions on speech, and maximalist use of the legal system as a response. But it's neither the first nor the most important example of projecting power extraterritorially in response to perceived risks. One of the core challenges businesses will face in the years ahead is the unruly elevation of standards because one jurisdiction goes first—ensnaring global companies whether their home country likes it or not.

Dispersion and Extraterritoriality

Governments have effectively failed to regulate the growth of technology companies and the dispersion of their innovations to date. The speed and haphazardness with which the U.S. government, in particular, is rolling out export controls and regulation of artificial intelligence (AI) is a case in point. It's not like governments should be surprised by AI, which has received huge investment in the recent decade. Nor should they be surprised that the tools new technology creates can be used against them, as the history of conventional warfare has many parallels. Instead, governments like the United States are attempting to execute a massive pivot away from mostly free markets for technology to entirely regulated markets for technology. That shift creates a sense that the rules of the game for commerce are completely unsettled.

That shift gives rise to a few implications. First, for governments to make up for lost time, they need to overreact, which can undermine rule of law in their borders and beyond. In effect, governments can knock out business models overnight by deciding they are too dangerous. And given sprawling supply chains, even the slightest exposure to a jurisdiction is increasingly viewed as justification to bring a foreign corporation under its purview. National security reviews of corporations are at an all-time high. So are restrictions on their ability to sell anything remotely dual-use abroad. This is the United States exporting its geopolitical challenge.

In 2022, the United States implemented a new export control regime that projected its authority onto most high-end technology in the world because in some way the supply chain of that product likely touched the United States. These U.S. measures dramatically expanded the scope of the 1959 Foreign Direct Product Regime. It went beyond controlling the export of items made in the United States, or items made outside the United States incorporating U.S.-made parts to include items made entirely outside the United States that incorporated U.S. technology or software, and even items made with equipment containing U.S. technology or software.[15] This increasingly recursive definition of "U.S.-origin inputs" put companies like Dutch chipmaker ASML, which makes lithography machines for high-end chipmaking, in the position of having to sacrifice business in China to comply with U.S. restrictions. It also put the Dutch government in a position to have to follow suit on similar controls, which the Dutch eventually did, rather than cede regulatory authority to the United States.[16] But beyond this, we also seem to be seeing an expansive definition of the very idea of technological vulnerability (or primacy) beyond high-end technology. Efforts to rebuild domestic supply chains have led to increased concern about China's dominant position in legacy chip-making that might hobble the economics of potential U.S. competitors. Meanwhile, such dominance in less sophisticated chips could still give Chinese entities the cashflow to increase investment in cutting-edge technologies. In effect, market share and fungible revenue streams are increasingly seen as another powerful dual-use technology.[17] These developments make it even harder to predict who or what might be next in the regulatory firing line.

The extraterritorial regulation with the widest recognizable reach in recent years is the EU-driven "cookie-clicker" that resulted from the European Union's General Data Protection Regulation (GDPR). This E.U. measure, the GDPR, was inspired by concerns over privacy and imposed stiff penalties for any company that violated its provisions and touched the European economy in any way. While U.S. companies scrambled to figure out how to comply in Europe to avoid penalties, the act from Brussels also shifted U.S. politics on the issue. Once a jurisdiction sets a high bar, it doesn't necessarily matter what other countries do unless they set a higher one. So if GDPR requires very specific things in terms of data management and another jurisdiction, say the U.S. state of Montana, sets a low, laissez-faire bar for how to manage personal data, in practice global companies have to comply with GDPR for all their customers, so Montana residents gain the protections enshrined in GDPR whether they want them or not. And as localities like California layer on additional restrictions through their own privacy laws, it only raises the global bar higher as companies that have exposure to Europe and to California now follow both.

The biggest question with rules like this is whether government will enforce them. Sometimes it will—and it will be expensive. Meta, for instance, was fined $1.3 billion for running afoul of GDPR, a law that many think arose to regulate it in the first place.[18]

While this chapter is about technology regulation, it's important to recognize this dynamic of falling behind and then asserting even stronger regulatory authority, which often can manifest in more analog ways because of rules driven by fear of innovation.

The United States has been particularly forceful in such an approach with respect to financial crime. As the use of sanctions increases, more and more countries and entities are sanctioned. There are still people in the world who want to transact with those entities. When those people or companies move money from one foreign location to another in U.S. dollars, in effect they need to use a U.S. correspondent bank to complete the transaction. That momentary electronic exposure to the United States, as money passes through, suddenly opens the company up to U.S. jurisdiction.[19]

China has gone further with its Hong Kong National Security Law, which doesn't even require exposure to Hong Kong or China for an act to be considered a crime. In effect, it punishes speech wherever it occurs in the world, in part driven by the ability of Chinese abroad to stoke unrest via social media. Under the law, there are stiff penalties for crimes like subversion or terrorism, and Article 38 of the law authorizes the punishment of offenders regardless of where the crime took place or where the offenders are from. This means anyone who calls for Hong Kong independence is a criminal and can be arrested and prosecuted the minute they set foot in China—even if that call came in a conversation, say, between two Brazilians in Brazil. This has a chilling effect not just on Chinese students abroad who are afraid to discuss these issues even when they are in countries that otherwise have broad free speech protections but also on foreign critics who may have been vocal about all types of public affairs issues and are now criminals the minute they arrive for a single sentence they said on the other side of the world.

As the world becomes increasingly fragmented, this type of extraterritorial approach to legislation and enforcement will become increasingly prominent.

A PARALLEL ECONOMY

What this ends up creating is a set of existing technology companies that function almost in a parallel economy where their market power is so strong they can move faster than government and have the resources to win when government catches up.

While market concentration is usually used for antitrust analysis, it's helpful to think about your own personal tech stack. In a given day, you might listen to this book via the audio app Audible while shopping at

Whole Foods, scrolling software apps built on Amazon Web Services as you walk home to watch your favorite show on Amazon Prime. Or you might use Apple CarPlay to guide you to your gym, where you will swim with an Apple Watch tracking your health data, before you go home and do work on your Macbook.

As technology companies become bigger and bigger, the average citizen will interact with fewer and fewer technology parents. With governments trailing far behind on legislation, those companies will determine the rules of engagement—often forcing customers to sacrifice legal rights through terms and conditions they don't understand.

I recently took an autonomous Waymo taxi around Los Angeles. When the car made a couple of herky-jerky movements, I started thinking about who would be responsible in the event of an accident. If I was injured, did I have any idea who would be at fault?

The honest answer is I have absolutely no idea. I can see how the car manufacturer or the autonomous ride-hailing app would have liability for failures or mistakes they could make. I could see how any of the riders could be liable if we physically interfered with the car. I could imagine the software being hacked in ways that could leave any of us or none of us at fault. But the simple fact was that I was rolling around town in a vehicle that could put my life and others' lives and property at risk without really understanding the terms and conditions.

This is a state of the world today that is hard to avoid. Research by Deloitte found 91% of consumers accept terms and conditions without reading them—even higher for younger consumers.[20] Thinking through this reminded me of the television show *Black Mirror*, in particular an episode titled "Joan Is Awful."[21] In that episode, the main character Joan discovers her life can be re-created by streaming service Streamberry because she agreed to that in the terms and conditions of joining the streaming service. Bad thing after extremely bad thing happens to Joan while a stream of lawyers tell her she can't sue because she agreed to the terms.

It sounds outlandish that a person could cede authority to their life through terms and conditions for a video service, but actually a major streaming service asserted something similar in mid-2024. After a man's wife had a fatal allergic reaction from eating at a restaurant on a property owned by Disney, the man included Disney in his lawsuit against the restaurant operator. Disney initially argued that the man must submit to arbitration instead of going to court because he had once taken a Disney+ streaming trial and agreed to a term there that "any dispute between you and us, except for small claims, is subject to a class action waiver and must be resolved by individual binding arbitration."[22] Disney eventually reversed course.

Much like companies may have exposure to the U.S. extraterritorial regime in ways they don't anticipate, customers have similar exposure to a very small number of sprawling companies increasingly in control of more and more of their lives.

It's possible these companies could take consent for something like binding arbitration in the context that has the lowest bar and apply that in ways the customer would never have contemplated. For instance, that Waymo I was riding was owned by Alphabet, the parent of Google. If it crashed and injured me, did I cede my rights to a jury trial when I signed up for Gmail more than a decade prior? If it veered across the street and hit someone following Google Maps directions on their phone, did their assent to the mapping app jeopardize their claim for injury?

These may seem like edge cases, but we live in a world of great consolidation. In the context outlined here—where governments are woefully behind on regulating technology—companies will increasingly fill the space of some of the most important legal agreements affecting citizens' lives. However, the sense that customers are following corporate-made rules is both novel and gives a further dimension to how law is changing in society.

To solve this problem, Professor Gillian Hadfield has suggested creating a private market of for-profit regulators who are up to the task of regulating technology.[23] In effect, these private regulators will be able to pay top dollar to top talent to come and design "rules for a flat world," as her book on the subject is called. Such for-profit regulators would compete with each other to capture economic gains from designing the best regulation and evolving it. Otherwise, we seem to just be left with technology companies acting as regulators in the absence of clear regulatory will, expertise, or muscle.

This is a novel solution and one that could work well to solve the expertise gap at the government level. However, it could also further erode the powers of government.

FIGHTING BACK

Government is woefully behind on regulating emerging tech, something that will be further exacerbated with the scale and pace of the AI revolution. If you think of the law as a street sign, there are often stop signs where things are clearly illegal and you can't proceed without fully braking until the situation is safe. Technology companies don't blow through the stop signs and risk an accident: they do the equivalent of a "California stop"— they pull up to these stop signs, slow down to make sure there's no clear hazard approaching, and keep going. Now imagine you were racing that car and you stopped at every sign. You're going to lose the race.

Most corporations are used to this dynamic in their core business and choose their risk tolerance accordingly. And there are lots of areas where you should be cautious rather than cavalier about rule-breaking. But what many are failing to grasp is that just like today the distinction between traditional companies and Internet companies makes little sense, all companies that survive over the next decade will become AI companies. To have any chance of winning the race, these companies are going to have to accept more risk.

Waiting until the rules of AI regulation are clear to embrace AI in your core business will be a guaranteed losing strategy. Instead, companies will need to figure out how they can behave more like tech companies so they can outpace their competitors, which, more and more, will be a small number of ever-expanding tech behemoths, especially as tech leaders like Elon Musk earn political power by bringing such techniques to electoral politics.

This is not to say that you should break the law outright to win in the market—that is like running all the stop signs, which is a great way to cause an accident. But realizing that government will be spending the next few years defining what is and is not acceptable in the case of AI opens up an opportunity today to outpace competitors who are too cautious.

CHAPTER NINE

UNRULY TRUTH: DEEPFAKES AND THE LIAR'S DIVIDEND

Imagine being a mid-level employee and being invited to a meeting with your CFO to discuss a secret deal that requires you to immediately and discreetly transfer about $25 million via 15 transactions to five bank accounts. All sorts of alarm bells would be going off in your head that this can't possibly be legitimate.

But then imagine showing up to the video meeting and realizing it's not a one-on-one call with the CFO—a call where a scammer could trick you using deepfake technology—but instead it was a group of your colleagues who were all assembled to discuss the deal with the CFO. In that case, you'd be reassured you're attending a real meeting and your actions were needed for the betterment of the company. You'd be more worried about not completing a secret transaction requested by the top financial officer than about questioning it any further.

The scenario requires imagination, but it was not imagined: a clerk working for the Hong Kong branch of U.K. engineering company Arup fell victim to such a scam involving a real-time group deepfake and made the requested transactions before discovering he had been faked out.[1]

50 Cent once rapped, "I hate a liar more than I hate a thief / A thief is only after my salary / A liar's after my reality."[2] Reflecting on the Arup story, I realized losing the ability to distinguish real from fake is much more costly than any set of transactions.

DEEPFAKES AND ELECTIONS

Deepfakes are one form of manipulation malicious actors can use to gaslight any of us into believing something fake is real. What if a deepfake video of a presidential candidate in any election in the world dropped days before voting day showing them in a compromising position? It could be them in cahoots with a foreign leader, insulting the general population, or participating in a sex act—use your imagination. Assume the candidate loses the election.

Would the election be invalidated and rerun? Would there be claims that there's no precedent to nullify an election because of actual fake news? It's not at all clear other than that it would be a mess emblematic of the unruly world we live in today.

To start to appreciate the level of risk of something like this, we need to dive a bit deeper into the technology and politics of such manipulation.

As Jason Cade of BAE Systems points out, malicious actors can operate at different levels to force electoral outcomes favorable to them or just to sow discord within societies. They can use "influence" to interfere and change turnout. They can use "disruption" to sabotage election infrastructure. They can "undermine" trust in the electoral process and give the perception the entire electoral system is failing.[3]

A number of foreign powers tried to influence the 2024 U.S. election, all the way up to election day when false bomb threats at polling sites in swing states were traced back to Russia.[4] Russia, whose role in the 2016 election is documented elsewhere in this book, was long known to be a threat and is believed to have engaged in support of Trump's return to power. Details emerged about a Russian-run disinformation group, CopyCop, which "alters articles from mainstream and conservative-leaning U.S. and U.K. media as well as from Russian state-affiliated outlets and spreads them to U.S. election-themed websites, all within 24 hours of the original articles being posted."[5]

Furthermore, conspiracy theories surrounding a nearly-successful attempt on President Trump's life were promoted on fake U.S. news sites, run by pro-Russian sources, one of which published an AI-generated audio deepfake that seemed to showcase former President Obama and an aide discussing the assassination attempt, suggesting that the Democratic Party orchestrated the attack. As David Salvo, managing director of the Alliance for Securing Democracy at the German Marshall Fund, told me, the whole point of tactics like this is to get this misinformation in the mainstream and amplified by influencers with hopes that it goes viral and is not traced back to Russia.[7]

Iran launched a campaign focused on undermining Trump, probably because he scrapped a nuclear deal and killed one of their top scientists. In August 2024, news broke of a suspected Iranian hack of the

Trump campaign and attempted hack of the Biden-Harris campaigns. Iran's attempted interference in the Trump campaign was a complicated, lengthy process, with Tehran laying the foundation to do so from 2020 when its hackers sent voters threatening emails to scare them away from the polls.

In 2024, the attack had two main components. First, it attempted to influence voters, especially in swing states, by sending misinformation about trending topics. Second, it tried to get intelligence about the campaigns themselves. To achieve the first, the Iranian hacking group Storm-235 operated a number of websites posing as legitimate U.S. news sites, writing about topics like LGBTQ+ rights and the Israel-Hamas war. To achieve the second, Iran sent spear-phishing emails to campaign staff, which resulted in Trump's campaign being hacked. A source called "Robert" then leaked internal Trump documents to the press, including a vetting file on Trump's vice-presidential choice, JD Vance.

Meanwhile, China has long been a practitioner of such techniques. It recently came under the spotlight for its interference in the Taiwanese elections, by using deepfakes and fake online accounts to promote conspiracy theories, including about topics like "egg shortages, Taiwan's submarine production, political and sex scandals, and Taiwan's readiness for war, fueling fears over conscription and young people being forced to fight, as well as casting doubt over the US's support."[8] China also tried its hand at influencing the 2024 U.S. presidential election, with Chinese-run social media accounts pretending to be members of the Republican Party and Trump supporters, pushing false narratives. Chinese social media company TikTok is under investigation for allegedly being used by China to influence U.S. elections, by disseminating pro-Chinese content that capitalizes on partisan divisions, all of which can be considered a threat to U.S. democracy.

THE LIAR'S DIVIDEND

So that's the landscape—a world of threat actors trying to manipulate elections to achieve their own policy goals or simply cause disorder. The current combination of deepfakes, foreign state manipulation, and election interference being used to undermine political processes has had immense implications on the legitimacy of democracy and its institutions. When politicians intentionally promote AI-generated images and audio recordings and trade accusations of promoting fake images, it creates the sense that anything could be fake—even things that are really real. As such, the use of AI in elections "destabilizes the concept of truth itself," with no truth baseline, meaning that politicians and their supporters can pick and choose which alternate reality they believe and choose to align themselves with.[9]

This is simply an extension of the "post-truth" era where citizens trust nothing and question everything. People are already wary of trusting media organizations owned by tech titans; for instance, Jeff Bezos owns the *Washington Post*, and Elon Musk owns X (formerly Twitter)—and an increasing number of people get their news from social media. With citizens unsure which forms of media to trust and which politicians they can trust, traditional institutions lose credibility.

Bill Henderson, editor of legaltech blog *Legal Evolution* and professor at Indiana University Maurer School of Law, told me that the January 6, 2021, storming of the U.S. Capitol was a turning point for him in understanding society.[10] He realized that people were angry enough to storm Congress because "the system" didn't work for them—an anger with the status quo that would deliver Trump back to the White House in late 2024. But Bill's core insight is that the system is not just political. It is also legal.

There is a lot to say about access to justice and the legal system, which I will get into in the LegalAI part of this book. However, the societal challenge looming in the backdrop is that there can be no justice or fairness if there is no agreed upon sense of truth. And both a political culture shift against elites and common sources of truth in favor of social media and user-based content generation undermine the idea that we all live with a singular shared truth. The law is there to codify society's values, and if there are varying definitions of what those values are, it becomes hard for law to do its job.

This is starting to show up in the courtroom. In recent years, the availability of and ease with which deepfakes can be created has made prosecutors, defense attorneys, and judges' jobs in the courtroom all the more challenging because of the likelihood of including "falsified evidence ... and causing an unjust result" increases and as does the likelihood that "the opposing party will challenge the integrity of evidence, even when they have a questionable basis for doing so".[11] Attorneys have started to lean into the "deepfake defense" strategy, through which they argue that genuine video or audio evidence is unreliable because there is no guarantee that it is unaltered.[12]

This practice gives rise to the "liar's dividend," since "a skeptical public will be primed to doubt the authenticity of real audio and video evidence," as law professors Robert Chesney and Danielle Keats Citron have argued.[13] In effect, when you see so much fake stuff, you start thinking real stuff is fake, which benefits the liar. It makes sense, and it is a chilling thought.

These strategies were recently used by lawyers in a case involving January 6th protestors and in a case involving Elon Musk's statements on Tesla's self-driving cars. The lawyers of two defendants on trial for their participation in the January 6th riots questioned the validity of videos that showed the men inside the capitol and at the protests, arguing that the jury should therefore move to acquit the men.[14] In Elon Musk's case, a similar argument was made, with his lawyers arguing that Musk's claims about Tesla's self-driving abilities captured on video several years ago were actually inaccurate and amounted to a deepfake video.[15] In both cases, these arguments were unsuccessful, with judges vehemently rejecting the attorney's claims.

However, the judge in Musk's case wrote that the arguments were "deeply troubling" and that the court was "unwilling to set such a precedent by condoning Tesla's approach here."[16] As Jonathan A. Porter, a partner at law firm Husch Blackwell, argues, these examples show that "categorical denunciation of evidence because deepfakes exist is not a wise strategy" and that such defenses "should be brought only when there is something the defense can point to that would suggest that the evidence is fake."[17]

Part of the challenge is that due to the fallibility of memory, courts have generally elevated video and audio evidence in recent decades. To introduce audio or visual evidence, the courts currently use a "fair and accurate portrayal" standard, which law professor John P. LaMonaga says "sets an extremely low bar," since "the witness need only testify that the depiction is a fair and accurate portrayal of her knowledge of the scene."[18] Nonetheless, many experts have expressed a need for further regulation on permitted evidence, especially with the possibility of AI-generated or manipulated evidence.

An increasingly AI-rife evidence base will have implications for juries. For example, juries might be more skeptical toward audio or visual evidence, meaning that the plaintiff's lawyers will need to work harder to prove that the evidence is real, resulting in increased costs, which could create a financial burden for some individuals seeking to take legal action.[19] You could argue the jury's increased skepticism will likely benefit the defendant, but of course a jury could be presented with completely fake evidence that it believes for some reason.

At a time when public trust in U.S. courts is already very low, the inclusion of deepfakes in the courtroom further erodes this trust, as it blurs the line between what is real and what is fake. Controversy over deepfake evidence eliminates our shared base of common facts, from which the justice system should be able to secure, if not advance, the truth and justice. If juries can no longer trust evidence presented in the courtroom, citizens will likely not trust the court's final decision on a case, resulting in a loss of trust in the judicial system and an overall loss of trust in democratic institutions as a whole.

FIGHTING BACK: TALK LESS, SMILE MORE

So, public trust in elites is cratering and will continue to be undermined by new tools that will raise doubts about what's real and what's fake. Plus, your employees are soft targets for scammers who will trick them to take irreversible actions that will inflict economic and public relations damage on your company. What are you to do?

As a corporate actor, you can't solve all of this, but you should use the tools you have at your disposal. You can start by making sure your employees are constantly updated on new techniques attempting to manipulate them into damaging scams. But more importantly, you need to work to re-establish your business as a trusted voice.

As elites, you should assume the general public does not trust you or your company, even if it likes your products. If you want to lessen the liar's dividend and the chance it manifests negatively against your firm, you must work harder to establish yourself as a paragon of truth.

Companies have found themselves in trouble of late by commenting too little or too much about politics and societal issues. As the pendulum swings away from values-based orientations, companies risk being caught in the middle of an increasing number of politicians who will punish them for such positioning and some percentage of customers who will view them as hypocritical when they hedge their bets.

When we think of fighting back, we often think of active strategies. But one way of fighting back is to refuse to be pulled into the fray. The case for remaining silent on noncore issues is increasingly attractive.

Businesses get themselves in trouble when they take public positions they don't really believe. Standing with Israel after the horrific attacks of October 7, 2023, seemed like a no brainer. Until that raised the question of whether they were still standing with Israel a week or a year later. Similarly, standing with Ukraine when it was invaded by Russia raised expectations those businesses might stand with Taiwan amid ongoing provocations from China. Or stand with oppressed minorities in every geography where the business operates. Did those businesses really mean to sign up to narrate global affairs with play-by-play opinions?

As the world becomes more complex, it's increasingly unlikely you can pick and choose engagement with politics on your terms—doing so creates an expectation you will keep doing so. And doing so poorly undermines your credibility when your business is on the receiving end of deepfakes and fake news.

Many companies take their ESG, sustainability, and political positions seriously and seek to implement their vision of change. But many don't and have subscribed to such views publicly for performative purposes—or perhaps because they felt nervous about not commenting on breaking news when their competitors were. Employees and customers can detect inauthenticity, and those who care will increasingly hold this against its perpetrators.

Authenticity matters in a world where politics is increasingly anti-elite. As the data from Edelman's 2024 Trust Barometer shows, nearly two-thirds of the population worries that government leaders, business leaders, and journalists purposely try to "to mislead people by saying things they know are false or gross exaggerations."[20] Forget deepfakes; the public is worried about good old elite gaslighting.

Why shouldn't the public be? After all, as Alison Taylor wrote in *Harvard Business Review*, "Making a public statement is often a way to compensate for, or distract from, a lack of meaningful action, and it is increasingly the norm. For instance, the Carbon Disclosure Project recently reviewed 4,100 corporate commitments on climate change and found that fewer than 100 were credible."[21] Citizens have learned to worry about this because it happens all the time.

Businesses have gotten smarter about the need for a "social license to operate" but can often miss that performative gestures undermine this rather than support it. The public isn't stupid and has access to a lot of data. If it doubts your authenticity, it is unlikely to support you when a crisis strikes. That crisis could be amid economic turmoil when a costly government intervention is needed. Or it could be when a jury is considering a claim against you and you need jurors to see you as sympathetic—or even just to believe your evidence isn't fake.

This gets even more complicated when you have global exposure and need to balance your authentic position in one geography with risks in another. Standing with democracy or human rights might seem like a simple position to take in a Western context, but if you do a heavy business in China, for instance, you might increase the target on your back. While we often think about the target as a political one (you'll fall out of favor), it can actually ignite some serious legal consequences in markets where political speech is illegal or severely restrained.

Moreover, as your unpopularity in a jurisdiction increases, the ability of competitors to use the courts against you increases, as does the chance regulatory authorities scrutinize you further. This can present serious problems when your public relations positions end up contradicting your operational decisions.

Businesses are a critical stakeholder group in society and are a force for good. They provide employment, economic growth, and consumer choice. They have a right to be represented and to make their views known. They simply need to consider when doing so actually supports their goals and when doing so might create expectations that undercut those goals.

Stepping back, it makes sense to me that businesses become increasingly selective in picking and choosing where to comment. Arguably, it is better for businesses to take a page from the musical *Hamilton* and "talk less, smile more" by selecting to comment on only those issues central to their vision.[22]

CHAPTER TEN

UNRULY WAR-BOTS: THE INTERNET OF WEAPONS

O
n September 17, 2024, Fatima Abdallah Jaafar returned home after her first day of fourth grade. A child not much older than my own, she heard her father's pager going off on a table in the kitchen. Much like my kids might do, she carried it to her dad. It exploded in her hands, killing her.[1]

The attack—widely reported to be conducted by Israel—crippled militant group Hezbollah's communication infrastructure by infiltrating the supply chain of the pagers and implanting explosives. It also crippled or killed thousands of Lebanese who possessed or were near the exploding booby-trapped pagers and walkie-talkies over a two-day period. Such an attack set aside any concerns about collateral damage and also set aside international law protections against booby-trapping civilian devices.

It's not hard to see how the Internet of Things—those connected devices from fridges to phones—can be turned into the Internet of Weapons. This is why there are increasing national security rules being implemented about everything from TikTok to Chinese software in autonomous vehicles.

In the new world of war, if you fail to secure your devices, it can lead to catastrophic consequences. And those devices don't just need to blow up: one of the big concerns about Chinese electric vehicle imports into the United States is that if the United States and China were one day in direct conflict, China could simply disable them causing massive havoc. This is unruly war, where the risks of Artificial Politics are on display at every turn.

ARTIFICIAL POLITICS AND WAR

In Part II, I covered the Geolegal Risk implications of conflict in an unruly world. In short, the United States and China are trying to leverage their economies and international power to split the world into spheres, while Russia vies for increased influence and much of the rest of the world tries to navigate the fallout of the three. Now let's think about conflict from an Artificial Politics point of view.

New technologies are allowing countries to fight war like they never have before. And companies are increasingly caught in the middle because they have significant stakes in critical industries that are integral to a state's national security. This means there are more vectors of threat as conflicts become protracted and smaller actors use technology to inflict damage, while companies enabling battle directly or indirectly become targets.

Drones

Artificial Politics brings us innovations like drones that level the war field. Just as every company is today part of geopolitical conflict, now even smaller, less well-funded militaries can take part in advanced military tactics. For advanced militaries like the United States, drones have yielded many advantages, but most are around the ways a machine can outperform a human. Most importantly, a drone can be shot down, and no family has to hold a funeral. But also humans have physical limits in terms of both attention spans and life support needs. Drones can fly around and around a single spot for hours waiting for a specific convoy to attack.

Looking at the way Ukraine and Iran have deployed drones, it is clear they can equalize a battlefield. Building a capable air force is complex, is expensive, and takes decades. A drone can be purchased at Walmart and deployed to the battlefield after some relatively simple modifications.[2] These drones serve a somewhat different tactical purpose than bombers, but in today's battlefield, being able to deploy surveillance and missile-armed drones gives countries with essentially no air force—or at least no air force that can compete with the air power of the United States and many other NATO militaries—unprecedented capabilities.

The value proposition makes air power more accessible too. For decades, air power could cost hundreds of millions of dollars for a single bomber. Even high-end drones could cost tens of millions of dollars. The drones Ukraine is using against Russia cost far less. Iran is using cheap drone power to project influence in Iraq, Syria, Lebanon, Yemen, Sudan, and likely elsewhere, no longer needing to foot the bill to stand up local militias.

While I will get to key implications for companies in the following sections, the critical insight here is that battles can go on longer because countries and nonstate actors can use cheap weapons with limited casualty risk on their side to prolong conflicts. As a result, there's a greater chance for companies to be caught in the middle or for smaller powers to inflict serious damage against larger ones.

AI Weapons

Greater use of artificial intelligence (AI) in warfare was inevitable as soon as machine learning models advanced to the point where they could be integrated into military systems. These advances would make militaries and intelligence gathering faster and potentially more accurate. But just as the world was acclimatizing to computer scripts fighting alongside warriors, generative AI (GenAI) came into the public domain. Just as GenAI can finish a high schooler's term paper, it can also write code to execute a drone attack based on whatever inputs it gets. GenAI is not especially explainable, and getting it to repeat tasks precisely can be inconsistent. This is important when it comes to lethal force in warfare.

One of the biggest fears about AI is that it will become entangled with warfare in a way that leads to autonomous weapons with a mind of their own. Recent research about large language models powering the GenAI revolution scares the life out of me: five LLMs applied to wargames showed a predilection for escalation, even to the point of nuclear war.[3] The danger is that AI is an irrational six-year-old with a PhD in nuclear physics and a military budget.

For now, it appears that AI is being proven on the battlefield in more restrained ways. Ukraine, for instance, uses AI to identify targets that will have the biggest psychological impact and to connect disparate pools of data for counterintelligence purposes. Israel is reportedly using algorithms that assess whether humans are militants and whether buildings may be potential targets. U.S. spending on AI in the military has increased exponentially. American programs have similar aims to those outlined in Ukraine or Israel, where the systems are tracking and helping to attack targets. China, too, is using AI for similar purposes though public reporting tends to emphasize its use on trawling information. We'll increasingly see AI used for wargaming and high-level knowledge tasks in and around war, if not for the direct initiation of strikes at the moment.

The critical point to note today is that all governments claim there are human decision-makers in the loop; while systems may surface threats, it's ultimately humans who are deciding whether to strike. The problem is that this is an unstable equilibrium. Humans are slow and often unavailable, even in wartime. Think about algorithmic stock trading, for instance: allowing computers to "do their thing" can create untold advantages simply based on reaction times and processing times.

Do we really believe governments will keep AI decision-making off-limits in the long run? I don't. Countries will increasingly see the benefits of training AI to react faster than humans ever could. In the Cold War, mutually assured destruction meant countries would not attack each other because they could be obliterated in return. With AI, it is possible to get to a point of decisive advantage—to determine that there is a single unmissable instance where launching the first strike could be decisive but the window for attack is so small that only a machine could act on the opportunity. If you think your enemy might do this, then you might do this too.

The only way to constrain such behavior is to tie hands against it. But the international community can barely agree on toothless declarations let alone verifiable mechanisms. The UN General Assembly approved its first resolution in October 2023 combating Lethal Autonomous Weapons systems with notable objections from India and Russia and abstentions from China, Iran, Israel, and Saudi Arabia. The United States proposed its own declaration on Responsible Military Use of Artificial Intelligence and Autonomy at a summit in the Hague in 2023, but many of the same countries would not even sign on to a nonbinding call to action. If we can't agree there's a problem, we're unlikely to find a solution.

Personal Electronic Devices

In all our pockets we carry smartphones, massively powerful mini-computers that have parts sourced from around the world and carry incredibly complex software. These devices are essential now for our personal and professional lives; but they are an always-on vector for adversaries to steal our personal and company data. The Israeli company NSO Group's Pegasus software is a surveillance tool that requires no careless action by the user. Once a message is received, the device is infected. This caused a widespread scandal in 2021 when it was revealed how frequently countries had infected other heads of state, with the Moroccan hacking of French President Emmanuel Macron's phone with Pegasus perhaps being the most prominent.[4]

And of course, there's the example of exploding pagers that opened this chapter. If every person carries an electric device on them at all times, the ability of adversaries to infect, track, or even explode those devices increases.

COMPANIES AS COMBATANTS

In today's world, companies are being pulled into global conflicts not only as pawns, but as partisans. Major companies have long been pawns in geopolitics, to their advantage and disadvantage. Despite being private companies, the California-Arabian Standard Oil Company (later Arabian American Oil Company or ARAMCO, and still later, Saudi Aramco) and Anglo-Persian Oil Company were integral to the U.S. and U.K. national strategy of securing oil supplies. The nationalization of the Anglo-Persian Oil Company during Iran's short-lived Mohammad Mosaddegh government before the U.S.-backed coup in 1953 into the National Iranian Oil Company certainly tracked with global politics, but for the company that would later become BP, it was firmly treated as an extension of the British Crown.

Today companies are still tethered to their home governments in ways that helps and hurts their business. Huawei comes under scrutiny in the

United States because it is Chinese; Coca-Cola and Starbucks face periodic boycotts because they are symbols of the United States. These sorts of dynamics are likely to continue. What is new is that companies will increasingly be actors in geopolitical disputes rather than appendages. CEOs who realize that they are part of the theater of conflict will thrive; others will be felled.

When the Ukraine war began, the U.S. government put significant pressure on Elon Musk's Starlink to provide satellite Internet access for Ukraine's military.[5] For most companies, aligning with the U.S. government's stated objectives and showing your product off on a global stage in the most critical circumstances might not be a difficult business decision. Musk's mercurial personality made this decision to provide the Internet to the Ukrainian military more fraught than it might have otherwise been because it made Starlink part of the conflict, as distinct from a formal contractor for the government. Starlink claimed that it was only for defensive purposes and that Musk personally refused to enable Starlink for offensives and escalations. A military analysis published by West Point indicates that Starlink could be legally targeted by Russia (or, in the future, China) under certain circumstances even if doing so would have ramifications for civilian employees, for civilians who rely on the same satellites (like the country of Tonga), and even if it causes environmental degradation.[6]

If your products are part of a war, you risk being treated like a warrior.[7] Trevor Hehn, an emerging technology lawyer who I interviewed, has gone further to raise the idea that since technology is so ubiquitous in war, it is reasonable that technology is providing advantages to countries fighting each other without any intention of the technology company to do so.[8] In such a case, operations, facilities, *and* employees of the company could potentially be targeted in the battlefield or elsewhere in the globe by one of the hostile countries.

There is a raft of complexity as to whether such targeting would be legitimate. Jonathan Horowitz of the Red Cross, for instance, engages with this in depth in the *Chicago Journal of International Law* and generally highlights that the company must actively choose to be involved in order to lose its civilian protections under the laws of war.[9] However, the reality is that if a hostile power thinks it has legal cover to attack foreign civilians helping their enemy, it may do it. With so much technology functionally dual use nowadays, it's worth considering that governments seeking an advantage not only might be willing and able to attack third-country corporations but that they might feel like they have legal cover for doing so.

Becoming a player in geopolitical conflict is going to be increasingly common for companies either in critical industries or with a massive user base. The Taiwan Semiconductor Manufacturing Company (TSMC) and TikTok are two companies operating at the nexus of the U.S.-China conflict. Neither of these companies makes core products explicitly for the military. But TSMC is in the middle of the battle for advanced AI applications with huge military and economic implications.

TikTok's perceived national security threats became a rare example of bipartisan agreement in the United States during the Biden administration. Appearing innocuous enough, TikTok is a video sharing app, not unlike Google-owned YouTube. However, TikTok appears to have cracked the algorithm for videos, and U.S. kids (and adults) quickly became enthralled by the app, scrolling endless videos that were programmatically curated for maximum screen time. Being owned by a Chinese-linked parent company, as TikTok took over the social media space, national security officials in the United States grew increasingly concerned.

Under Chinese law, companies operating in China must hand over any data they have to the government, and it is widely believed that for practical purposes companies must put Chinese state interests above their own commercial ones when asked. While TikTok claims no data on U.S. users is stored in China, U.S. politicians are skeptical. In rare bipartisan votes in 2024, the U.S. Congress demanded that TikTok's parent company ByteDance either divest TikTok's U.S. subsidiary or risk being banned from operating in the United States. Putting aside the constitutional issues of the U.S. government banning use of an app, this puts TikTok in an almost unprecedented position—and one that may be instructive for other companies that either find themselves in such situations or want to avoid them in the first place.

From TikTok's perspective, the company has not done anything wrong. They made a wildly successful app that has an enormous U.S. user base that includes companies, celebrities, content creators, loads of teenagers, and even presidential candidates. But the possibilities for abuse are significant. Like nearly every app, TikTok tracks its users' interests, connections, and locations. In aggregate it understands when new topics among different geographic and demographic groups are emerging. It understands which viewpoints get traction with what types of users. In short, it provides insights into a vast swath of the United States.

TikTok, of course, is not the only company that has this type of data. Companies like Facebook, Google, and X (formerly Twitter) use this data to improve their products and find new commercial opportunities. That comes with its own list of concerns for many people (especially in Europe), but those concerns are presumably much smaller than if TikTok, through its parent ByteDance, provided all of that data to the government of China. There is no publicly available evidence that this is happening, but assumptions that Beijing has a backdoor into every data repository within ByteDance's companies are far from unreasonable.

This is not the only risk, though, with Chinese-influenced TikTok. Because its recommendation algorithm is so good, users tend to scroll through video after video. The assumption is that given TikTok's business model—like all social media—its objective is to capture your eyeballs for as long as possible and providing videos you find interesting. But what if the Chinese government decided that it wanted to leverage TikTok to inject more positive media about China and more negative media about the outlook for the United States? TikTok could shift its algorithm just slightly in ways that do that. This might decrease its revenues since some people might not like the change, but the objective here is not to increase profits—as Facebook does—but rather to serve a geopolitical interest. By putting its thumb on the algorithmic scale, China could push societies, and especially the youth within them, in directions that served Beijing's interest.

Of course, Russia has long done this, most recently with bots on Twitter and paying influencers on YouTube. With the exception of its television channel RT (formerly Russia Today), Moscow does not own the platforms and therefore has to engineer the existing algorithm to find eyes and ears. And when they get caught, they get thrown off the platforms and have to start fresh. With TikTok the call is coming from inside the house.

This may not seem like war at the moment. But when war takes hold, such tools could be the most important weapons.

Walking in Through the Digital Front Door

While foreign intelligence agencies can occasionally turn an asset inside a rival government's intelligence agencies, those individuals tend to be highly loyal and well trained to spot an attempt to compromise them. In contrast, a company employee whose job is highly technical and has only had an annual online training course on cybersecurity and protecting the company's data is a far softer target.

Even better, why go to the trouble of hacking a company's IT through a naive employee when you could simply have your own agent apply for a job at that company? North Korea appears to have done so on various occasions and other states likely do too. While North Korea may be more interested in leveraging telework to get remote jobs and collect paychecks for their cash-strapped government, in other cases countries could gain footholds on internal networks.[10]

In the Cold War, spies could use infiltration into private companies that worked with the government as a way to penetrate government secrets. Today, though, some of the most valuable innovative work with national security implications is being done in the private sector. Silicon Valley innovates faster than the Pentagon, and it thrives on an open exchange of information. Engineers love open-source data. Kaggle and Wikidata can be more exciting places to test new ideas and approaches than the closed—but vastly more secure—world of the national security apparatus. Adversaries increase their return on investment by seeking out softer-target corporations that innovate key technologies and maintain critical infrastructure.

This is not to say that there isn't massive collaboration between companies and the government in this competition. Certainly Russia, China, and even France actively partner with corporations that are seen as national champions to advance their national interest. Indeed even in the United States, public-private information exchange around security has become common, though it is focused on defending against threats more than making them. But these sorts of relationships are analogous to the past corporations that enjoyed deep political and military support, like the British East India Company or the United Fruit Company. Now it is relentless phishing emails to entire corporate organizations where the critical parts of the network could come under threat if just one of the thousands of employees lazily clicks. It is monitoring and training traveling employees to ensure they do not compromise their devices and therefore open vectors into the company's digital assets.

This theater of the conflict is rarely included in geopolitics and war, but it has become a key element of it and is as much a part of global competition as the front-page headlines about Ukraine, Iran, and North Korea. Today it is mostly a part of corporate IT security, travel security, and intellectual property protection. Companies are increasingly aware of this, and a new field, often called threat intelligence, has emerged with companies hiring anywhere from an individual analyst to a small team to track how geopolitics and security threats could impact operations and employee safety. It is an important start, but small departments within companies do not have the resources or intel collection capabilities to match a determined state actor.

Cyber

Diverse types of risks tend to be grouped under "cyber risk," which conceals that although the vector might be in cyberspace, motivations and effects are rooted in politics, business, and conflict.

Cyber threats can be grouped into three nonmutually exclusive categories: stealing things, breaking things, and influencing things—all of which is being democratized.

Theft of IP through cyber attacks is happening on a mind-boggling scale. China alone reportedly steals several hundred billion dollars' worth of intellectual property annually from U.S. companies, mostly through cyber.[11] Ransomware attacks that lock down computers for payment are in a similar vein. Patching security flaws, locking down access points, and training employees on good cybersecurity practices can only be so effective. Many employees today are adept at recognizing typical email phishing attempts, which try to get a user to click a malicious link. This becomes harder to stop when combined with deepfakes and social engineering.

While ransomware can often look like countries trying to steal money, it can also be done simply to cause damage. The Russia-originated Not Petya malware seemed to ask for money to decrypt computers but actually just destroyed them, bringing one of the world's largest shipping companies to its knees.[12] Destruction can also take the form of simple retribution: When Sony Pictures planned to release a movie that offended North Korean leadership, that country hacked its computers and leaked sensitive information.

Indeed for adversaries like Russia, Iran, and North Korea, cyber has emerged as a theater in which they can demonstrate offensive capabilities against the United States without drawing a kinetic response. For companies in critical areas of the U.S. economy, though, this means efforts to break, disrupt, or embarrass are a threat.

One final note is that your internal threat assessments may not be enough: You do need to think about where else might be holding your sensitive data. Law firms are a telling example outside your four walls. They hold much of your sensitive information. They are increasingly pulled into the geopolitical fray, as they do work for or against sanctioned entities and warring powers. And they are even ripe targets for info-anarchists, like when the Panama Papers hack of a single law firm dumped 12 million documents exposing the illegal tax tactics of powerful corporate leaders and politicians. If you don't have a clear sense of where those law firms—or your consulting or accounting firms for that matter—actually do their back office processing or related outsourced work (India? Philippines?) and of their geopolitical positioning, you may find you are exposed to risks you'd rather not be taking.

FIGHTING BACK: RETHINK INSURANCE

Exploding pagers, cyberattacks, business interruption due to militarized drones, and being banned for national security purposes are all pretty big risks to companies whose employees and operations may become ensnared in war amid Artificial Politics.

Many CEOs assume that the impacts of an existing or emerging risk will be covered by their insurance program.[13] "All risks" policies were considered by executive committees and boards to be just that—covering any risk that could impact the business. Political risk coverage is available in a number of forms through specialist teams and markets, aimed at larger global companies. However, the risks now arising from the intersection of politics, law, and technology create new challenges. As a result, insurers and reinsurers are tightening up their coverage.

As the world becomes more unruly, it is harder to predict where, when, how, and how widespread a manifestation of risks may be. Restrictions and exclusions are used to retrofit outdated policy language into a changing risk landscape by cutting out risks insurers don't want to take, though with the benefit of clarity about what is actually covered. Underwriters who worry about correctly pricing loss ratios will charge more. Insurance firms concerned that risks will cut across many of their lines of business worry that they may not be fully covered by their own reinsurance and refuse to cover the risk. Regulators may fear that insurance company solvency is threatened, increasing reserve requirements, which would bring further pressure on cost and availability.

Such concern manifested with the invasion of Ukraine by Russia, when pricing for political violence insurance rose dramatically. In 2023, reinsurers imposed restrictions on renewal terms that forced many primary carriers to revise specific clauses and drove the restriction in "All Risks" policies and the creation of stand-alone covers for specific political and war-related perils. Many insurers involved in this market also reviewed their exposure to potential and actual conflict zones, often increasing premiums, restricting coverage, and, in some cases, even moving to monthly policy renewals.

In short, it's hard to model an unruly world when there's no historical dataset of such conditions. Yet herein lies the opportunity to fight back: AI can potentially leverage a vast amount of disparate internal and external data to create more agile, real-time pricing and loss models. More granular data offers the opportunity to not just model loss scenarios and price a portfolio more effectively but to also consider the individual risks of a customer, helping not just to tailor coverage but also to inform risk avoidance and mitigation for the client. An additional benefit may be to increase the scope of coverage from the larger organizations to smaller entities that have previously been unable to access protection.

But you're a CEO, not necessarily an insurance executive. The main thing you can do is appreciate the insurance environment is shifting and invest in alternatives until the market reaches a new equilibrium. This involves focusing on risk avoidance, risk management, and risk mitigation rather than relying on (possibly misplaced) ideas of risk transfer.

Yes, this will require more investment in threat and data analysis to make smarter decisions about the risks you are and are not willing to take. But as your competitors struggle with rising premiums and restricted coverage, you'll have confidence that you are choosing where you play in a better-informed way. That way when you do need insurance to cover potential losses, you'll be considered a better risk for your insurance company to take due to your superior data-driven insight and risk management.

Finally, there's also the opportunity to shift your thinking about insurance companies from simply a risk transfer mechanism or vendor of protection and instead to think of them as partners for modeling the future. The more you share your data with your insurance providers, the more likely those providers are to ultimately solve the challenge of how to model an unruly world.

CHAPTER ELEVEN

UNRULY VALUES: WHEN EVERYTHING IS ABOUT EVERYTHING

To expand Budweiser's consumer base to include Gen-Z, women, and the LGBTQ+ community and reinvent the brand's image to be one of inclusivity and modernity, Bud Light partnered with transgender TikTok celebrity Dylan Mulvaney. Mulvaney posted a promotional video for the brand on her Instagram page during 2023 March Madness basketball, with a few personalized beer cans that the brand had sent her. Believing Bud Light to be a brand "in decline for a very long time," with a "fratty, kind of out-of-touch humor" that needed to "evolve and elevate," executives approved the partnership to show the company's commitment to diversity and revamp its image.[1]

The marketing campaign backfired spectacularly. A massive boycott ensued against Bud Light and its parent company, Anheuser-Busch (AB InBev). Musician Travis Tritt lamented that Anheuser-Busch, "a great American company," was no longer "American owned" and had instead been "sold out to the Europeans and became unrecognizable to the American consumer."[2] Musician Kid Rock argued that Bud Light's miscalculation stemmed from its decision to leave "its roots in America's heartland," opting to relocate to New York City and then "hiring Ivy League progressives ... who don't know sh–t about working-class people or Middle America."[3] Florida Governor Ron DeSantis argued that Bud Light's campaign was "part of a larger thing where corporate America is trying to change our country, trying to change policy, trying to change culture."[4]

Social media lit up with objections to the campaign. Videos showing people destroying Bud Light beers became exceedingly popular. A number of bomb threats were also reportedly sent to Anheuser-Busch, resulting in the closure of some factories and the cancellation of several company events due to safety concerns.[5]

The boycott caused Bud Light to suffer devastating financial and reputational consequences. By May 1, 2023, just one month after the release of the marketing campaign, Bud Light's off-premise sales had fallen 26%, dragging down other AB InBev brands with it.[6] In total, it is estimated that the marketing campaign cost AB InBev close to $1.4 billion in sales.[7]

Bud Light's marketing efforts are part of a more comprehensive trend in which companies seek to satisfy activists and shed positive light on their operations. However, these attempts often fail to achieve this goal, and marketing missteps end up alienating both the company's core consumers and any potential new consumers by dragging the company into controversial political topics. In the case of Bud Light, the brand failed to properly defend Mulvaney in the face of backlash, with spokespeople arguing that the initiative was "one can, one influencer, one post, and not a campaign." AB InBev's CEO Brendan Whitworth shared a vague statement that did not directly state his support for the company's partnership with Mulvaney, which ended up irritating members of the LGBTQ+ community and thus also many potential new consumers.[8]

The trap that AB InBev fell into stemmed from technological, social, and political change. But it was fundamentally an Artificial Politics challenge where the shifting nature of communication intersected with divisive politics to create a crisis.

Previously, products like Bud Light were advertised mostly on large imprecise platforms such as TV (often during sports), billboards, and maybe some more niche magazines. There was no microtargeting the way platforms like Instagram and Google allow, so while ads were framed in ways to appeal to a certain type of consumer, they had to be generally acceptable to very broad audiences. Instagram and Google Search open incredible opportunities to target highly specific customer eyeballs based on an unnervingly long set of criteria that are demographic, geographic (including specific places recently visited), related to interests, and more. But the temptation to push much deeper in a particular marketing direction means not just more effective advertising but also vastly more opportunities to get yourself into trouble.

The last decade has witnessed a societal shift in which companies are seen by many to be a part of social and political discourses in ways they were largely separate from previously. While politics in the United States seem to be moving on from this, the emphasis remains in Europe.

It wasn't always that way. When the North Carolina–native basketball star Michael Jordan was asked in 1990 to endorse the African American Democratic candidate for U.S. Senate in his home state over the incumbent Republican Jesse Helms (who called the 1964 Civil Rights Act "the single most dangerous piece of legislation ever introduced in the Congress"), he refused. Later Jordan remarked that not only did he not know enough about politics to get involved but also that "Republicans buy sneakers too," in reference to his massively profitable deal with Nike and their Air Jordan brand.[9]

Today athletes, celebrities, and other public figures are increasingly comfortable weighing in on political and social issues, even at the cost of harming their own personal brand with large swaths of the population. From Taylor Shift to LeBron James, there is growing acceptance and even expectations that public figures express their political views.

This shift around the intersection between brands and politics extends increasingly to companies. This practice can be bad for business, as was the case with Bud Light, but it can also be good for business as Nike's use of Colin Kaepernick was or Chick-fil-A's CEO making statements opposing same-sex marriage in 2012 solidifying the brands as righteous in the mind of key customer groups.

But in many cases, it's simply unpredictable for companies. Stay silent on an issue and be criticized for not being a good corporate citizen, or speak out and risk the wrath of one side of a polarizing issue.

The roots of this deeper involvement of companies in social and political issues also have a less obvious origin at the intersection of politics and law: the 2010 Supreme Court decision *Citizens' United*, which gutted campaign finance laws and effectively allowed corporations to make unlimited campaign donations via Super PACs.[10]

On the surface, *Citizens' United* was an extraordinary decision for corporate America, which could use its formidable financial resources to influence electoral politics in profound ways.

Just as the separation of Church and State for America's founders was about keeping religion out of government and preventing the corrupting influence of politics on the church, *Citizens' United* undid limiting corporate influence on politics but also allowed for politics to influence corporations. According to OpenSecrets.org, Super PAC funding raised rose from just over $800 million in 2012 to more than $4 billion in 2024, often on issues like corporate taxes or financial rules.[11] But with that amount of money flying around, blowback is inevitable.

Companies typically donate to an issue- or electoral race–focused Super PAC with the intention of supporting candidates with positions that align with their business interests. But now such data is public, easily accessible, and easy for political enemies to weaponize. DoorDash, for example, contributed more than $600,000 to a Super PAC called the Republican Governors Association (RGA), a group that supported North Carolina Republican gubernatorial candidate Mark Robinson.[12] DoorDash's interest in North Carolina politics was fairly narrow but important to its business: in July 2024 the state legalized to-go and delivery cocktails.[13] After Mark Robinson made repeated disparaging remarks toward LGBTQ+ people, DoorDash came under fire for its previous donations. When CNN revealed in a report in September 2024 that Robinson had made anonymous online comments calling himself a "black Nazi," supportive of slavery, and about his history as a Peeping Tom,[14] DoorDash was suddenly associated with issues that it almost certainly did not actually support but also had nothing to do with its business.

With *Citizens' United* turning companies into explicit political actors and with social media allowing hot takes on corporate immorality to spread quickly and with scant evidence, there is likely to come a time when political donations will increasingly be subject to risk reviews—with risk flowing in many directions.

WOKENESS

While marketing and donations are one manifestation, many companies took to heart shifting political tides and actually worked to implement change within their core businesses. What is economic, social, and governance (ESG) excellence to one person is "wokeness" (said derisively) to another.

One of the main results of globalization was the elevation of values in the conversation about business and politics, leading to many of the political conflicts over ESG programs; diversity, equity, and inclusion (DEI); and whether companies ought to have views on social and political values.

At the international level this took the form of a focus on human rights and democracy promotion. For a period, it seemed like the world would continue to converge until capitalism and democracy had entrenched themselves so much that there was no turning back. Of course, that's not what happened.

But on national levels there's been a similar march toward societal values that was equally compelling. Anyone who takes an economics course learns about negative externalities generated by business. As countries get richer, voters start to care more about those externalities and exert pressure for change. For the most egregious cases, this was relatively uncontroversial. Should diamond and chocolate producers turn a blind eye to the ways their supply chain fund brutal rebel groups and employ child slave labor, respectively? Most everyone agrees corporates should not place profits over these risks, though the chocolate industry has made less progress than the diamond industry has. But not every values-based issue is quite so stark.

In the United States and Europe, there were rising demands for "responsible investing" and caring about the environment. Activist interest groups put pressure on large investors like pension funds and money managers to divest from pollutive industries as well as other value-laden criteria (gun manufacturers, defense companies, tobacco companies, and the like), and many investment companies seized the momentum to create ESG investment products. Companies, fearing share price declines and boycotts or protests, started to take steps to either support or look supportive of satisfying ESG criteria. They fell over each other to disclose, report, and improve their societal impact.

Black Lives Matter and the #MeToo movement also brought racial and gender diversity to the forefront initially as a moral issue, but it was embraced by many companies for business reasons in their belief that failing to recruit, promote, and support women and people of color in their organization meant losing out on potential talent. The term "woke," a shorthand for being aware of social injustices and fighting against them, took on new prominence in the wake of George Floyd's brutal murder. Arguments that it wasn't enough to be against racism but that one had to be actively anti-racist began to turn the agenda into something even more forceful.

In the United States, companies were quickly caught in the middle as it also triggered a massive backlash from conservatives who reappropriated and weaponized the term "woke," with promises to fight the "woke agenda." This move worked and mobilized voters in support of Republicans in the 2024 election cycle. Europe has largely stayed the course in building rules and norms to support corporate ESG agendas, which only complicates the picture further for global corporations.

BATTLING OVER VALUES

In places like the United States, politics of the environment or social equality is so divisive that a broad political consensus is well out of reach. Even in times when one party controls Congress and the White House, passing large-scale legislation seems like a pipe dream. When citizens and interest groups can't persuade the government to solve problems, they often put pressure on the private sector. As a result, those who view topics like climate change as a "crisis"—which is a diverse group of progressives, younger generations, and moderates—have turned their pressure and attention to the companies that they see as enabling it. The same is true with respect to corporate actors who have not prioritized gender or racial diversity.

Companies have a lot of reasons to self-regulate. In a world of divisive politics, a good defensive mechanism is to hold yourself to a higher standard so that when the pendulum swings toward regulation, you are not caught by surprise. Customers may boycott you for failing to do so; conversely, you can attract audiences by doing so ably. And, increasingly the ability to raise funding can be tied to good social behavior. It's better to meet a high standard crafted by those who understand the industry than one crafted by activists who may know nothing about it.

As a result, there was a march in the United States and Europe toward ESG factors that are akin to social responsibility. A lot of money poured into investment funds that had a socially focused mandate—inflows to sustainable funds rose from $5.4 billion in 2018 to $69.8 billion in 2021."[15]

But opposition to the ESG mantra never went away. Conservative politicians started to use ESG issues and "wokeness" as political boogeymen, threatening everyone who entered the fray.

The best example of this is the conflict between Disney and Florida Governor Ron DeSantis, who turned Disney's cozy regulatory environment inside out when the company said its goal was to counter his bill banning discussions of homosexuality and gender identity in some elementary school grades.[16] Disney took DeSantis to court claiming political retaliation. When it lost, Disney vowed to appeal because the case has "serious implications for the rule of law … if left unchallenged, this would set a dangerous precedent and give license to states to weaponize their official powers to punish the expression of political viewpoints they disagree with."[17] (The parties ultimately settled on terms reflecting the relative bargaining power of Disney and a major U.S. state—it was about an even split.)

Disney is not the only example. Law firm Morgan Lewis documented anti-ESG laws across the United States, including legislation that outlaws boycotting companies over ESG, discriminating against certain industries because of ESG, or even prohibiting ESG consideration in investment decisions.[18] A group of legislators in New Hampshire, as James

Surowiecki points out in the *Atlantic*, have even gone so far as to try to make it a felony for a state official to consider ESG in their investment decisions.[19] For Republicans who have historically been of the view that government should have limited influence over how companies run themselves, this is a radical reversal and, as with political donations, further erodes the line between government and business. It also suggests the ways that it is not only liberals using social wedges to affect corporate change but also demonstrates that conservatives are willing to at a minimum limit investment decisions in pursuit of social goals. No doubt the return to office of Donald Trump—whose son recently announced that he would be working at an "anti-ESG" investment fund—will raise the political stakes of this further.[20]

EVERYTHING IS ABOUT EVERYTHING

Matthew Yglesias has written about our current political climate that "the thing that really has increased is polarization and the accompanying 'everything is about everything' totalizing political conflict."[21] Most businesses would prefer that everything be about really only one thing: profits. But that's not the world we live in.

Companies must now consider how leveraging one influencer to increase business in one area is actually taking a stand on that influencer's social position. A decision to move corporate headquarters from California to Texas, as Tesla and Chevron have done, raises the question of whether its about tax and regulation or a broader political statement. A decision to contribute to the campaign (or affiliated Super PAC) of a politician who sits on a critical regulatory committee is only safe if the individual's views on #MeToo, race, Palestine, or any number of other highly polarized issues have been considered.

FIGHTING BACK: SAFETY IN NUMBERS

In a world where technology means everything is public, there can be safety in numbers. Companies know this, which is why they are part of industry groups. But many industry groups use their force just to water down rules and regulations to insulate members from political pressure, which may trigger activists to try even harder to get new regulations implemented.

Actually, industry groups can be a way to raise standards, which can provide both political and social benefits. On the former, governments are looking for companies to be responsible stakeholders in their societies, and often, companies get tripped up promising to do this but failing to deliver. On the latter, companies are under ESG pressure that often doesn't align with profit-motive or may trigger political backlash.

The mining industry, however, offers a glimpse of a new model—one in which an entire industry has come together to elevate their own standards. Approaches like these may be able to expand the breathing room of companies that are under attack for their values and performance in various jurisdictions.

The stakes for the mining industry are high as any: the energy transition is going to require more copper to be mined in the next 30 years than has been mined in the last 5,000 years.[22] Mining without guardrails can destroy natural environments and indigenous communities while also feeding a cycle of corruption and state capture.

Yet, the International Council on Mining and Metals (ICMM), the industry's opt-in standards body, has been able to achieve striking successes, like voluntary restraints on mining in world heritage sites or agreement among members to publish all mining contracts with governments and all taxes paid on a country-by-country basis. How do you get a raft of competitor firms, some with a reputation for being too cavalier about the societal costs of their businesses, to succeed together at elevating standards?

First, you need to tackle a traditional collective action problem where it's easier for companies to defect than to go along with higher standards. One way to get around this is to create critical mass in the industry toward change so that it is costly for companies to remain on the outside. ICMM's 24-firm membership represents roughly a third of mining industry revenue hailing from public and private sector companies in the United States, United Kingdom, Peru, China, Japan, and many other points on the globe. That's enough to generate meaningful commitments that can create a gravitational force for governments to contemplate codifying the rules and for nonmembers to bear some cost for being on the outside.

Second, you actually need decision-makers in the room. For ICMM, that means that CEOs themselves are the members. The CEOs meet and discuss the future direction of the industry and where it could go. As ICMM's CEO Rohitesh Dhawan noted, the second most important person in the room is ICMM's antitrust lawyer, who is there to make sure there's no actual collusion or any appearance as such given that some U.S. politicians have been fighting back on ESG via antitrust threats.

Third, you need to create a high but achievable bar for decision-making. For many years, ICMM operated under unanimity as a rule. Of course, this means fewer rules can be passed. Today, ICMM requires a 75% majority for decisions and then forces companies that don't join to either get on board or issue a public explanation why they are objecting to a particular standard. That public justification is there to prevent accusations of greenwashing by holding accountable their own members when they choose not to be onboard. It can often drag them into participating.

Finally, you need high standards for membership. Many industry groups are "broad churches"—they take on their own inertia driven less by impact and more by fees and, thus, welcome members of all stripes. For

ICMM, they accept about 10% of applicants and only those that can document clear performance on sustainability criteria before joining.

In a world where governments are less likely to agree on international treaties or agreements than ever before—and where national governments struggle to regulate because of political divisiveness and the likelihood of every regulation being litigated in court—this type of model makes a lot of sense. But in searching for parallels, it seems the imperative in mining—where social license to operate is critical—is unique at least for today.

Indeed, it is hard to find other industries that have something similar but others would be wise to consider it. After all, deflection of responsibility to a standard-setter can insulate oneself against critics while also biasing toward progress on values-based issues the public in many countries increasingly expects.

PART IV

LEGALAI: WHEN LAW AND TECHNOLOGY COLLIDE

CHAPTER TWELVE

UNRULY LAW: EMPOWERMENT THROUGH NEW LEGAL WEAPONS

A car crashed into our family van as we were stopped on the offramp of the I-10 freeway in Los Angeles. My kids were asleep and didn't register the impact. My wife was startled but fine. My head flew back and hit the headrest. It immediately started to hurt.

The other driver apologized and took responsibility for the accident. Over the course of the day, my head started to hurt more and more. An urgent-care nurse told me to go to the emergency room, where I failed to correctly give the receptionist my own phone number due to brain fog. The ER doctor diagnosed me with a concussion, confirmed again by my doctor two days later.

I heard from the other driver's insurance company soon thereafter. I provided them my emergency room report and the doctors' diagnoses. I assumed they would offer to cover my ongoing medical bills.

To my surprise, the insurance company attempted to pressure me to take a $600 settlement immediately via Venmo ("wouldn't you like to have $600 right now?!"). That would have granted them a full release for about the cost of a normal doctor visit. I told them I didn't yet know my medical exposure, though I assumed it was going to be at least 10 times their offer—I live in America after all. My head was still hurting, and I was worried of lingering effects. The insurance company then attempted to use legal technology against me: they sent their full release offer via a well-known e-signature platform that automatically reminded me every single day to sign it. The pressure had begun.

I rested the next few days, which messed up my whole routine. My intermittent fasting was out the window, and my writing came to a standstill. I had trouble concentrating and had to cancel a host of meetings. While I wasn't necessarily seeking compensation, there was a very direct cost to me from the other driver's negligence.

I was not gearing up for a fight about my concussion: just pay my medical, fix my car, and let me on my way. But then a letter arrived from the other driver's insurance company claims handler:

> "It was unlikely that there were any injuries related to this accident … if you continue to seek treatment, I will carefully review all medical expenses to determine if they are related to the accident, and any that are not will be your responsibility."[1]

Seriously? I had provided two separate diagnoses of a concussion, and I was planning to just move on with my life. But this particular insurance company was attempting to create leverage for itself by trying to gaslight me into believing I wasn't hurt and by implying that I might want to think twice about seeking further medical treatment.

The insurance company's behavior was logical for the current legal era, which we will soon be exiting. Most claimants would be persuaded to have $600 right now rather than get tied up with the legal system. Where an average concussion claim might be worth a few thousand dollars, it requires wanting a fight and finding a lawyer who advertises on billboards to help you get that settlement. Those billboards, of course, aren't free, so the settlement would be a pittance once received. And it would be a lot of work and emotion in the process.

But technology is leveling the playing field. No longer would I need an ambulance chaser to negotiate my claim. Cars drive themselves nowadays, so surely car insurance lawyers can be automated too.

AUTOMATED LAW

The world of law is about to get turned on its head by robotic disputes and automatic legal weapons. In fact, the way we think of law today—where companies look at their top legal risks as stand-alone events—is going to look quaint. Legal risk is soon going to look like cyber risk—where there are hundreds of attacks at any moment aimed at your organization.[2] And you have even more exposure because the geopolitical shifts I've outlined in prior chapters mean you will have more enemies than you have had previously.

I refer to this intersection of technology and law as LegalAI Risk, a synthetic risk that is advancing rapidly. This risk will change how companies use the law, how the law is used against them, and what the law even means. It will change how lawyers work and how lawyers are used.

Today, the rich and powerful have many advantages in the legal system. They lean on employees to sign one-sided agreements. They drag out legal battles because they can afford it. They pay spin masters to tell their story, and they mobilize lobbyists to change rules that are not to their advantage.

This is why employees who may have valid claims against their employers are afraid to bring them. This is why wealthier spouses have the upper hand in a divorce, large companies have the advantage when in court with smaller companies, and debt collectors can take painful actions against their indebted clients.

This is both a cause and a function of the so-called justice gap—the difference between the legal needs of citizens and the resources they have available. Legal aid funding in the United States is roughly half of what it was in constant dollars 40 years ago.[3] Seventy-five percent of civil matters in the United States find one side representing themselves even though lawyers are nearly half a percent of the population.[4]

But technology has the potential to change all of this. The question is whether it will be used for good or evil or, less hyperbolically, justice or injustice. The answer is probably for both—sometimes at the same time.

Companies cannot miss the sea change that is coming in the disputes arena. Today, when boards talk about litigation pending against their company, they are generally focused on the biggest ticket items. Smaller cases don't rise to board level. But legal is an increasingly digital good. That is to say that while the law has historically been hard to access, software is making it less so. The ability to upload chapters of federal law in order to have AI parse them is table stakes. The ability to ask AI for ideas of how to defend yourself from criminal charges in those pages is here today, too.

As goods become digital, the cost of each additional unit starts to approach zero—like copying music or photos. What does this mean for the law? It means that it will become cheaper and cheaper to take digital legal action.

Think about the personal tax industry of the past. Anyone with a whiff of complexity on their taxes used to pay for an accountant. TurboTax stepped in with software that made the filing of taxes a templated exercise that anyone can follow along. Now the majority of Americans are filing taxes on their own.[5]

As the cost of legal declines, and as AI begins to take on more and more of the litigation process-chain, the bar to filing a dispute will drop. More and more cases will be filed for a variety of motivations. Companies will need tools to grapple with a world where legal attacks are pervasive. It will be the aggregation of a great many new claims that will serve as the biggest risk for companies, not the single big-ticket litigation they faced in the past. This will call for new methods to identify and manage risk related to the cases themselves and to government regulation of AI in legal upstream.

My New Weapon

I was upset that an insurance company was downplaying an injury I had, but I didn't want to pick a fight. However, a friend of mine suggested I check out a company called ZAF Legal, which stands for "Zero Attorney Fees."[6] The company is a traditional injury law firm that was licensed in the state of Utah to provide an AI-powered accident claim app. I answered a few questions about the accident, my symptoms, the name of the other driver, and the like. Within minutes the system generated a demand letter I could send to the other insurance company. For free.

Suddenly, I was no longer encumbered by the decision of lawyering up or letting it go. Where I might otherwise not have pursued my claim, I was able to do so in such an easy fashion that there was no reason not to. To create my own leverage, I used ChatGPT to generate a full complaint I could have filed for me in a court of law if I so chose.

Now the insurance company and I are having a much different conversation. The upshot of this is not the outcome of the settlement, which will be determined as the insurance company volleys back and forth with my AI-generated responses over the two years California allows for resolution of a personal injury claim. Rather, the fact is that instead of folding, I'm fighting. I wouldn't be doing that without technology. And this has profound implications for the way we think about the risk of legal action more broadly.

What if every insurance incident resulted in a well-informed claimant accurately framing the damages of their case such that the insurance company on the receiving end had to take it into account? That's the vision of Ty Brown, the CEO at ZAF Legal, whose AI helped me with my claim.[7]

ZAF's AI tool was developed to solve the real information asymmetry that exists between a regular person who hopes to never have to file an insurance claim and an insurance company who hopes to never pay more than it needs to. The AI helps the claimant understand their rights and frame it into a demand letter the insurance company generally must acknowledge. Part of that is a process of the AI estimating what their claims could be worth for both economic (car damage) and non-economic (sleepless nights) claims. If a person understands that the claim is worth more than they expected, they may proceed further with the negotiation process than they might otherwise have—if it is less so, they may be willing to accept a settlement without legal action. And, like me, they are better able to articulate the value of the claim in their demands and assessment of offers.

The insurance settlement process itself is not a legal process—it's a negotiation to avoid legal action. In the current market, a claimant turns over their claim to a personal injury lawyer who will immediately threaten to litigate in order to build leverage over the claim and inflate the value of the claim, which is not necessarily better for society as a whole given that insurance prices go up when claims cost more than they should.

In the new scenario, the claimant approaches the insurance company with more of an optimization problem: You know you owe me some money. Here's a demand that lets you know I know you owe me money. Let's cut to the chase and get this thing settled. That can result in justice for the claimants and fewer cases going to court.

While zero-dollar legal may seem like something of the future, AI is already bringing the cost of traditional legal down substantially. Hundreds of millions of dollars flow into legaltech for productivity and efficiency purposes each year, allowing lawyers to do more work with and for less. This will make it easier for those who use human lawyers to consume more human legal time for the same dollar spent. Already, companies like LegalZoom offer all-you-can-eat subscriptions to legal advice; for instance, their Assist package is $199 for a year of unlimited 30-minute calls on new issues, a library of forms, and legal document review.[8] That's about the cost of a streaming music or movie service.

But the bigger disruption will be for people and use cases that can bypass those phone calls fully. Why not ask the same questions to an intelligent computer program that can answer them for me or take action on my behalf?

Generative AI is increasingly able to provide the self-service legal work I am describing here. As the law becomes digitized—through products that ingest what the law is to tools that are built on top of it to comb it for advantages—the cost of accessing and interrogating the law will eventually become negligible.

I'm already able to access a playlist of the world's best songs. Soon I'll be able to access a playlist of the best legal attacks and defenses. This means that I'm more likely to threaten legal action or to stand up and defend myself than ever before. And so are others.

One implication that is often missed is that we're also able to better probe the extent of the law. I got a parking ticket recently when I misunderstood a confusing sign. I was inclined to pay it because the transaction cost of fighting it didn't seem to outweigh the low probability of dismissal. But what if the cost of fighting was nothing? Software company DoNotPay includes in their monthly subscription the ability to challenge parking tickets. So, I answered a few questions from their AI and out comes a letter I can file with my city to dispute my parking ticket.[9]

Now, the city must review whether the ticket was issued fairly. It may turn out there was some other reason it was invalid than the one I expected, which disempowered me from effectuating my full rights. Perhaps I've been receiving tickets that were invalid all along but I could never discover this.

Or it may mean the city becomes overwhelmed with exponentially more parking ticket disputes to deal with. If they can't give due consideration to each of these tickets, they may have to excuse them. In scenarios like that, AI shifts power to the individual.

This is a narrow, personal version of a broader tool that will soon enter the business toolkit. We often think about governments enforcing against business for violations, but governments trample on the legitimate rights of businesses all the time. And often this restricts the businesses' ability to grow. As the price for identifying such occurrences drops, and the prices for communicating it through legal channels does too, businesses will be able to police governments for advantages—especially small businesses that try to minimize legal spend.

CATCH YOU IF I CAN

This new environment is particularly challenging for companies that bank on their power dynamics or think of legal as something they can handle episodically. It's one thing for customers to press every claim they have against you, which can erode margin. It's another for competitors or police to go on a fishing expedition to find the things you may have done to break the law—knowingly or not.

Supreme Court Justice Neil Gorsuch makes the case in his 2024 book, *Over Ruled: The Human Toll of Too Much Law*, that there are so many laws and rules in the world that we can't even keep track.[10] How many federal crimes are there? Thousands but nobody knows how many. As a result, every citizen has probably broken one of them. If that's true, then the question about who goes to jail and who doesn't becomes one of enforcement and of means of defense.

In his book he tells the story of a fisherman of modest means who was convicted of violating the Sarbanes-Oxley Act—a law that deals largely with destroying financial evidence, passed in the wake of the Enron scandal. However, the fisherman wasn't cooking the books—he was accused of throwing back underweight fish that were evidence supporting the claim he had fished illegally. By the time he was convicted, his fishy action wouldn't have even been a crime under revised rules. It was the complexity of the law itself and federal agency interpretation of it that led to such an outlandish outcome. The man was sentenced to jail and lost his livelihood before the Supreme Court overturned the case years later.

But the analysis of legal complexity is a story half told. In a prior technological era, that type of story might make your head spin but was likely to affect only unlucky individuals or businesses that are in the wrong place at the wrong time. Today's technology changes this considerably by enabling governments to catch you each time you do something wrong and by enabling your enemies to try to enforce the same.

What if we take technology and law to its logical conclusion? Abdi Aidid and Benjamin Alarie in *The Legal Singularity: How Artificial Intelligence Can Make Law Radically Better* make the case that we are on a pathway to the law becoming fully predictable.[11] That is to say, when everyone has the same legal data and computing power, all legal actors—judges, lawyers, accused, defendants, private adjudicators—will know the way the law will be interpreted in advance making the law effectively automatic and allowing incomparable efficiency and fairness.

To give you a sense of what this world would look like, consider this. What if the world was all red light cameras everywhere you step? That is to say, what if the Internet of Things and government surveillance systems were designed to report on you every time you broke a rule or simply issue you fines? If you speed in your car, it is connected to highway patrol, so a ticket is automatically issued. If you burn down your house by burning your toast, the toaster reports this to the authorities and your insurance company, so your liability is clear.

Or, even better, the authors give an example where the law says you should drive your car at a "safe speed," so it's not clear just how fast you can drive. In the legal singularity, your car takes into account how many years of experience you have, weather conditions, and the state of your car to guide you to the safest speed for that moment. The law becomes automatic because it is predictable—you don't have to guess.

A variation of this is that the law may become more personalized. As Ariel Porat and Omri-Ben Shahar argue in their book *Personalized Law: Different Laws for Different People*, there's no reason why individuals can't all have laws tailored live for each of us.[12] So in the car example, instead of there being an objective "safe speed," what if the car understood my safe speed differently from my wife's safe speed in real time based on how much sleep one of us had the night before as recorded by our smartwatches? That achieves the law's ultimate goals in a tailored and more precise way.

Examples like these feel like Big Brother, and Western societies will balance concerns about privacy against movement in that direction. But it is undeniable the technology will exist to do this, if it doesn't already. These are radically different future legal environments that businesses need to contemplate.

SOLVING ACCESS TO JUSTICE

As discussed earlier, some of society's discontents come from a failing or highly gatekept legal system. Could LegalAI solve this?

Many lawyers talk about how their work can't be automated—every client problem is a special body that needs a custom suit made for it. But, as Richard Susskind has argued for decades, the reality is that much legal work is not actually legal work.[13] It is document assembly and management. It is legal research. It is contract drafting. It is court testimony transcription and analysis. AI is really good at all of these things lawyers charge their clients for.

As AI eats those jobs, law firms will initially benefit from an efficiency gain that they can capture or pass on in savings to their clients. Over time, a competitive market will reach a new equilibrium where the more repetitive tasks that humans perform disappear and the legal profession becomes narrower.

A big piece of the puzzle is how fast regulation of the legal sector shifts. There's a general bias against full-scale AI adoption among the predominantly self-regulatory bodies that oversee the legal sector. But U.S. states like Utah have opened the door, and once tools like that which I used to fight the insurance battle or query my parking tickets are released for public consumption, they build up constituencies of users and advocates who will see AI as leveling the playing field. Over time, it seems inevitable to me that these tools will do more and be broadly available.

As legal sector expert Jordan Furlong told me:

"Lawyers and judges like to say: 'No one is above the law.' Regardless of whether that's true in practice, I think the question we should be asking is: 'What about all the people who are *beneath* the law?' What about the 90% of us who have no realistic, effective means to enforce our rights and obtain our entitlements through the legal system? Because if you're a corporation or a rich person, the rule of law works great as a floor. But if you're anyone else, the rule of law is a ceiling that limits our rights. Imagine if we said instead: 'These are all the rights and privileges that the law affords, and no one is entitled to *less*.' That's where we should be going. And that's what AI and other technologies can do: Give people the ability to change the rule of law from a ceiling to a floor, and then to keep on raising it higher."[14]

As I discussed with legal thought leader Damien Riehl, new AI tools will empower the vast majority of people who end up in court unrepresented.[15] Today, individuals who can't afford an attorney will still represent themselves in child custody cases or evictions. Yet, all they are able to do is use a search engine and some online forums to try to build their argument. While they may have a valid claim, often they are unable to navigate the court process, and their claim is tossed out because it doesn't use the right language or the right format.

But in a world where they can use AI, their valid claim is filed correctly, and the court accepts it. Now they are able to defend themselves. In a world where governments do not want to foot the bill for legal aid budgets, it's easy to imagine that they warm to bots that can do similar work. They may even fund them as a utility citizens can draw upon.

Technology absolutely provides the opportunity to enhance access to justice, and perhaps it will deliver on the promise of building a more harmonious society too. Connecting access to the law to political peace and security is not a new idea. As Bridget McCormack, former chief justice of the Michigan Supreme Court and president and CEO of the American Arbitration Association, told me, tools like arbitration originated in part to bring peace more generally to communities. Around 100 years ago, one of the founders of her organization put forward the idea of "arbitration as a means of increasing the peaceful resolution of conflicts among people, organizations, governments and eventually nations," believing that "a process that allows people to have more agency over what the resolution of a particular dispute increases peace more generally in their community and their world."[16] Today, the cost of arbitrations will decline as they go increasingly digital, which may allow more communities to experience related positive impacts.

Many focus on the challenge of hallucinations from AI as a reason to hold back progress. But technology gets better and better over time, and I'd rather see larger populations get access to some justice than wait until the technology is perfect.

However, the core risk we need to keep our eyes open to is that AI may create a two-tier legal system, as Drew Simshaw, assistant professor at Gonzaga University School of Law, argues. For instance, the rich might continue to use human lawyers who are now super-powered by AI support, while all funding for the poor goes to AI products that are not as good.[17] That's a real risk but also a manageable one once society determines it views automated law as an opportunity to expand access to justice.

ROBOT LOBBYISTS

It's not just lawsuits and traditional legal work that will be amplified by AI; it is political influence via lawmaking as well. The work that human lobbyists do can be automated much like the work of other knowledge professionals. AI, as Stanford fellow John Nay has written, can be used to identify whether a proposed law is relevant to a corporation by digesting its public filings and automatically trigger a letter from the company to a member of Congress or a regulator triggering changes.[18] In fact, Sarah Kreps and Doug Kriner of Cornell University sent 30,000 letters to more than 7,000 state legislators to see if they were more or less likely to respond to AI-generated letters. While they found the response to AI was statistically less likely to generate a response, on some topics there were no differences and on some topics the AI actually did better.[19]

In fact, a group of hacktivist lawyers proved this point in 2024 as well, when the LexPunkArmy's Treasury Raid—an AI bot released publicly to generate comments on a proposed Treasury Department crypto rule—elicited 120,000 comments. Ultimately the U.S. Treasury Department made concessions in the direction the raiders were pushing.[20]

Nathan E. Sanders and Bruce Schneier take this a step further in *MIT Technology Review* by explaining how AI can be used to build a "micro-legislator" or a lobbying robot that digests proposed legislation, understands the smallest and least-detectable changes to legislation that could benefit a particular interest, and then strategizes how to get that language inserted by pulling levers of power.[21]

There are some real concerns about automated influence. The government may start to lock down avenues for public comment if it feels like AI is manipulating those pathways, which could ultimately shut out certain interests who feel they have no choice but to turn to disruptive protests. Robot lobbyists could reinforce power dynamics where the strong get even more advantage because they can invest in these tools.

But the reality is that technology will become an increasingly important part of getting your corporate message across in the future, especially when interacting with government and the legal system. Planning early for a strategy to harness it will be critical to amplifying your message in the future. Otherwise, your competitors will, and they will get an edge.

FIGHTING BACK: FIGHT AI WITH AI

To succeed in today's world, you need to begin thinking about legal from both defensive and offensive points of view.

To defend yourself, you're going to need to invest in new tools for litigation management, matter management, and the like. Such tools will need to accurately be able to assess whether incoming legal threats are legitimate or legal spam. That will be necessary but not sufficient.

To really thrive, you will need new tools that are able to go upstream to identify policy changes or other vectors of change that raise your legal risk. And that involves breaking down corporate silos to deal with the multifaceted nature of such risks.

One way to do this is to stand up large, sophisticated risk intelligence teams. But that is costly and generally not within the core competence of the company.

Instead, first you can leverage artificial intelligence and machine learning tools built by software companies to filter incoming developments and determine what risks and opportunities arise. A single event has security, legal, and regulatory implications—or maybe it has no meaningful impact at all. Sophisticated data models allow for synthesizing data in more dimensions, so you can look at 12 things happening at once.

Entrepreneurs like myself are building those tools but they will drive an impact only if customers can conceive of the boundary-busting nature of such risks and work on their own ability to drive collaboration between legal, risk, government affairs, and public affairs.

The other way to fight back against this vector of unruliness is to go on the offense. An old formulation of "offensive legal" is to weaponize intellectual property to win and maintain markets as well as aggressively monetize ideas and other intangible assets, as Kevin Rivette and Daniel Kline argue in *Rembrandts in the Attic* from 1999.[22] A new formulation might be to use technology to digest public data and see opportunities to quickly and regularly assert legal rights. In the past this was the bastion of big companies. Now companies of all sizes can do this.

To the extent discernable, do your competitors have public law compliance risk issues? Do they have private contract issues? Do they have vulnerabilities that may emerge if you pay attention to them? Now you can use AI to find out and move quickly.

In 2011, Park City Mountain Resorts forgot to renew their "sweetheart" lease on a mountain and they lost in court to the landlord who was perfectly glad to find a new tenant at a more lucrative rent.[23] That's a small mistake that cost a lot to the resort company, and it was a lucky break for the landlord. Now, imagine being able to discover your customers or your competitors making such mistakes and being able to capitalize on it at scale. Technology will make you much more efficient at that.

Moreover, you can use AI to see where your competitors may be boxed out of a market or unable to sell to certain governments due to legal or political issues. In the past, that type of competitive monitoring would be costly, but it won't be anymore. You can then place a bigger bet on that market if you are unencumbered.

To be sure, it is hard to forecast exactly how LegalAI Risk and opportunity will manifest. But I do know that if you don't start thinking about plausible risks today, you will be crushed by competitors who weaponize these tools against you.

PART V

FIGHTING BACK

CHAPTER THIRTEEN

FIGHTING BACK: UNRULY DOOM LOOPS AND FLYWHEELS

Most books on global affairs are oriented toward the policy community, so they typically end with recommendations to lawmakers and governments. Where current events books are geared toward business leaders, such books usually urge caution or focus on general advice like "building resilience."

But it's a lot harder to build resilience to 100-year hurricanes or megaquakes if they happen every year. Risk-transfer mechanisms like insurance will break down, and it's very costly to prepare to weather the disaster. The same is true of 100-year political, legal, or technological storms. And when they combine into Geolegal "hurriquakes" or LegalAI tsunamis, it's even more challenging.

Yet unlike natural phenomena, where all you can do is prepare, you are actually an empowered player in the unruly world. You can fight back and influence outcomes. You can fight back through a mindset that recognizes risks ahead and knows that you will be successful only if you are honest with yourself about your exposures. You can fight back using the specific techniques I outlined at the end of each chapter both for the specific risks highlighted and for new challenges that emerge from all sides of the Unruly Triangle.

The good news is that you have runway to prepare for many of the risks outlined. If the point of this book was to scare you, I'd tell you that unruliness threatens to kill your business soon. But not only is that unlikely, it's not actually the way risk is manifesting. Instead, Geolegal, Artificial Politics, and LegalAI Risk vectors are interacting to bleed your profitability. While that may kill you over a long enough time horizon, you are able to take steps today to fight back.

The same forces that are shifting the world are forces that empower you for battle. This is not just about fighting back to preserve the status quo. In fact, once you understand the shape of the unruly world, you'll realize you are empowered to use these to navigate it better than your competitors.

In this chapter, I'll conclude this book by reminding you that you can fight back only if you know yourself and know your world. With that information, I'll explain how you can avoid the worst manifestation of unruliness—the Unruly Doom Loop—by creating your own Unruly Flywheel.

THE SHAPE OF RISK

Taking in the totality of the book, we realize the shape of risk is changing. Traditional risk management approaches are very good at focusing resources on risks that are both likely and consequential. This is why boards typically hear about politics only when there is a crisis or lawsuits only when they reach a material threshold.

And when the three vertices of the Unruly Triangle—geopolitics, technology, and law—crop up at the board level, prescriptions are often narrowly scoped against that conception of the risk. If there's legislation that would be catastrophic for your business, you should lobby hard against it. If technology is upending your market, then you need to invest rapidly to innovate your way out. If you face a lawsuit, you need to both fight the lawsuit with the best lawyers you can find and have them check your legal protections to make sure you don't face it again.

But that's not what the future will look like. The future really is characterized by a host of somewhat likely risks that all bring low or medium pain coming from the intersection of geopolitics, technology, and law. To be sure, there is the potential for cataclysmic events. But a lot of managing risk in the unruly world is about anticipating the second-order effects of big issues that happen somewhere else in the world—whether a war hits your supply chain or a political change puts you on the wrong side of a public relations nightmare. That's because the old guardrails and rules have fallen away, but corporate exposures have not. The world is still globalized even as the underpinning of globalization has eroded. And everything, including innovation and the law, has been hyper-politicized.

The idea of single-channel approaches—fighting legal with legal—is born out of the siloing of the corporate world. But in the unruly world, the right technology strategy (innovation) may run counter to evolving political regulations. The right legal strategy (sue a powerful competitor) may cause a political challenge. If you want to fight back, you need integrated strategies. And they can't just be top down: they will require mobilizing the whole organization to fight back.

And those strategies need to be dynamically tested. There is no stable equilibrium between politics, law, and technology because all are evolving quickly. No longer can a one-off risk assessment build confidence for investing in a jurisdiction or a technology. That confidence needs to be dynamically tested in the light of constant changes in the three major vectors tackled in this book. Because investment decisions embed expectations of the future, those expectations need to be ratified (or not) by signposts. Priorities need to be made and remade. Ideally, this would happen not in a wholly reactive fashion but rather in accordance with plans for when a foreseen lower-probability outcome suddenly becomes a paramount concern—or an opportunity.

Throughout the book, I've highlighted a whole host of techniques you can use to analytically engage with an unruly world. Scenario planning that cuts across all the key risks of the Unruly Triangle will help you anticipate what the world could look like. But it is valuable only if the implications of the exercise will actually be implemented. Horizon scanning, no doubt, is a critical technique, but it is effective only if the dots on the horizon are connected to understand integrated risks and take action. Using robot lobbyists or partnering with your insurance companies may or may not suit the shape of your business today, but the idea of patrolling the intersection of technology and political tools that can help you, or of strategically allying with your vendor ecosystem to drive innovative solutions, can be applied in more suitable contexts.

THE SHAPE OF YOU

To fight back effectively, you need to know where you stand. That involves two challenges. First, you need to know yourself and your exposures.

Second, you need to be able to make sure that understanding doesn't drift as the unruly world changes around you.

The first step calls for a much deeper understanding of your mission, footprint, and advantages than you have ever had before. Answering the following questions and confirming your understanding multiple times a year is critical. The questions can be grouped into a few categories:

- What do you stand for?
  - What is non-negotiable for your business from a commercial perspective?
  - What drives you from a philosophical perspective?
- What and where are your critical operations?
  - What are your key business assets?
  - Where do you have people?
  - Are you highly dependent on certain countries or regions? Or on certain politicians or regulatory philosophies?
  - Where are you most vulnerable to disruption and where is disruption most costly?
  - Where are you most exposed to political or legal changes, and where will technology shift that exposure?
- Who are your customers, and what do they buy?
  - Are your products resilient to disruptions, or do people stop buying when there are economic, political, and technological shifts?
  - What geographic risks are they exposed to?
  - What political factors could make them less likely to buy?
  - What could cause them to stop being a client? Or stop existing?

- What are your sources of capital?
  - Could you face a shock as unruliness impacts your public market or private investors?
  - Could you use unruly dislocations to your advantage and tap new sources of capital?
- How do you think of competitors?
  - Where can you get an edge because of their exposure to unruliness?
  - What parts of your business are you prepared to cede to competition or to sacrifice for political gain?

If you do not understand yourself at least on a deeper level, then even if you have perfect monitoring of the world, you are not going to have a good sense of what to prioritize, when, and what to do about it. Instead, you will be prioritizing all of your actions based on external factors, which is a great way to get tossed around in an increasingly volatile global environment.

Once you understand yourself, you are able to focus on what matters most. And you can begin to monitor how such vulnerabilities change over time.

MONITORING YOUR WORLD

Today, you are probably pretty good at understanding legal and regulatory rules of the game to guide your decision-making. Modern government affairs, legal and compliance departments are built to do this well. But this takes for granted that the political or bureaucratic process works in a location, even if it doesn't always produce welcome results. When key localities are undergoing shifts, traditional monitoring techniques may not detect this until it is too late. When many localities are undergoing simultaneous shifts, this is exponentially harder.

Human analysts provide a critical piece of the puzzle. One useful technique is to conceive of your advisors—whether legal, political, or technological—as an integrated knowledge supply chain. And with all supply chains, you want to invest upfront in optimization and resilience.

Key questions include:
- Who will you call when Geolegal Risk manifests?
  - Where there are single analysts that understand the intersection of politics and legal risk, how do you make sure they will accept your call before that of your competitor? Can you identify who they are today and get to know them? How about putting in place a nondisclosure agreement or, better yet, an exclusive service contract?
  - Where there are emergent risks, how will you bring together your best-in-breed legal and political advisors to monitor risk evolution and help you design your strategy? And who will own this?
- With respect to Artificial Politics Risk, who is watching this for you?
  - Does your internal technology team have an interface with your threat team to make sure employees aren't falling victim to new fraud techniques, like deepfakes?
  - Is your public affairs team equipped to disprove the provenance of fake news about your company—or, better, are they working to build trust consistently so this is easier?
  - Does your company have a strategy for how AI will reshape the economy, not just your business?

- When it comes to LegalAI Risk, how is your team structured?
  - Have you built out a legal operations team that you trust to implement best-in-class technology solutions from defensive and offensive perspectives?
  - Is that team integrated with legal leadership and interfacing with senior executives in the company to understand whether weaponized legal technology will be aimed at the business—and how will it be aimed?

The answers to the above questions will depend on the size, nature, and global footprint of your business. But the key point is that if you don't build up the right knowledge supply chain today, you will struggle to do so in a reactive way in the future. And if those knowledge assets are not monitoring the unruly world for change, you risk being surprised.

Of course, technological advancement can make such monitoring easier. More information is at our fingertips than ever before. But sorting through what actually matters is much harder.

To use technology to fight back in an unruly world, you should make sure the software is designed to provide advice that is relevant to you. That means the software must be able to understand who you are, integrate your company context, and keep that up to date. There are just as many risks to acting on noise as there are to missing the signals.

UNRULY DOOM LOOPS AND UNRULY FLYWHEELS

The world is unruly and it is unruling around us. Throughout the book I've used the concept of the Unruly Triangle to orient you to think about intersections of risk dyads like law and politics or law and technology. The critical insight of this book is that to fight back you need to correctly identify that some of today's risks may be coming from a siloed vertex of politics, law, or technology, but most are not. The most worrisome risks are intersectional and thus require different techniques to fight back.

However, there's a final way these risks manifest that is worth considering, which is as a flywheel effect as shown above. The holy grail of fighting back is to build an Unruly Flywheel where politics, law, and technology can feed on each other to build momentum for your business. These elements can go in any order, and of course the opposite can occur: an Unruly Doom Loop can emerge whereby the same factors pick up fatal momentum.

Let's unpack this. Jim Collins popularized the concept of flywheels and doom loops in his business classic *Good to Great*.[1] Collins looked at a wide selection of companies, filtering for those that delivered the best performance. In isolating how those companies performed so well, Collins introduced the concept of a "flywheel effect"—a number of smaller factors that compound momentum and reinforce each other, contributing to growth many times faster than any single factor would have allowed. To describe Amazon's flywheel, for instance, he wrote how lower prices would bring customers and third-party vendors, which would enable Amazon to expand its store and distribution. Growing revenues would allow it to lower more prices and do the same again.[2]

Companies that failed to build a flywheel risked getting caught in a "doom loop," whereby they would try to gain momentum by taking a series of disconnected steps. Bad results would lead to companies trying to find a silver bullet; when that fails they then try something completely different. Eventually the company stops its own momentum. And such momentum could spin in reverse, cratering the business.

Unruliness presents companies with a doom loop of risk. No more are companies facing individualized risks from political, legal, or technological change. The interconnected nature of politics, technology, and law can set in motion risks that can disrupt even the most successful companies. Technology can provide companies with an edge that politics can amplify and translate permanently into law. Or, companies relying on the law to maintain advantages may find that politics is eroding it and they are vulnerable to a competitor's innovations.

To break out of the Unruly Doom Loop, companies need to correctly diagnose the challenges they face are coming from the accelerated interaction of these risks. They need to understand the order in which these risks are flowing and then figure out the way the factors are interacting with each other based on the issue at hand. They can then take steps to slow down momentum of the doom loop and neutralize the risk.

However, the most successful companies will create their own Unruly Flywheel that jumpstarts momentum by harnessing the power of these factors, leaving their competition to be subject to unruliness that they no longer face. Integrated strategies to harness one's own technological advances through political and legal channels will create feedback loops and momentum other companies cannot catch.

To build that flywheel instead of a doom loop, we need to remind ourselves that risk is coming at business from three different perspectives.

First, politics is more volatile than at any point in recent memory. Western economies—once known for political stability—are more unpredictable than ever before. Conflicts—whether live wars, proxy military battles, or strategic standoffs—characterize the landscape. Cross-border meddling or projections of power are commonplace. Targeting of companies for political gain is no longer unusual.

Second, technology is progressing in unpredictable ways. Artificial intelligence tools that can barely be explained by their creators are being innovated at a previously unthinkable speed. These new technologies are being deployed to overhaul entire industries at the same time they are being used for surveillance and weaponry. Productivity booms could lift entire economies. Or they could render large parts of the working population unemployed. They could even enable enemies to inflict massive—or decisive—damage, leading to calls to restrict them.

Third, the law is both eroding and being used as a weapon rather than a safeguard. Political actors are using legal tactics as an end run around politics, increasing societal divergence. Traditional rules of war or politics are no longer constraining. AI-powered litigation will be weaponized against companies at an alarming rate.

These factors intersect and build momentum in ways that have concrete business consequences.

Let's take the example of Huawei Technologies. As a domestic Chinese company, Huawei has exceptional advantages—the Unruly Flywheel works in its favor. Huawei is a political favorite that curries massive government support. As it innovates breakthrough technologies, it engenders further political support, which becomes enshrined in a favorable regulatory climate that disadvantages its competitors at home.

But as an international actor, Huawei is stuck in an Unruly Doom Loop that it is struggling to free itself from and that will challenge its domestic progress. U.S. politics has resulted in Huawei being declared a national security threat. As a result, rules and laws are put in place that restrict everything it can do in the U.S. economy. As Huawei innovates new technology—for instance, 5G technology—political concern grows further. Such concern results in the United States pressurizing European countries to cut Huawei out of their supply chains, and to restrict access to advanced technologies that allow for more innovation not just by Huawei but by Chinese companies more broadly. When Huawei announces a new smartphone with a chip that's more powerful than Western companies thought possible given restrictions, another cycle of investigation and restriction begins. Soon, the long arm of U.S. law will restrict much of Huawei's global market opportunity and damage its ability to innovate products for its core market.

In this way, politics, technology, and law continue to spin in a negative direction. There are a number of strategies available to a company like Huawei to break free of such a doom loop, but none of them would work if it doesn't realize the challenge. To date, the company has focused on running nonintegrated strategies of political lobbying and debuting new products, failing to realize it is precisely its innovation that is leading the harshest restraints.

A strategy of exporting its older technology rather than its cutting-edge technology might create a political narrative about restricting its own market opportunity to be a responsible actor. Or, a decision to exit Western markets completely and focus on the emerging world would tone down the core political and legal momentum against it, allowing it to use its new technologies to win market share in many global markets that might otherwise increasingly become off-limits.

The Unruly Flywheel

Microsoft provides an example of a company that has broken free from an Unruly Doom Loop and created its own Unruly Flywheel. Twenty years ago, Microsoft was being pursued by regulators for antitrust violations—accused of giving its own software applications primacy inside its operating system. Microsoft ultimately settled these cases and adapted business practices to accommodate political pressure, breaking the doom loop.

Microsoft began to support open-source software and innovated new products focused on cloud licenses and artificial intelligence, building political and commercial support in various corners. Microsoft has grown closer to the U.S. government, emerging as somewhat of a national champion, providing both direct solutions and also support for national security concerns as they arise. For instance, when Microsoft invested in Emirati AI company G42, the U.S. government was reportedly at the table and forced G42 to stop using Chinese technology to secure the investment. While Microsoft still faces legal challenges from time to time, they are of a muted political tenor that reflects the fact that the company is politically aligned with U.S. strategic direction and innovating solutions politicians want created in America.

Microsoft and Huawei provide interesting contrasting examples of how politics, technology, and law intersect to create positive or negative momentum for some of the world's biggest businesses. But the same is true for businesses of all sizes. Take a step back and consider how you can shift your political, legal, and technology strategies to be mutually reinforcing and pick up momentum. Your competitors won't understand what happened to them as you accelerate through an unruly world that holds them back.

FROM UNRULY TO RULY

It has always struck me that political risk analysts spend most of their time focusing on downside risk while their clients spend their days looking for opportunities. Telling a customer to watch out because there's a lot of uncertainty due to regulatory change misses the fact that such changes could be a really bad thing for that customer or it could be absolutely splendid. If the customer is miles ahead of their competitors and can afford to comply with new regulations while their competitors will all be held back—well, that's a good scenario. The shutting down of shipping channels could create material advantages for companies that have invested in redundancy and optionality when their competitors haven't. An unpredictable and bombastic president coming into office could still result in lower taxes, massive subsidies, and other protections.

This book is meant to serve as a wakeup call that we—as the broader business community—risk sleepwalking into a world that is more volatile and less well governed than ever before. If we don't open our eyes to the fact that these challenges are coming for our businesses and, in some cases, our personal lives, then we may well wake up with some of the more dystopian risks I've outlined. But these challenges come at a time of great innovation when real global problems are being solved.

While I've spent a lot of time on how that could go wrong, those advances also present a chance to "get it right" by remedying the inequalities that are at the root of the discontent driving much of today's unruliness. There are terrific opportunities for society and the economy in these new technologies. To believe otherwise would be to believe that things are currently as good as they are ever going to get. I am not nearly so pessimistic.

Computers today can perform unbelievable feats and no doubt I underestimate the extent to which they will progress in my lifetime. Tremendous productivity gains present the chance to innovate the modern world out of so many societal challenges while untold economic growth awaits those individuals, companies, and countries that create and build upon such innovations. Advances in healthcare could far exceed our wildest imaginations. While I've highlighted the risk that eroding law and new technology allow politicians to creep toward authoritarianism, such technologies can be democratizing and increase access to justice for many as well.

It is up to us to fight back against unruliness—not just for business survival but for the sake of our civilizations and future generations. There are no easy solutions to smoothing over fractures in society, but it costs nothing to be hopeful. So despite the ink I've spilled warning you about what lies ahead, you can count me as an optimist. Consider me ready to be enlisted alongside you to fight back against unruliness.

NOTES

INTRODUCTION

1. Peters, Jeremy W, and Shaila Dewan. "A Cantor Effect for Businesses and the G.O.P." Nytimes.com. *The New York Times*, June 14, 2014. https://www.nytimes .com/2014/06/15/business/for-businesses-and-the-gop-a-cantor-effect.html.
2. Yaqoob, Adam. "Quotation of the Day: Fleeing Sudan Conflict, Only to Find in England a Mob Menacing Them." *The New York Times*, August 14, 2024. https://www.nytimes.com/2024/08/14/pageoneplus/quotation-of-the-day-fleeing-sudan-conflict-only-to-find-in-england-a-mob-menacing-them.html.
3. Duntsova, Yekaterina S. "Quotation of the Day: Russians in the Kursk Region 'Were Living Our Lives,' Until the Incursion." *The New York Times*, August 16, 2024. https://www.nytimes.com/2024/08/16/pageoneplus/quotation-of-the-day-russians-in-the-kursk-region-were-living-our-lives-until-the-incursion .html.
4. Awada, Mohamad. "Quotation of the Day: Netanyahu Vows 'Severe' Reaction to Rocket Strike." *The New York Times*, July 30, 2024. https://www.nytimes .com/2024/07/30/pageoneplus/quotation-of-the-day-netanyahu-vows-severe-reaction-to-rocket-strike.html.
5. Tooze, Adam. "Welcome to the World of the Polycrisis." *Financial Times*, October 28, 2022. https://www.ft.com/content/498398e7-11b1-494b-9cd3-6d669dc3de33.

6. Bautzer, Tatiana, and Nupur Anand. "JPMorgan CEO Jamie Dimon Says 'It's Time to Fight Back' on Regulation." *Reuters*, October 29, 2024. https://www.reuters.com/business/finance/jpmorgan-ceo-says-its-time-fight-back-regulation-2024-10-28/.

CHAPTER 1

1. Bremmer, Ian. 2012. *Every Nation for Itself: Winners and Losers in a G-Zero World*. Portfolio.
2. World Justice Project. "World Justice Project Rule of Law Index 2024 Insights." (2024). Accessed November 3, 2024. https://worldjusticeproject.org/rule-of-law-index/downloads/WJPInsights2024.pdf.
3. Miliband, David. "Opinion | Our Age of Impunity." Nytimes.com. *The New York Times*, February 17, 2023. https://www.nytimes.com/2023/02/17/opinion/ukraine-corruption-human-rights.html.
4. For instance, see Levitsky, Steven, and Daniel Ziblatt. 2018. *How Democracies Die*. Crown.
5. Global Citizen. "The Richest 1% Own Almost Half the World's Wealth & 9 Other Mind-Blowing Facts on Wealth Inequality." January 19, 2023. https://www.globalcitizen.org/en/content/wealth-inequality-oxfam-billionaires-elon-musk/#:~:text=The%20richest%201%25%20own%20almost%20half%20of%20the%20world's%20wealth,the%20world%20own%20just%200.75%25.

CHAPTER 2

1. "What Is the WTO?" The World Trade Organization. Accessed November 19, 2024. https://www.wto.org/english/thewto_e/thewto_e.htm.
2. Timberg, Craig, and Ellen Nakashima. "Agreements with Private Companies Protect U.S. Access to Cables' Data for Surveillance." *The Washington Post*, July 6, 2013. https://www.washingtonpost.com/business/technology/agreements-with-private-companies-protect-us-access-to-cables-data-for-surveillance/2013/07/06/aa5d017a-df77-11e2-b2d4-ea6d8f477a01_story.html.

3. Carrel, Paul. "U.S. Spy Agency Tapped German Chancellery for Decades: WikiLeaks." *Reuters*, July 9, 2015. https://www.reuters.com/article/world/us-spy-agency-tapped-german-chancellery-for-decades-wikileaks-idUSKCN0PI2AD/.

4. Freifeld, Karen, and Steve Stecklow. "Exclusive: HSBC Probe Helped Lead to U.S. Charges against Huawei CFO." *Reuters*, February 26, 2019. https://www.reuters.com/article/world/exclusive-hsbc-probe-helped-lead-to-us-charges-against-huawei-cfo-idUSKCN1QF1IA/.

5. West, Sean. "Manufactured Housing Finance and the Secondary Market." *Community Development Innovation Review, Federal Reserve Bank of San Francisco*, no. 1 (2006): 35–47. Accessed September 21, 2024.

6. Gill, Dee. "Where China's Stimulus Program Went Wrong." *Chicago Booth Review CBR—Summer 2017* (2017). Accessed September 21, 2024. https://www.chicagobooth.edu/review/where-chinas-stimulus-program-went-wrong.

7. Moss, Todd, Sarah J. Staats, and Julia Barmeier. "The ABCs of the General Capital Increase." *Center for Global Development*, (2011). Accessed September 21, 2024. https://www.cgdev.org/sites/default/files/archive/doc/IFI/IFI_Briefs_GCI-FINAL.pdf.

8. Rosenberg, Matthew, Nicholas Confessore, and Carole Cadwalladr. "How Trump Consultants Exploited the Facebook Data of Millions." *The New York Times*, March 17, 2018. https://www.nytimes.com/2018/03/17/us/politics/cambridge-analytica-trump-campaign.html.

9. Detrow, Scott. "What Did Cambridge Analytica Do During The 2016 Election?" *NPR*, March 20, 2018. https://www.npr.org/2018/03/20/595338116/what-did-cambridge-analytica-do-during-the-2016-election.

10. Barry, Ellen. "Cambridge Analytica Whistle-Blower Contends Data-Mining Swung Brexit Vote." *The New York Times*, March 27, 2018. https://www.nytimes.com/2018/03/27/world/europe/whistle-blower-data-mining-cambridge-analytica.html.

11. Mueller, Robert S. Rep. *Report on the Investigation Into Russian Interference in the 2016 Presidential Election* Vol. I of II. Washington, D.C.: U.S. Department of Justice, 2019. https://www.justice.gov/archives/sco/file/1373816/dl

12. Ruy, Donatienne. "Did Russia Influence Brexit?" Center for Strategic and International Studies, July 21, 2020. https://www.csis.org/blogs/brexit-bits-bobs-and-blogs/did-russia-influence-brexit.

13. "India's Foreign Minister on Ties with America, China and Russia." *The Economist*, June 15, 2023. https://www.economist.com/asia/2023/06/15/indias-foreign-minister-on-ties-with-america-china-and-russia.

14. Klar, Rebecca. "Trump: 'Fake News Media,' Democrats Working to 'Inflame the CoronaVirus Situation.'" *The Hill*, March 9, 2020. https://thehill.com/homenews/administration/486559-trump-fake-news-media-democrats-working-to-inflame-the-coronavirus/.

15. Abouzzohour, Yasmina. (2022). The Amplification of Authoritarianism in the Age of COVID-19. 47 (POMEPS Studies: COVID-19 in the MENA: Two Years On): 12–17.

16. Ibid.

17. Kennedy, Scott, and Wang Jisi. "America and China Need to Talk." *Foreign Affairs*, April 6, 2023. https://www.foreignaffairs.com/china/america-and-china-dialogue-need-lack-risk-conflict.

18. https://www.bbc.com/news/av/world-us-canada-53173436

19. Bing, Chris, and Schectman Joel. "Pentagon Ran Secret Anti-Vax Campaign to Incite Fear of China Vaccines." *Reuters*, June 14, 2024. https://www.reuters.com/investigates/special-report/usa-covid-propaganda/

20. "Qualified Immunity." Cornell Law School. Accessed September 23, 2024. https://www.law.cornell.edu/wex/qualified_immunity.

21. Gamio, Lazaro, and Karen Yourish. "A Timeline of Trump's Attempts to Overturn the 2020 Election Results." Nytimes.com. *The New York Times*, January 8, 2024. https://www.nytimes.com/interactive/2024/01/08/us/trump-2020-overturn-timeline.html.

CHAPTER 3

1. "World Justice Project (WJP) Rule of Law Index 2024." World Justice Project, October 23, 2024. https://worldjusticeproject.org/rule-of-law-index/insights.

2. Lange, Jason. "Voters Narrowly Support Trump's Tariff Pitch, Reuters/Ipsos Poll Finds." *Reuters*, September 15, 2024. https://www.reuters.com/world/us/us-voters-narrowly-support-trumps-tariff-pitch-reutersipsos-poll-finds-2024-09-15/.

3. Jordan, Miriam. "Voters Were Fed Up Over Immigration. They Voted for Trump." *The New York Times*, November 6, 2024. https://www.nytimes.com/2024/11/06/us/trump-immigration-border.html.

4. See, for example, Howe, Amy. "Supreme Court Strikes Down *Chevron*, Curtailing Power of Federal Agencies." *SCOTUSblog*, June 28, 2024. https://www.scotusblog.com/2024/06/supreme-court-strikes-down-chevron-curtailing-power-of-federal-agencies/.

5. *Trump v. United States*, 23–939 (2024).

CHAPTER 4

1. Hughes, Laura, Andrew England, and Najmeh Bozorgmehr. "Nazanin Zaghari-Ratcliffe Arrives Back in UK after Release by Iran." *Financial Times*, March 16, 2022. Hughes, Laura, Andrew England, and Najmeh Bozorgmehr . "Nazanin Zaghari-Ratcliffe Arrives Back in UK after Release by Iran." *Financial Times*, March 16, 2022. https://www.ft.com/content/cdbeaf46-a4d8-4e54-8d7f-c0eaf088af7e.

2. Debusmann, Bernd Jr. "What Happened to US Citizens like Otto Warmbier Detained in North Korea?" *BBC*, July 18, 2023. https://www.bbc.com/news/world-us-canada-66236989.

3. Zaru, Deena. "Timeline of Brittney Griner's Detention in Russia as US Secures Her Release." *ABC News*, December 8, 2022. https://abcnews.go.com/US/timeline-brittney-griners-detention-russia-us-vows-secure/story?id=87925739.

4. Light, Felix, and Mark Trevelyan. "Who Is Evan Gershkovich, US Journalist Released in Russia Prisoner Swap?" *Reuters*, August 1, 2024. https://www.reuters.com/world/evan-gershkovich-russia-reporter-who-became-story-2024-08-01/.

5. Specia, Megan. "Jamal Khashoggi's Killing: Here's What We Know." *The New York Times*, October 19, 2018. https://www.nytimes.com/2018/10/19/world/middleeast/jamal-khashoggi-case-facts.html.

6. Harding, Luke. "'A Chain of Stupidity': The Skripal Case and the Decline of Russia's Spy Agencies." *The Guardian*, June 23, 2020. https://www.theguardian.com/world/2020/jun/23/skripal-salisbury-poisoning-decline-of-russia-spy-agencies-gru.

7. Meacham, Sam. "Weaponizing the Police: Interpol as a Tool of Authoritarianism." *Harvard International Review*, April 11, 2022. https://hir.harvard.edu/weaponizing-the-police-authoritarian-abuse-of-interpol/.

8. U.S. Department of Justice. "Eight Individuals Charged with Conspiring to Act as Illegal Agents of the People's Republic of China." *Justice.gov*, October 28, 2020. https://www.justice.gov/opa/pr/eight-individuals-charged-conspiring-act-illegal-agents-people-s-republic-china.

9. Mahtani, Shibani, Meg Kelly, Cate Brown, Cate Cadell, Ellen Nakashima, and Chris Dehghanpoor. "How China Extended Its Repression into an American City." *The Washington Post*, September 3, 2024. https://www.washingtonpost.com/world/interactive/2024/chinese-communist-party-us-repression-xi-jinping-apec/.

10. Murphy, Jessica. "Three Arrested and Charged over Sikh Activist's Killing in Canada." *BBC*, May 4, 2024. https://www.bbc.com/news/world-us-canada-67836968.

11. Radford, Antoinette. "Roman Protasevich: Belarus Pardons Activist Hauled off Flight." *BBC*, May 22, 2023. https://www.bbc.com/news/world-europe-65670820.

12. Google.com. "Google Books Ngram Viewer," 2022. https://books.google.com/ngrams/graph?content=lawfare&year_start=1800&year_end=2022&corpus=en&smoothing=3.

13. Fatf-gafi.org. "Jurisdictions under Increased Monitoring—June 2024," 28 June 2024. https://www.fatf-gafi.org/en/publications/High-risk-and-other-monitored-jurisdictions/increased-monitoring-june-2024.html.

14. 4 Ezra. 4-12 (New International Edition).

15. Farrell, Henry, and Abraham Newman. 2022. *Underground Empire: How America Weaponized the World Economy*. Henry Holt and Co.

16. Vallée, Shahin. "Reserves Freeze Sends Shivers through Moscow." *Official Monetary and Financial Institutions Forum*, March 8, 2022. https://www.omfif.org/2022/03/reserves-freeze-sends-shivers-through-moscow/.

17. Saul, Jonathan, and Carolyn Cohn. "Exclusive: Lloyd's of London Leads Insurers Tightening Taiwan Cover as Conflict Risks Rise." *Reuters*, August 10, 2023. https://www.reuters.com/business/finance/lloyds-london-leads-insurers-tightening-taiwan-cover-conflict-risks-rise-2023-08-10/.

CHAPTER 5

1. "China Tells Bankers to Be More Patriotic." *The Economist*, February 29, 2024. https://www.economist.com/china/2024/02/29/china-tells-bankers-to-be-more-patriotic.

2. "China's Xi Urges Private Firms to 'Be Rich and Loving.'" *The Straits Times*, March 6, 2023. https://www.reuters.com/world/china/chinas-xi-urges-private-firms-be-rich-loving-pursuit-prosperity-all-2023-03-06/.

3. Tian, Yew Lun. "China's Xi Calls for Nurturing of Patriotic Scientists." *Reuters*, September 28, 2021. https://www.reuters.com/world/china/chinas-xi-calls-nurturing-patriotic-scientists-2021-09-28/.

4. Matthews, Owen. "Xi Jinping Says Companies Must Be More Patriotic." The China Project, July 22, 2020. https://thechinaproject.com/2020/07/22/xi-jinping-says-companies-must-be-more-patriotic/.

5. He, Laura. "Xi Jinping Hits out at US as He Urges China's Private Firms to 'Fight' alongside Communist Party." *CNN*, March 7, 2023. https://www.cnn.com/2023/03/07/economy/china-two-sessions-xi-jinping-speech-us-challenges-intl-hnk/index.html.

6. Gbedemah, Luke, and Kevin Allison. "A $1.5 Billion Deal with Microsoft Won't Rupture the UAE's Ties to China." Inferences by Minerva Technology Policy Advisors, April 22, 2024. https://minervainferences.substack.com/p/a-15-billion-deal-with-microsoft.

7. Trueman, Charlotte. "US Government Revokes Intel and Qualcomm's Huawei Export Licenses." Data Center Dynamics, May 9, 2024. https://www.datacenterdynamics.com/en/news/us-government-revokes-intel-and-qualcomms-huawei-export-licenses/.

8. Eichensehr, Kristen, and Cathy Hwang. "National Security Creep in Corporate Transactions" (123 Colum. L. Rev. 549 (2023)), September 4, 2022. https://papers.ssrn.com/sol3/papers.cfm?abstract_id=4211540#.

9. Carroll, Kevin, Michael Huneke, and Sean Reilly. "Whack-a-Mole Sanctions Compliance Can Benefit From War Lessons." *Bloomberg Law*, February 29, 2024. https://news.bloomberglaw.com/us-law-week/whack-a-mole-sanctions-compliance-can-benefit-from-war-lessons.

10. Sankaran, Karthik. "Government Push for Champions Could Have Firms Champing at the Bit." Foreign Policy Research Institute, July 31, 2023. https://www.fpri.org/article/2023/07/government-push-for-champions-could-have-firms-champing-at-the-bit/.

11. Somerville, Heather. "As Silicon Valley Pivots to Patriotic Capital, China Ties Linger." *The Wall Street Journal*, May 12, 2024. https://www.wsj.com/finance/investing/as-silicon-valley-pivots-to-patriotic-capital-china-ties-linger-7030bf93.

12. Congress of the United States House of Representatives, Select Committee on the Chinese Communist Party. Letter to Roelof Botha and Don Vieira. Washington, D.C.: 548 Cannon House Office Building, October 17, 2023. https://selectcommitteeontheccp.house.gov/sites/evo-subsites/selectcommitteeontheccp.house.gov/files/evo-media-document/2023.10.17-letter-to-sequoia-capital.pdf.

13. *Helvering v. Gregory*, 69 F.2d 809 (2d Cir. 1934), Justia. https://law.justia.com/cases/federal/appellate-courts/F2/69/809/1562063/#:~:text=We%20agree%20with,L.%20Ed.%20830.

14. Carter, Allison. "Why More CEOS Keep Getting Called to Testify before Congress – and The Role Comms Must Play." *PR Daily*, February 14, 2024. https://www.prdaily.com/why-more-ceos-keep-getting-called-to-testify-before-congress-and-the-role-comms-must-play/.

15. Publication. The Evolving Global Foreign Direct Investment and National Security Review Landscape. Dechert LLP, May 2023. https://docs.dechert.com/view/322665140/#zoom=true.

16. "Article: July 2019: Legal Challenges to CFIUS Reviews." Quinn Emanuel Urquhart & Sullivan, LLP, July 30, 2019. https://www.quinnemanuel.com/the-firm/publications/article-july-2019-legal-challenges-to-cfius-reviews/.

17. "Committee on Foreign Investment in the United States Annual Report to Congress (Report Period: CY 2022)." US Department of the Treasury, July 2023. https://home.treasury.gov/system/files/206/CFIUS%20-%20Annual%20Report%20to%20Congress%20CY%202022_0.pdf

18. Leonhardt, David. "TikTok's Pro-China Tilt." *The New York Times*, April 24, 2024. https://www.nytimes.com/2024/04/24/briefing/tiktok-ban-bill-congress.html#:~:text=TikTok%20as%20propaganda,allied%20with%20China.

19. West, Sean. "Legal Industry Rules on Cusp of Sea Change as Tech Forces Gather." *Bloomberg Law*, November 29, 2023. https://news.bloomberglaw.com/us-law-week/legal-industry-rules-on-cusp-of-sea-change-as-tech-forces-gather.

20. Stevastopulo, Demetri. "US Lawmakers Tune out TikTok Lobbying to Advance Bill to Ban App." *Financial Times*, March 7, 2024. https://www.ft.com/content/ce22dd51-9410-4245-8556-f9b4a4bf5ada.

21. Peters, Jay. "Grindr Has Been Sold by Its Chinese Owner after the US Expressed Security Concerns." *The Verge*, March 6, 2020. https://www.theverge.com/2020/3/6/21168079/grindr-sold-chinese-owner-us-cfius-security-concerns-kunlun-lgbtq.

22. Fung, Brian. "Biden Just Signed a Potential TikTok Ban into Law. Here's What Happens Next." *CNN*, April 24, 2024. https://edition.cnn.com/2024/04/23/tech/congress-tiktok-ban-what-next/index.html.

23. Smith, Ryan, and Connie O'Connell. "Direct Investment by Country and Industry, 2022." US Department of Commerce Bureau of Economic Analysis, July 20, 2023. https://www.bea.gov/sites/default/files/2023-07/dici0723.pdf.

24. Quote from email interview between author and Lewis Sage-Passant on December 16th, 2024. For those who want to learn more about private-sector intelligence teams, I recommend *Beyond States and Spies: The Security Intelligence Services of the Private Sector*, Edinburgh University Press, 2024.

CHAPTER 6

1. "Muswell Hill, London—best places to live in the UK 2020." *The Sunday Times*, March 20, 2020. https://www.thetimes.com/article/muswell-hill-london-best-places-to-live-in-the-uk-2020-x35n3p5w2.
2. Hoeven, Emily. "Gavin Newsom Wants S.F. to Enforce the 'damn Laws.' What Does That Mean?" *San Francisco Chronicle*, July 8, 2023. https://www.sfchronicle.com/opinion/article/gavin-newsom-sf-18180150.php.
3. Thomas, Merlyn, and Mike Wendling. "Trump repeats baseless claim about Haitian immigrants eating pets." BBC News, September 15, 2024. https://www.bbc.com/news/articles/c77l28myezko.
4. Blood, Michael R., and Jonathan J. Cooper. "Trump Animates California Republicans with Calls to Shoot People Who Rob Stores." *AP News*, September 29, 2023. https://apnews.com/article/donald-trump-california-republicans-desantis-e2f59e579f106c03aaf6189ea1079f11.
5. Alemán, Marcos. "El Salvador Is Gradually Filling Its New Mega Prison with Alleged Gang Members." *AP News*, October 12, 2023. https://apnews.com/article/el-salvador-prison-gangs-bukele-42315f24691e0a3136d005ab7c0bee6a.
6. Janetsky, Megan. "The President Jailed 1% of El Salvador's Population. Their Children Are Paying the Consequences." *AP News*, February 9, 2024. https://apnews.com/article/el-salvador-bukele-central-america-crime-gangs-60c3a34c571dfdbdf0a203deb85abf71.
7. Dela Cruz, Kimberly. "The Sunday Story: Life in the Shadow of the Philippines' Drug War." *NPR*, May 19, 2024. https://www.npr.org/2024/05/19/1198912731/philippines-drug-war-duterte-marcos.
8. "How Many People Have Been Killed in Rodrigo Duterte's War on Drugs?" *The Economist*, November 22, 2021. https://www.economist.com/graphic-detail/2021/11/22/how-many-people-have-been-killed-in-rodrigo-dutertes-war-on-drugs.
9. IBISWorld. "Market Size of Security Services in the United States from 2012 to 2023 (in billion U.S. dollars)." April 30, 2024. https://www.statista.com/statistics/294206/revenue-of-security-services-in-the-us/.

10. McCarthy, Craig. "Wild Video Shows Walgreens Security Guard Getting Hit by Shoplifter—and He's the One Arrested." *New York Post*, May 1, 2023. https://nypost.com/2023/05/01/walgreens-guard-arrested-for-stopping-shoplifter-to-sue-papd/.

11. "Lidl GB Becomes First Supermarket to Roll Out Body-Worn Cameras Across All Stores." Lidl Great Britain, November 8, 2023. https://corporate.lidl.co.uk/media-centre/pressreleases/2023/body-worn-cameras.

12. Kavilanz, Parija. "Lululemon Stands by Decision to Fire Employees Who Intervened in Robbery." *CNN Business*, June 7, 2023. https://edition.cnn.com/2023/06/06/business/lululemon-fires-employees-stop-robbery/index.html.

CHAPTER 7

1. Autor, David, David Dorn, and Gordon H. Hanson. "On the Persistence of the China Shock." *National Bureau of Economic Research NBER Working Paper Series*, (2021). Accessed September 29, 2024. https://doi.org/10.3386/w29401.

2. Venkatu, Guhan. "Rust and Renewal: A Pittsburgh Retrospective." *Federal Reserve Bank of Cleveland*, February, 2018. https://www.clevelandfed.org/regional-analysis/pittsburgh-retrospective.

3. Ellingrud, Kweilin, Saurabh Sanghvi, Gurneet S. Dandona, Anu Madgavkar, Michael Chui, Olivia White, and Paige Hasebe. "Which Jobs Will Be in Demand? Which Ones Are Shrinking? And Which Ones Could Be Hardest to Fill?" *McKinsey Global Institute*, July 26, 2023. https://www.mckinsey.com/mgi/our-research/generative-ai-and-the-future-of-work-in-america#/.

4. "Generative AI Could Raise Global GDP by 7%." Goldman Sachs, April 5, 2023. https://www.goldmansachs.com/insights/articles/generative-ai-could-raise-global-gdp-by-7-percent.

5. Kochhar, Rakesh. "Which U.S. Workers Are More Exposed to AI on Their Jobs?" *Pew Research Center*. July, 2023. https://www.pewresearch.org/social-trends/wp-content/uploads/sites/3/2023/07/st_2023.07.26_ai-and-jobs.pdf.

6. Treisman, Rachel. "The Fastest Ever Laundry-folding Robot Is Here. And It's Likely Still Slower than You." *National Public Radio*, October 2, 2022. https://www.npr.org/2022/10/22/1130552239/robot-folding-laundry.

7. Verma, Pranshu, and Gerrit De Vynck. "From Airlines to Hollywood, Workers Are Fighting to Keep AI at Bay." *The Washington Post*, June 8, 2024. https://www.washingtonpost.com/technology/2023/06/08/labor-unions-fight-ai/.

8. Stewart, Heather. "Calls for Stricter UK Oversight of Workplace AI amid Fears for Staff Rights." *The Guardian*, April 16, 2023. https://www.theguardian .com/law/2023/apr/16/calls-stricter-oversight-workplace-ai-fears-staff-rights#:~:text=Calls%20for%20stricter%20UK%20oversight%20of%20 workplace%20AI%20amid%20fears%20for%20staff%20rights,-This%20 article%20is&text=Campaigners%2C%20trade%20unions%20and%20 MPs,its%20effect%20on%20staff%20right.

9. Gordon, Anna. "Why Protesters Around the World Are Demanding a Pause on AI Development." *Time Magazine*, May 13, 2023. https://time.com/6977680/ ai-protests-international/.

10. Conway, Ed. "The Paradox Holding Back the Clean Energy Revolution." *The New York Times*, February 22, 2024. https://www.nytimes.com/2024/02/22/ opinion/vegas-sphere-energy-efficiency.html.

11. Rosalsky, Greg. "What if AI Could Rebuild the Middle Class?" *National Public Radio*, May 9, 2023. https://www.npr.org/sections/money/2023/05/09/11749 33574/what-if-ai-could-rebuild-the-middle-class.

12. Rosalsky, Greg. "What if AI Could Rebuild the Middle Class?" *National Public Radio*, May 9, 2023. https://www.npr.org/sections/money/2023/05/09/ 1174933574/what-if-ai-could-rebuild-the-middle-class.

13. McArdle, Megan. "AI Is Coming for the Professional Class. Expect Outrage — And Fear." *The Washington Post*, April 29, 2024. https://www.washingtonpost .com/opinions/2024/04/29/ai-professional-class-low-skill-jobs/.

14. Khogali, Hisham O., and Samir Mekid. "The Blended Future of Automation and AI: Examining Some Long-term Societal and Ethical Impact Features." *Technology in Society 73*, no. May 2023 (2023). Accessed September 29, 2024. https://doi.org/10.1016/j.techsoc.2023.102232.

15. Reuters. "Microsoft May Pay Constellation Premium in Three Mile Island Power Agreement, Jefferies Says (Sept 23)." *Reuters*, September 24, 2024. https://www.reuters.com/markets/deals/microsoft-may-pay-constellation-premium-three-mile-island-power-agreement-2024-09-23/.

16. "What Is UBI | Stanford Basic Income Lab." The Stanford Basic Income Lab, 2016. https://basicincome.stanford.edu/about/what-is-ubi/.

17. Samuel, Sigal. "Everywhere Basic Income Has Been Tried, in One Map." *Vox*, October 20, 2020. https://www.vox.com/future-perfect/2020/2/19/21112570/ universal-basic-income-ubi-map.

18. Francese, Maura, and Delphine Prady. "What Is Universal Basic Income?" International Monetary Fund. December 1, 2018. https://www.imf.org/en/ Publications/fandd/issues/2018/12/what-is-universal-basic-income-basics.

19. *"What Is UBI | Stanford Basic Income Lab." The Stanford Basic Income Lab, 2016.* https://basicincome.stanford.edu/about/what-is-ubi/.

20. Francese, Maura, and Delphine Prady. "What Is Universal Basic Income?" International Monetary Fund. December 1, 2018. https://www.imf.org/en/Publications/fandd/issues/2018/12/what-is-universal-basic-income-basics.

21. Francese, Maura, and Delphine Prady. "What Is Universal Basic Income?" International Monetary Fund. December 1, 2018. https://www.imf.org/en/Publications/fandd/issues/2018/12/what-is-universal-basic-income-basics.

22. "What Is UBI | Stanford Basic Income Lab." The Stanford Basic Income Lab, 2016. https://basicincome.stanford.edu/about/what-is-ubi/.

23. Samuel, Sigal. "Finland Gave People Free Money. It Increased Their Trust in Social Institutions." *Vox*, April 6, 2019. https://www.vox.com/2019/4/6/18297452/finland-basic-income-free-money-canada.

24. Samuel, Sigal. "Everywhere Basic Income Has Been Tried, in One Map." *Vox*, October 20, 2020. https://www.vox.com/future-perfect/2020/2/19/21112570/universal-basic-income-ubi-map.

25. Samuel, Sigal. "Everywhere Basic Income Has Been Tried, in One Map." *Vox*, October 20, 2020. https://www.vox.com/future-perfect/2020/2/19/21112570/universal-basic-income-ubi-map.

26. Samuel, Sigal. "Everywhere Basic Income Has Been Tried, in One Map." *Vox*, October 20, 2020. https://www.vox.com/future-perfect/2020/2/19/21112570/universal-basic-income-ubi-map.

27. Torkington, Simon. "Does 'Universal Basic Income' Work? These Countries Are Putting It to the Test." *World Economic Forum*, March 9, 2024. https://www.weforum.org/agenda/2023/06/children-care-guaranteed-income/.

28. Jarow, Oshan. "Artificial Intelligence Isn't a Good Argument for Basic Income." *Vox*, July 22, 2024. https://www.vox.com/future-perfect/361749/universal-basic-income-sam-altman-open-ai-study.

29. The Economist. "Universal Basic Income Gains Momentum in America." *The Economist*, August 6, 2020. https://www.economist.com/united-states/2020/08/08/universal-basic-income-gains-momentum-in-america?utm_medium=cpc.adword.pd&utm_source=google&ppccampaignID=17210591673&ppcadID=&utm_campaign=a.22brand_pmax&utm_content=conversion.direct-response.anonymous&gad_source=1.

30. The Economist. "Universal Basic Income Gains Momentum in America." *The Economist*, August 6, 2020. https://www.economist.com/united-states/2020/08/08/universal-basic-income-gains-momentum-in-america?utm_medium=cpc.adword.pd&utm_source=google&ppccampaignID=17210591673&ppcadID=&utm_campaign=a.22brand_pmax&utm_content=conversion.direct-response.anonymous&gad_source=1.

31. Wharton Staff. "Why Alaska's Experience Shows Promise for Universal Basic Income." *Knowledge at Wharton*, (2018). Accessed September 29, 2024. https://knowledge.wharton.upenn.edu/podcast/knowledge-at-wharton-podcast/alaskas-experience-shows-promise-universal-basic-income/.

32. Doar, Robert. "Universal Basic Income Would Undermine the Success of Our Safety Net." *George W. Bush Institute: The Catalyst*, no. 10 (2018). Accessed September 29, 2024. https://www.bushcenter.org/catalyst/are-we-ready/doar-universal-basic-income#:~:text=Universal%20Basic%20Income%20(UBI)%20would,national%20debt%20(or%20both).

33. Klein, Christopher. "The Original Luddites Raged against the Machine of the Industrial Revolution." History.com, January 4, 2019. https://www.history.com/news/industrial-revolution-luddites-workers.

34. Clarke, Colin, Mollie Saltskog, Michaela Millender, and Naureen C. Fink. "The Targeting of Infrastructure by America's Violent Far-Right." *Combatting Terrorism Center at West Point* 16, no. 5 (2023). Accessed September 29, 2024. https://ctc.westpoint.edu/the-targeting-of-infrastructure-by-americas-violent-far-right/.

35. Clarke, Colin, Mollie Saltskog, Michaela Millender, and Naureen C. Fink. "The Targeting of Infrastructure by America's Violent Far-Right." *Combatting Terrorism Center at West Point* 16, no. 5 (2023). Accessed September 29, 2024. https://ctc.westpoint.edu/the-targeting-of-infrastructure-by-americas-violent-far-right/.

36. Piazza, James A. "The Determinants of Domestic Right-Wing Terrorism in the USA: Economic Grievance, Societal Change and Political Resentment." *Conflict Management and Peace Science* 34, no. 1 (2017): 52–80. https://www.jstor.org/stable/26271447.

37. Rosenbach, Eric and Katherine Mansted. "Can Democracy Survive in the Information Age?" *Belfer Center for Science and International Affairs, Harvard Kennedy School.* October 2018. https://www.belfercenter.org/publication/can-democracy-survive-information-age.

38. Fukuyama, Francis. "The End of History?" *The National Interest*, no. 16 (1989): 3–18. http://www.jstor.org/stable/24027184.

39. "Once Considered a Boon to Democracy, Social Media Have Started to Look like Its Nemesis." *The Economist*, November 4, 2017. https://www.economist.com/briefing/2017/11/04/once-considered-a-boon-to-democracy-social-media-have-started-to-look-like-its-nemesis.

40. Bischoff, Paul. "Internet Censorship 2024: A Map of Restrictions by Country." Comparitech, October 16, 2023. https://www.comparitech.com/blog/vpn-privacy/internet-censorship-map/.

41. Rosenbach, Eric and Katherine Mansted. "Can Democracy Survive in the Information Age?" *Belfer Center for Science and International Affairs, Harvard Kennedy School.* October 2018. 2018. https://www.belfercenter.org/publication/can-democracy-survive-information-age.

42. Rancy, Amaris. "Big Question: How Does Digital Privacy Matter for Democracy and Its Advocates?" National Endowment for Democracy, January 22, 2024. https://www.ned.org/big-question-how-does-digital-privacy-matter-for-democracy-and-its-advocates/.

43. Rancy, Amaris. "Big Question: How Does Digital Privacy Matter for Democracy and Its Advocates?" National Endowment for Democracy, January 22, 2024. https://www.ned.org/big-question-how-does-digital-privacy-matter-for-democracy-and-its-advocates/.

44. Pearson, J.S. "Defining Digital Authoritarianism." *Philosophy and Technology* 37, 73 (2024). https://doi.org/10.1007/s13347-024-00754-8

45. Pearson, J.S. "Defining Digital Authoritarianism." *Philosophy and Technology* 37, 73 (2024). https://doi.org/10.1007/s13347-024-00754-8

46. Morgus, Robert, and Justin Sherman. "How U.S. Surveillance Technology Is Propping up Authoritarian Regimes." *The Washington Post*, January 17, 2019. https://www.washingtonpost.com/outlook/2019/01/17/how-us-surveillance-technology-is-propping-up-authoritarian-regimes/.

47. Rancy, Amaris. "Big Question: How Does Digital Privacy Matter for Democracy and Its Advocates?" National Endowment For Democracy, January 22, 2024. https://www.ned.org/big-question-how-does-digital-privacy-matter-for-democracy-and-its-advocates/.

48. Rancy, Amaris. "Big Question: How Does Digital Privacy Matter for Democracy and Its Advocates?" National Endowment For Democracy, January 22, 2024. https://www.ned.org/big-question-how-does-digital-privacy-matter-for-democracy-and-its-advocates/.

49. Miyamoto, Inez. "Surveillance Technology Challenges Political Culture Of Democratic States." Edited by Alexander L. Vuving. *Hindsight, Insight, Foresight: Thinking About Security in the Indo-Pacific.* Daniel K. Inouye Asia-Pacific Center for Security Studies, 2020. http://www.jstor.org/stable/resrep26667.9.

50. Nissenbaum, Helen. Symposium, *Privacy as Contextual Integrity*, 79 WASH. L. REV. 119 (2004). https://digitalcommons.law.uw.edu/wlr/vol79/iss1/10.

51. Miyamoto, Inez. "Surveillance Technology Challenges Political Culture Of Democratic States." Edited by Alexander L. Vuving. *Hindsight, Insight, Foresight: Thinking About Security in the Indo-Pacific.* Daniel K. Inouye Asia-Pacific Center for Security Studies, 2020.

52. Miyamoto, Inez. "Surveillance Technology Challenges Political Culture Of Democratic States." Edited by Alexander L. Vuving. *Hindsight, Insight, Foresight: Thinking About Security in the Indo-Pacific*. Daniel K. Inouye Asia-Pacific Center for Security Studies, 2020.

53. Rancy, Amaris. "Big Question: How Does Digital Privacy Matter for Democracy and Its Advocates?" National Endowment For Democracy, January 2, 2024. https://www.ned.org/big-question-how-does-digital-privacy-matter-for-democracy-and-its-advocates/.

54. "What Is the Rule of Law?" World Justice Project. Accessed September 29, 2024. https://worldjusticeproject.org/about-us/overview/what-rule-law.

55. "China's Efforts to Subvert Norms and Exploit Open Societies." *U.S.-China Economic and Security Review Commission*, (2023). Accessed September 29, 2024. https://www.uscc.gov/sites/default/files/2023-11/Chapter_2_Section_1-Chinas_Increasingly_Global_Legal_Reach.pdf.

56. Thayer, Bradley A., and Lianchao Han. "'People's War of Surveillance' Ensures China Will Never Be Free." *The Hill*, December 22, 2019. https://thehill.com/opinion/international/475064-peoples-war-of-surveillance-ensures-china-will-never-be-free/.

57. Yang, Zeyi. "The Chinese Surveillance State Proves that the Idea of Privacy Is More "Malleable" than You'd Expect." *MIT Technology Review*, October 10, 2022. https://www.technologyreview.com/2022/10/10/1060982/china-pandemic-cameras-surveillance-state-book/.

58. Bereja, Martin, Andrew Kao, David Y. Yang, and Noam Yuchtman. "AI-TOCRACY." *The Quarterly Journal of Economics* 138, no. 3 (2023): 1349–1402. Accessed September 29, 2024. https://doi.org/10.1093/qje/qjad012.

59. Greenberg, Andy. "Facebook Report Shows It Denies U.S. Surveillance Requests More Often Than Google." *Forbes*, August 27, 2013. https://www.forbes.com/sites/andygreenberg/2013/08/27/facebook-first-report-on-government-data-requests-shows-it-denies-u-s-surveillance-demands-more-often-than-google/.

60. Greenberg, Andy. "Facebook Report Shows It Denies U.S. Surveillance Requests More Often Than Google." *Forbes*, August 27, 2013. https://www.forbes.com/sites/andygreenberg/2013/08/27/facebook-first-report-on-government-data-requests-shows-it-denies-u-s-surveillance-demands-more-often-than-google/.

61. Agustin, Francis. "The US Government Requests — And Is Granted — the Most User Data from Tech Companies Compared to Countries like the UK, France, and Japan: Report." *Business Insider*, September 21, 2021. https://www.businessinsider.com/us-gov-requests-more-user-data-report-2021-9.

62. Woollacott, Emma. "U.S. Government Requests Most User Data From Big Tech Firms." *Forbes*, August 28, 2024. https://www.forbes.com/sites/emmawoollacott/2024/08/28/us-government-requests-most-user-data-from-big-tech-firms/.

63. Google. "Number of user data requests issued to Google from U.S. federal agencies and courts as of 1st half 2023." Chart. July 1, 2023. Statista. Accessed September 30, 2024. https://www.statista.com/statistics/273815/global-data-requests-from-google-by-federal-agencies-and-governments/

64. "Customer Letter." Apple. Accessed September 29, 2024. https://www.apple.com/customer-letter/.

65. "Israeli Firm Helping FBI to Open Encrypted IPhone: Report." *Reuters*, March 23, 2016. https://www.reuters.com/article/technology/israeli-firm-helping-fbi-to-open-encrypted-iphone-report-idUSKCN0WP17J/.

66. Austin, Patrick L. "Apple Is Once Again Under Pressure to Help the FBI Unlock a Shooter's IPhone. Here's What to Know." *Time*, January 16, 2020. https://time.com/5765771/apple-fbi-pensacola/.

67. Satter, Raphael, "Governments spying on Apple, Google users through push notifications - US senator", *Reuters*, December 6, 2023. https://www.reuters.com/technology/cybersecurity/governments-spying-apple-google-users-through-push-notifications-us-senator-2023-12-06/.

68. Levitsky, Steven, and Daniel Ziblatt. 2018. *How Democracies Die*. Crown.

69. Reid, Tim. "Trump Tells Christians They Won't Have to Vote after This Election." *Reuters*, July 28, 2024. https://www.google.com/url?q=https://www.reuters.com/world/us/trump-tells-christians-they-wont-have-vote-after-this-election-2024-07-27/&sa=D&source=docs&ust=1727715649769204&usg=AOvVaw0hvp1F7KyvkJEZiVJnyLsn.

70. Halmai, Gábor. "Coping Strategies of the Hungarian Constitutional Court since 2010." Verfassungsblog, September 27, 2022. https://verfassungsblog.de/coping-strategies-of-the-hungarian-constitutional-court-since-2010/.

71. Halmai, Gábor. "Coping Strategies of the Hungarian Constitutional Court since 2010." Verfassungsblog, September 27, 2022. https://verfassungsblog.de/coping-strategies-of-the-hungarian-constitutional-court-since-2010/.

72. Garcia Cano, Regina, and Joshua Goodman. "Maduro Is Declared Winner in Venezuela's Presidential Election as Opposition Claims It Prevailed." *Associated Press*, July 29, 2024. https://apnews.com/article/venezuela-presidential-election-maduro-machado-edmundo-5ce255ae90614162590bfe1207d2e1d0.

73. "CHP Holds Urgent Meeting over Court Case against Istanbul Mayor." *Hürriyet Daily News*, September 24, 2024. https://www.hurriyetdailynews.com/chp-holds-urgent-meeting-over-court-case-against-istanbul-mayor-200899.

74. Ellis-Petersen, Hannah. "India's Supreme Court Suspends Rahul Gandhi's Two-year Defamation Jail Term." *The Guardian*, August 4, 2023. https://www.theguardian.com/world/2023/aug/04/rahul-gandhi-wins-supreme-court-appeal-against-defamation-conviction.

75. Godbole, Tanika. "India: Can Opposition Leader Kejriwal Make a Comeback?" *DW News*, September 23, 2024. https://www.dw.com/en/india-can-opposition-leader-kejriwal-make-a-comeback/a-70302318.

76. Grimshaw, Jeff, Tanya Mann, Lynne Viscio, and Jennifer Landis. "Why It Pays To Be Long-Term Greedy." Chief Executive. Accessed November 19, 2024. https://chiefexecutive.net/ceos-pay-long-term-greedy/.

77. Caminiti, Susan. "AT&T's $1 Billion Gambit: Retraining Nearly Half Its Workforce for Jobs of the Future." *CNBC*, March 13, 2018. https://www.cnbc.com/2018/03/13/atts-1-billion-gambit-retraining-nearly-half-its-workforce.html.

CHAPTER 8

1. My example was made up, but for a good explanation of Starbucks app gamification, see Scrimmage, "How Starbucks Perfected its Addictive Rewards Program," https://scrimmage.co/how-starbucks-perfected-its-addictive-rewards-program/. Accessed 8 November 2024.

2. Queen, Jack. "Pennsylvania Judge Allows Elon Musk's $1 Million Voter Giveaway." *Reuters*, November 4, 2024. https://www.reuters.com/legal/judge-weighs-challenge-elon-musks-1-million-voter-giveaway-2024-11-04/.

3. West, Sean and Jae Um. Sean West Interview with Jae Um. Personal, October 8. 2024.

4. For private sector: Bindley, Katherine. "The Fight for AI Talent: Pay Million-Dollar Packages and Buy Whole Teams." *The Wall Street Journal*, March 27, 2024. https://www.wsj.com/tech/ai/the-fight-for-ai-talent-pay-million-dollar-packages-and-buy-whole-teams-c370de2b. For government: "Salary Table 2024-GS Incorporating the 4.7% General Schedule Increase Effective January 2024." United States Office of Personnel Management. Accessed November 19, 2024. https://www.opm.gov/policy-data-oversight/pay-leave/salaries-wages/salary-tables/pdf/2024/GS.pdf.

5. Canfield, Grace A. "How Uber's Regulatory Success in the United States Slowed Its International Expansion." *Penn State Journal of Law and International Affairs* 10, no. 1 (February 2022). https://elibrary.law.psu.edu/cgi/viewcontent.cgi?article=1308&context=jlia.

6. Author interview with Casey Flaherty on December 11, 2024.

7. Holden, Michael. "Explainer: Why Are There Riots in the UK and Who Is behind Them?" *Reuters*, August 7, 2024. https://www.reuters.com/world/uk/why-are-there-riots-uk-who-is-behind-them-2024-08-07/. And Cruz, Manon, and Kylie Maclellan. "UK Charges 17-Year-Old Boy with Murder in Southport Child Killings." *Reuters*, August 1, 2024. https://www.reuters.com/world/uk/clashes-uks-southport-after-killing-three-girls-leaves-many-police-injured-2024-07-31/.

8. Wilmot, Claire. "Did Russian Disinformation Fuel the Southport Protests?" The Bureau of Investigative Journalism, August 2, 2024. https://www.thebureauinvestigates.com/stories/2024-08-02/did-russian-disinformation-fuel-the-southport-protests/.

9. "A Riot in Southport Shows How the British Far Right Is Changing." *The Economist*, July 31, 2024. https://www.economist.com/britain/2024/07/31/a-riot-in-southport-shows-how-the-british-far-right-is-changing.

10. "A Riot in Southport Shows How the British Far Right Is Changing." *The Economist*, July 31, 2024. https://www.economist.com/britain/2024/07/31/a-riot-in-southport-shows-how-the-british-far-right-is-changing.

11. Holden, Michael. "Explainer: Why Are There Riots in the UK and Who Is behind Them?" *Reuters*, August 7, 2024. https://www.reuters.com/world/uk/why-are-there-riots-uk-who-is-behind-them-2024-08-07/.

12. PA Media. "Chester Woman, 55, Arrested over False Posts about Southport Murders." *The Guardian*, August 8, 2024. https://www.theguardian.com/uk-news/article/2024/aug/08/chester-woman-55-arrested-over-false-posts-about-southport-murders.

13. Davies, Caroline. "Pakistan Police Arrest Man over Southport Attack Disinformation." *BBC News*, August 21, 2024. https://www.bbc.com/news/articles/c05je6yz0q1o.

14. News Wires. "UK Slams Elon Musk for 'Civil War' Comments on Far-Right Riots." France 24 August 7, 2024. https://france24.com/en/europe/20240807-uk-government-elon-musk-civil-war-comments-far-right-riots-stabbing-misinformation.

15. Hill, Steven F., Guillermo S. Christensen, Jeffrey Orenstein, Stacy J. Ettinger, Jerome J. Zaucha, and Catherine A. Johnson. "U.S. Government Imposes Significant New Export Controls on Semiconductor, Semiconductor Manufacturing Equipment, and Supercomputer-Related Transactions Involving China and Chinese Entities." K&L Gates, October 21, 2022. https://www.klgates.com/US-Government-Imposes-Significant-New-Export-Controls-on-Semiconductor-Semiconductor-Manufacturing-Equipment-

and-Supercomputer-Related-Transactions-Involving-China-and-Chinese-Entities-10-21-2022.

16. Kharpal, Arjun. "Netherlands Takes on U.S. Export Controls, Controlling Shipments of Some ASML Machines." *CNBC*, September 6, 2024. https://www.cnbc.com/2024/09/06/netherlands-expands-export-curbs-on-advanced-chip-tools.html.

17. Shivakumar, Sujai, Charles Wessner, and Thomas Howell. "The Strategic Importance of Legacy Chips." CSIS, March 3, 2023. https://www.csis.org/analysis/strategic-importance-legacy-chips.

18. Satariano, Adam. "Meta Fined $1.3 Billion for Violating E.U. Data Privacy Rules." *The New York Times*, May 22, 2023. https://www.nytimes.com/2023/05/22/business/meta-facebook-eu-privacy-fine.html

19. Cipriani, Marco, Linda S. Goldberg, and Gabriele La Spada. "Financial Sanctions, SWIFT, and the Architecture of the International Payments System" (Federal Reserve Bank of New York Staff Reports, no. 1047), January 2023. https://www.newyorkfed.org/medialibrary/media/research/staff_reports/sr1047.pdf.

20. "2017 Global Mobile Consumer Survey: US Edition." Deloitte, 2017. https://www2.deloitte.com/content/dam/Deloitte/us/Documents/technology-media-telecommunications/us-tmt-2017-global-mobile-consumer-survey-executive-summary.pdf.

21. Heritage, Stuart. "Joan Is Awful: Black Mirror Episode Is Every Striking Actor's Worst Nightmare." *The Guardian*, July 13, 2023. https://www.theguardian.com/tv-and-radio/2023/jul/13/joan-is-awful-black-mirror-striking-actors-nightmare.

22. Burke, Minyvonne. "Disney Says Man Can't Sue over Wife's Death Because He Agreed to Disney+ Terms of Service." *NBC News*, August 14, 2024. https://www.nbcnews.com/news/us-news/disney-says-man-cant-sue-wifes-death-agreed-disney-terms-service-rcna166594.

23. Hadfield, Gillian K. *Rules for a Flat World*. 1st ed. Oxford University Press, 2016.

CHAPTER 9

1. Original HK police story: "Deepfake colleagues trick HK clerk into paying HK$200M", RTHK, April 2, 2024" https://news.rthk.hk/rthk/en/component/k2/1739119-20240204.htm. Confirmation of company name here: Leng, Cheng and Chan Ho-him, "Arup lost $25mn in Hong Kong deepfake video conference scam," Financial Times, 16 May 2024 https://www.ft.com/content/b977e8d4-664c-4ae4-8a8e-eb93bdf785ea.

2. 50 Cent, "I'm a Hustler," lyrics accessed November 11, 2024 on Genius.com (https://genius.com/50-cent-im-a-hustler-lyrics).

3. BAE Systems | International. "The Cyber Impact on Elections: Safeguarding Democracy in 2024," February 20, 2024. https://www.baesystems.com/en/blog/the-cyber-impact-on-elections-safeguarding-democracy-in-2024.

4. FBI Statement on Bomb Threats to Polling Locations, FBI, November 5, 2024. https://www.fbi.gov/news/press-releases/fbi-statement-on-bomb-threats-to-polling-locations.

5. Woollacott, Emma. "AI-Powered Russian Influence Network Targets U.S. Elections." *Forbes*, June 27, 2024. https://www.forbes.com/sites/emmawoollacott/2024/06/24/ai-powered-russian-influence-network-targets-us-elections.

6. Agence France-Presse. "Pro-Russia 'news' Sites Spew Incendiary US Election Falsehoods." *France24*, August 19, 2024. https://www.france24.com/en/live-news/20240819-pro-russia-news-sites-spew-incendiary-us-election-falsehoods.

7. West, Sean, and David Salvo. Sean West Interview with David Salvo. Personal, August 20, 2024.

8. Helen Davidson, "Taiwan Presidential Election: China's Influence Looms Large." *The Guardian*, January 9, 2024, https://www.theguardian.com/world/2024/jan/09/taiwan-presidential-election-china-influence.

9. Verma, Pranshu, and Gerrit De Vynck. "AI Is Destabilizing 'the Concept of Truth Itself' in 2024 Election." *The Washington Post*, January 22, 2024. https://www.washingtonpost.com/technology/2024/01/22/ai-deepfake-elections-politicians/.

10. West, Sean, and William Henderson. Sean West Interview with William Henderson. Personal, September 20, 2024.

11. Ferraro, Matthew F., and Brent J. Gurney. "The Other Side Says Your Evidence Is a Deepfake. Now What?" WilmerHale, December 21, 2022. https://www.wilmerhale.com/insights/publications/20221221-the-other-side-says-your-evidence-is-a-deepfake-now-what.

12. Dixon, Herbert B. "The 'Deepfake Defense': An Evidentiary Conundrum." American Bar Association, June 11, 2024. https://www.americanbar.org/groups/judicial/publications/judges_journal/2024/spring/deepfake-defense-evidentiary-conundrum.

13. Bond, Shannon. "People Are Trying to Claim Real Videos Are Deepfakes. The Courts Are Not Amused." *National Public Radio*, May 8, 2023. https://www.npr.org/2023/05/08/1174132413/people-are-trying-to-claim-real-videos-are-deepfakes-the-courts-are-not-amused.

14. Porter, Jonathan A. "Will Juries Latch Onto Deepfake Concerns Like They Did To Scientific Evidence During The Infamous "CSI Effect"?" *American Bar Association Criminal Justice Section's White Collar Crime Committee*, no. Winter/Spring 2024 (2024). Accessed September 30, 2024. https://www.americanbar.org/content/dam/aba/publications/criminaljustice/2024/porter.pdf.

15. Bond, Shannon. "People Are Trying to Claim Real Videos Are Deepfakes. The Courts Are Not Amused." *National Public Radio*, May 8, 2023. https://www.npr.org/2023/05/08/1174132413/people-are-trying-to-claim-real-videos-are-deepfakes-the-courts-are-not-amused.

16. Bond, Shannon. "People Are Trying to Claim Real Videos Are Deepfakes. The Courts Are Not Amused." *National Public Radio*, May 8, 2023. https://www.npr.org/2023/05/08/1174132413/people-are-trying-to-claim-real-videos-are-deepfakes-the-courts-are-not-amused.

17. Porter, Jonathan A. "Will Juries Latch Onto Deepfake Concerns Like They Did To Scientific Evidence During The Infamous "CSI Effect"?" *American Bar Association Criminal Justice Section's White Collar Crime Committee*, no. Winter/Spring 2024 (2024). Accessed September 30, 2024. https://www.americanbar.org/content/dam/aba/publications/criminaljustice/2024/porter.pdf.

18. LaMonaga, John P. "A Break From Reality: Modernizing Authentication Standards for Digital Video Evidence in the Era of Deepfakes." *American University Law Review* 69, no. 6 (2020): A5. Accessed September 30, 2024. https://digitalcommons.wcl.american.edu/cgi/viewcontent.cgi?article=2221&context=aulr#:~:text=Because%20the%20technology%20to%20detect,the%20proponent%20of%20video%20evidence.

19. Bond, Shannon. "People Are Trying to Claim Real Videos Are Deepfakes. The Courts Are Not Amused." *National Public Radio*, May 8, 2023. https://www.npr.org/2023/05/08/1174132413/people-are-trying-to-claim-real-videos-are-deepfakes-the-courts-are-not-amused.

20. Salmon, Felix. "Media Trust Hits New Low." *Axios*, January 21, 2021. https://www.axios.com/2021/01/21/media-trust-crisis.

21. Taylor, Alison. "Corporate Advocacy in a Time of Social Outrage." *Harvard Business Review*, February 6, 2024. https://hbr.org/2024/02/corporate-advocacy-in-a-time-of-social-outrage.

22. Miranda, Lin-Manuel. *Hamilton*. Directed by Thomas Kail. Disney+, 2020.

CHAPTER 10

1. Based on reporting in: Mitrovica, Andrew. "The 'Brilliant' Way Israel Kills Innocents." Al Jazeera, September 25, 2024. https://www.aljazeera.com/opinions/2024/9/25/the-brilliant-way-israel-kills-innocents.

2. Bulos, Nabih. "Drones Sold at Walmart Help Keep Ukraine in the Battle for Bakhmut." *The Los Angeles Times*, April 14, 2023. https://www.latimes.com/world-nation/story/2023-04-14/drones-sold-at-walmart-help-keep-ukraine-in-the-battle-for-bakhmut.

3. Rivera, Juan-Pablo, Gabriel Mukobi, Anka Reuel, Max Lamparth, Chandler Smith, and Jacquelyn Schneider. "Escalation Risks from Language Models in Military and Diplomatic Decision-Making." In *Proceedings of the 2024 ACM Conference on Fairness, Accountability, and Transparency (FAccT '24)*, 836–898. New York: Association for Computing Machinery, 2024. https://doi.org/10.1145/3630106.3658942.

4. Pegasus spyware: French President Macron changes phone after hack reports, *BBC,* July 22, 2021. https://www.bbc.com/news/world-europe-57937867.

5. Copp, Tara. "Elon Musk's Refusal to Have Starlink Support Ukraine Attack in Crimea Raises Questions for Pentagon." *Associated Press*, September 11, 2023. https://apnews.com/article/spacex-ukraine-starlink-russia-air-force-fde93d9a69d7dbd1326022ecfdbc53c2.

6. Brown, Tara. "Can Starlink Satellites Be Lawfully Targeted?" Articles of War, Lieber Institute West Point, August 5, 2022. https://lieber.westpoint.edu/can-starlink-satellites-be-lawfully-targeted/.

7. Brown, Tara. "Can Starlink Satellites Be Lawfully Targeted?" *Articles of War,* Lieber Institute West Point, August 5, 2022. https://lieber.westpoint.edu/can-starlink-satellites-be-lawfully-targeted/.

8. "Sean West and Trever Hehn." Hence Technologies. May 13, 2024. Video, https://www.youtube.com/watch?v=KFOumoKv5Es.

9. Horowitz, Jonathan. "One Click from Conflict: Some Legal Considerations Related to Technology Companies Providing Digital Services in Situations of Armed Conflict." *Chicago Journal of International Law* 24, no. 2 (2024). https://doi.org/10.2139/ssrn.4470988.

10. Sabin, Sam. "North Korean IT Workers Game U.S. Companies' Hiring Practices." *Axios*, May 21, 2024. https://www.axios.com/2024/05/21/north-korea-it-workers-us-hiring.

11. Wiseman, Paul. "Counterfeiters, Hackers Cost US up to $600 Billion a Year." *Associated Press*, February 17, 2017. https://apnews.com/counterfeiters-hackers-cost-us-up-to-600-billion-a-year-2234bddc68c14ba18d4d403442187c59.

12. Greenberg, Andy. "The Untold Story of NotPetya, the Most Devastating Cyberattack in History." Wired, August 22, 2018. https://www.wired.com/story/notpetya-cyberattack-ukraine-russia-code-crashed-the-world/.

13. Much of this section resulted from an email interview with Ian Thompson, insurance industry executive at IMT Advisory, on September 30, 2024.

CHAPTER 11

1. Carbonaro, Giulia. "Who Is Alissa Heinerscheid? Bud Light's VP of Marketing Amid Trans Debate." *Newsweek*, April 10, 2023. https://www.newsweek.com/bud-light-vp-says-brand-was-out-touch-before-transgender-campaign-1793392.

2. Stewart, Emily. "The Bud Light Boycott, Explained as Much as Is Possible." *Vox*, June 30, 2023. https://www.vox.com/money/2023/4/12/23680135/bud-light-boycott-dylan-mulvaney-travis-tritt-trans.

3. Hetzner, Christiaan. "Bud Light Boycott Campaigner Kid Rock Changes His Tune on Protests: 'I Think They Got the Message. The Punishment at This Point Doesn't Fit the Crime.'" *Fortune*, December 14, 2023. https://fortune.com/2023/12/14/bud-light-boycott-kid-rock-anheuser-busch-tucker-carlson/.

4. Homans, Charles. "Man Vs. Mouse: Ron DeSantis Finds Taking On Disney Is a Dicey Business." *The New York Times*, April 26, 2023. https://www.google.com/url?q=https://www.nytimes.com/2023/04/26/us/politics/desantis-disney-republicans.html&sa=D&source=docs&ust=1727716421717733&usg=AOvVaw3-TU1MV2EtD28lovzc_D6J.

5. Stewart, Emily. "The Bud Light Boycott, Explained as Much as Is Possible." *Vox*, June 30, 2023. https://www.vox.com/money/2023/4/12/23680135/bud-light-boycott-dylan-mulvaney-travis-tritt-trans.

6. Bary, Andrew. "Bud Light Sales Fall 26% as Transgender Backlash Worsens." *Barron's*, May 1, 2024. https://www.barrons.com/articles/bud-light-sales-dylan-mulvaney-transgender-backlash-9d426f09.

7. Ziady, Hanna. "Bud Light Boycott Likely Cost Anheuser-Busch InBev over $1 Billion in Lost Sales." *CNN*, February 29, 2024. https://edition.cnn.com/2024/02/29/business/bud-light-boycott-ab-inbev-sales/index.html.

8. Valle, Jay. "Chicago Gay Bars Boycott Anheuser-Busch for Distancing Itself from Dylan Mulvaney." *NBC News*, May 10, 2023. https://www.nbcnews.com/nbc-out/out-news/chicago-gay-bars-boycott-anheuser-busch-distancing-dylan-mulvaney-rcna83537.

9. Lutz, Tom. "The Guardian." *Michael Jordan Insists 'Republicans Buy Sneakers Too' Quote Was a Joke*, May 4, 2020. https://www.theguardian.com/sport/2020/may/04/michael-jordan-espn-last-dance-republicans-sneakers-quote-nba.

10. *Citizens United v. FEC*, 558 U.S. 310 (2010) (U.S. Supreme Court January 21, 2010).

11. Calculated based on opensecrets.org dashboard for 2024: "2024 Outside Spending, by Super PAC." OpenSecrets. Accessed November 19, 2024. https://www.opensecrets.org/outside-spending/super_pacs/2024?chrt=2020&disp=O&type=S.

12. Legum, Judd. "These Companies Are Bankrolling a Multi-Million Dollar Effort to Elect Mark Robinson Governor of North Carolina." Web log. *Popular Information* (blog), September 23, 2024. https://popular.info/p/these-companies-are-bankrolling-a.

13. Sherman, Lucille, and Katie Peralta Soloff. "N.C. Legalizes Takeout and Delivery Cocktails." *Axios*, July 10, 2024. https://www.axios.com/local/raleigh/2024/07/10/north-carolina-legalizes-takeout-delivery-cocktails-roy-cooper-legislature.

14. Kaczynski, Andrew, and Em Steck. "'I'M a Black NAZI!': NC GOP Nominee for Governor Made Dozens of Disturbing Comments on Porn Forum." *CNN*, September 19, 2024. https://www.cnn.com/2024/09/19/politics/kfile-mark-robinson-black-nazi-pro-slavery-porn-forum/index.html.

15. "How ESG Became Part of America's Culture Wars." *The Economist*, June 21, 2023. https://www.economist.com/the-economist-explains/2023/06/21/how-esg-became-part-of-americas-culture-wars.

16. Whitten, Sarah. "Disney Vows to Help Repeal 'Don't Say Gay' Law, Says Florida Gov. DeSantis Shouldn't Have Signed It." *CNBC*, March 28, 2022. https://www.cnbc.com/2022/03/28/disney-vows-to-help-repeal-dont-say-gay-law.html.

17. Fineout, Gary. "Federal Judge Throws Out Disney's Lawsuit against DeSantis." *Politico*, January 31, 2024. https://www.politico.com/news/2024/01/31/federal-judge-throws-out-disneys-lawsuit-against-desantis-00138852.

18. Behbin, Mana, Elizabeth S. Goldberg, and Rachel Mann. "ESG Investing Regulations across the 50 States." Morgan Lewis, July 21, 2023. https://www.morganlewis.com/pubs/2023/07/esg-investing-regulations-across-the-50-states.

19. Surowiecki, James. "The War on 'Woke Capital' Is Backfiring." *The Atlantic*, January 31, 2024. https://www.theatlantic.com/ideas/archive/2024/01/republicans-woke-capital-esg-investment/677294/.

20. Betts, Anna. "Donald Trump Jr. to Join Venture Capital Firm Rather than Father's Administration." *The Guardian*, November 12, 2024. https://www.theguardian.com/us-news/2024/nov/12/donald-trump-jr-1789-capital

21. Yglesias, Matthew. "The 'Misinformation Problem' Seems like Misinformation." Web log. *Slow Boring* (blog), February 15, 2022. https://www.slowboring.com/p/misinformation-myth.

22. West, Sean, and Rohitesh Dhawan. Sean West Interview with Rohitesh Dhawan. Personal, August 7, 2024.

CHAPTER 12

1. Insurance Company, mail to the author, May 13, 2024.

2. Stephen Heitkamp and I go into this in-depth in "Gen AI Makes Legal Action Cheap – and Companies Need to Prepare." *Harvard Business Review Online*, October 3, 2024 accessible here: https://hbr.org/2024/10/gen-ai-makes-legal-action-cheap-and-companies-need-to-prepare?ab=HP-hero-latest-text-1

3. Reich, David. "Additional Funding Needed for Legal Service Corporation." Center on Budget and Policy Priorities, February 1, 2021. https://www.cbpp.org/blog/additional-funding-needed-for-legal-service-corporation.

4. "SRLN Brief: How Many Srls? (SRLN 2019)." Self-Represented Litigation Network, August 25, 2024. https://www.srln.org/node/548/srln-brief-how-many-srls-srln-2015.

5. Allcot, Dawn. "75% of Americans Plan To File Their Own Taxes — Why This Is a Good Money Move." *Yahoo Finance*, March 12, 2024. https://finance.yahoo.com/news/75-americans-plan-file-own-183553544.html?guccounter=2.

6. "You've Been Injured Now What?" ZAF Legal—Personal Injury, Zero Attorney Fees, AI Assistant. Accessed September 30, 2024. https://www.zaflegal.com/.

7. West, Sean, and Ty Brown. Sean West Interview with Ty Brown. Personal, August 27, 2024.

8. "Legal Assist Provides Affordable Legal Advice You Can Trust." LegalZoom. Accessed September 30, 2024. https://www.legalzoom.com/attorneys/legal-plans/personal.html.

9. "Save Time and Money with Donotpay!" DoNotPay. Accessed September 30, 2024. https://donotpay.com/.

10. Gorsuch, Neil, and Janie Nitze. *Over Ruled*. Harper Collins, 2024.

11. Aidid, Abdi, and Benjamin Alarie. 2023. *The Legal Singularity: How Artificial Intelligence Can Make Law Radically Better*. University of Toronto Press.

12. Ben-Shahar, Omri, and Ariel Porat. *Personalized Law: Different Rules for Different People.* New York, NY: Oxford University Press, 2021.

13. Susskind, Richard. 2023. *Tomorrow's Lawyers: An Introduction to Your Future.* 3rd ed. Oxford University Press.

14. West, Sean and Jordan Furlong. Sean West Interview with Jordan Furlong. Personal, September 6, 2024.

15. West, Sean, and Damien Riehl. Sean West Interview with Damien Riehl. Personal, September 16, 2023.

16. West, Sean and Bridget McCormack. Sean West and Bridget McCormack interview. Personal. October 9, 2024.

17. Shimshaw, Drew. "Access to A.I. Justice: Avoiding an Inequitable Two-Tiered System of Legal Services." *Yale Journal of Law & Technology* 24, no. 150 (2022). Accessed September 30, 2024. https://yjolt.org/access-ai-justice-avoiding-inequitable-two-tiered-system-legal-services.

18. Nay, John J. 2023. "Large Language Models as Corporate Lobbyists." *arXiv preprint*, January 2023. https://arxiv.org/abs/2301.01181.

19. Kreps, Sarah, and Douglas L. Kriner. 2023. "The Potential Impact of Emerging Technologies on Democratic Representation: Evidence from a Field Experiment." *New Media and Society*, forthcoming. https://ssrn.com/abstract=4358982.

20. Hamilton, Jesse. "IRS 'raided' by Crypto Investors as Industry Puts up Fight against U.S. Tax Proposal." CoinDesk Latest Headlines RSS, November 13, 2023. https://www.coindesk.com/policy/2023/11/13/irs-raided-by-crypto-investors-as-industry-puts-up-fight-against-us-tax-proposal/. And also see my article in Harvard Business Review with Stephen Heitkamp cited above.

21. Sanders, Nathan E., and Bruce Schneier. "How AI Could Write Our Laws." *MIT Technology Review*, March 13, 2023. https://www.technologyreview.com/2023/03/14/1069717/how-ai-could-write-our-laws/.

22. Rivette, Kevin G., and David Kline. 1999. *Rembrandts in the Attic: Unlocking the Hidden Value of Patents.* Harvard Business Review Press.

23. Adhav, Taj. "Losing a Mountain over a Molehill." Leasecake, December 3, 2019. https://leasecake.com/blog/losing-a-mountain-over-a-molehill.

CHAPTER 13

1. Collins, Jim. *Good to Great: Why Some Companies Make the Leap...And Others Don't (Good to Great, 1).* 1st ed. Harper Business, 2001.

2. Collins, Jim. *Turning the Flywheel: A Monograph to Accompany Good to Great (Good to Great, 6).* Harper Business, 2019.

ACKNOWLEDGMENTS

This book happened quite quickly—it went from an idea to a manuscript in a few months. None of that would have been possible without the support of family, colleagues, and friends as I burrowed deep into the writing process.

My wife has been an unwavering source of strength and love through all of the crazy professional decisions I've made, like writing a book in such a short period of time. My kids have been amazing as I've skipped sunrise games of chess and Uno for time at the keyboard. I think they've awaited completion of this book more than anyone. I'm grateful to have shared the journey with my parents who have inspired me to think globally since I was a small child.

While I get to put my name on the cover, this book is a "mindmeld" from an exceptional braintrust of folks I've relied on for ideas, feedback, research, and articulation. If Karthik Sankaran, David Bender, Dan Currell, Mia Tellmann, or Varun Oberoi tell you they've co-authored this book with me, you should believe them. Seriously. This book would not have been completed without their unwavering dedication and all-around brilliance.

My Hence Technologies co-founder Steve Heitkamp has been an unending source of ideas and support as I've produced this book in parallel with our navigation of some of the most strategic decisions the company has ever made. I'm extremely grateful for the weight he has carried as I've gotten this done and for his all-around brilliance as a collaborator and business partner.

Special thanks as well to my co-founder Arun Shanmuganathan who constantly forces me to check my own biases and to never lose track of a true north of societal impact. And, of course, special thanks to the full family of Hencers who have inspired me along our journey and have created an exceptional community—and built exceptional technology.

Hence Technologies and this phase of my career would not have happened without the unwavering support of Daglar Cizmeci, who backed us even as COVID took hold and stuck with us as the start-up funding environment turned inside-out. A number of friends have supported us with investment and as clients or thought partners—I'm deeply grateful for your belief in everything we've been building and for your ideas along the way. Lama Kanazeh, Michael Syn, Ian Thompson, Christian Shelton, Brian Riley, Kevin Kamer, Manish Vekaria, and Charlie Ferry have served as idea champions from day one, while Nate Dalton, Matthew Ruesch, Lisa Shu, Matthew Layton, Andy Bird, Al Giles, Christy Clark, John Romeo, Jake Cusack, Paul Gamble, Jeff Enslin, Marcus Watson, Gaidi Faraj, Nicholas Hu, Dirk Eller, Michael Kovacs, Michael Brunt, Oliver Ratzesberger, Karin Knox, and Peter Smith have made huge impact along the journey.

I will forever owe a debt of gratitude to Ian Bremmer who taught me how to think about the world and how to build a business that spans it. Ian showed me the power of being timely, consistent, counterintuitive, and provocative, leveraging humor and levity to engage audiences. Robert Johnston and David Gordon took big bets on me while at Eurasia Group, which enabled me to transform as both an executive and an analyst, and I am so grateful for their support and friendship. Without my time at Eurasia Group, I wouldn't be writing this book today full stop.

Intellectually, I've drawn inspiration from a few core sources that helped me conceptualize the world we are heading into. First, conversations with Mustafa Suleyman many years ago piqued my interest in the intersection of politics and AI; his latest book, *The Coming Wave*, reinforced that for me. Azeem Azhar's missives and book *Exponential* served as consistent sources of inspiration and guidance in the new exponential age. Richard Susskind and Daniel Susskind's book *The Future of the Professions* caused the "aha" moment for me that I wanted to create technology for the evolution of knowledge work and to study the professions myself. Bjarne Tellmann's *Building an Outstanding Legal Team* helped me ground my views in the reality of top legal departments.

Thanks is in order to Bill Falloon at Wiley for scooping up my concept for this book so quickly and fast-tracking publication. And thanks to Marko Papic, whose analysis of the world is mind-bogglingly insightful and who also introduced me to Bill at Wiley. Thanks to Julie Kerr for her collaboration through editing process as well as to Susan Cerra, Katherine Cording, and the rest of the Wiley team for their work to bring this book to the world. Special thanks to Tracy Feldman for her work on so many of the interviews that underpin this book as well as the beautiful artwork within it.

I'm grateful to Liam Dillon who read this manuscript and provided exceptional feedback, occasionally in autonomous vehicles. Similarly, Juan Pujadas' strategic feedback on the manuscript has shaped this book to be much more compelling than it otherwise would have been. Finally, I've benefitted a lot from authors who have come before me like Brody Mullins, Bilal Baloch, Noah Waisberg, and Andrew Cooper who took the time to share with me their experiences and tactics for making their first book a success.

I've written this book on a boundless journey across the world. I spent a month working on this book from beautiful Kotor, Montenegro. I've drafted text in Rwanda, Uganda, Kenya, and Ethiopia. I've snuck away from the beach in the Maldives and from the city in Singapore to keep writing. And, of course, I've written a lot of this at home in California and London. I would have written a weaker book without everyone I traded ideas with in each of these amazing places.

Finally, I want to acknowledge everyone working to make the world a better place. This book shouldn't be depressing—it is a call to action for all of us to care about the unruly world we are otherwise sleepwalking into.

—SW

Santa Monica, California

ABOUT
THE AUTHOR

Sean West is an entrepreneur, analyst, educator, and author. He is co-founder of Hence Technologies (www.hence.ai), an award-winning software company bridging geopolitical and legal risk. Prior to that, he spent more than a decade at Eurasia Group, the leading global affairs firm, where he was the Deputy CEO and an advisor to top CEOs, general counsels, and investors. He is author of *GeoLegal Notes* (geolegal.substack.com), the only weekly newsletter tracking the intersection of geopolitics, law, and technology read by thousands of readers. He also lectures at Berkeley Law Executive Education on Geolegal Risk. Sean's work has been published in most major print outlets. His debut book, *Unruly* explores the complex interplay of the forces shaping our world in the next decade.

INDEX

Page numbers followed by *f* refer to figures.